The Science of Flavor

DR. STUART FARRIMOND

The Science of Flavor

Unlock the secrets
of flavorful cooking

CONTENTS

Introduction	6
A Route to Flavor	8
Flavor and the Brain	46
Activating Flavor	64
Flavor Directory	86
Index	216
About the Author	222
Acknowledgments	222

INTRODUCTION

There are two types of people in this world: those who see food as fuel, and those for whom food is one of life's greatest pleasures. For those of us in the second camp, food is a joy around which we celebrate, commiserate, find comfort when times are hard, forge new friendships, and even fall in love. For food lovers, great meals are the punctuation points of life—moments when our most precious memories are made. We connect with other cultures and our senses can be whisked to far-flung lands. In fact, my wife tells me she fell in love with me the evening I cooked her a dish of pan-fried salmon wrapped in Italian cheese, bay leaf, and prosciutto—served on a bed of fresh pasta!

Eating does more than excite the taste buds—all our senses are drawn together to create flavor, an all-immersive, multifaceted jewel through which this book shines a scientific light, projecting a delicious rainbow, which we will learn is made from a food's appearance, aroma, and taste, as well as its sound, our emotions, and even the surrounding ambiance. Whether you are an amateur cook, chef, or foodie—or simply curious about the food we eat—this book explores each facet, letting us appreciate and savor food on a deeper level and also making us better cooks and more mindful eaters. Leaving needless jargon in the compost bin, this book is designed to teach you how to extract every morsel of flavor out of everyday ingredients, build delicious pairings, and gain inspiration for your exciting new creations. And this is all, hopefully, seasoned with handfuls of tasty facts and tidbits to dine out on.

The words flavor and taste are sometimes used interchangeably, but they are subtly different. Taste is just what our tongues detect—sweetness, saltiness, sourness, bitterness, umami, and a few other oral sensations. Flavor is the entire experience—a blending of taste with aroma, texture, temperature, and even sound.

This is neither a textbook with dry theory nor a recipe book with rigid instructions. Rather, it is a guide to getting flavor out of every crumb and to cooking more confidently and creatively. It teaches us to tune in to each of the notes and aromas of an ingredient, helping us better savor every mouthful. Don't let the chemical names throughout this book baffle you, but use them as keys to unlocking your creativity, discovering harmonious ingredients, and crafting uniquely delicious dishes out of the ingredients you have in your pantry. In the first three chapters, you will discover that flavor is an illusion created in the brain and how substances called flavor compounds are its foundation. After learning about taste and flavor, chapter 4—the largest part of the book—is a tour of everyday ingredients, and I hope it will serve as a go-to resource when you are lacking inspiration. Got an eggplant and unsure how to get the most out of it? Turn to page 92. Or perhaps the leafy greens languishing at the bottom of the fridge need to be used up (page 98)? Whether it's elevating humble carrots (page 100) or unlocking the depth of umami in mushrooms (page 142), let this book be your trusted companion in the kitchen.

This is my fifth book, and it means a lot to me. While I was writing it, my previously removed brain tumor decided to make an unwelcome return, requiring months of chemotherapy and radiotherapy to keep it at bay. But with the amazing love and support of my wife, family, friends, and church, I managed to finish this book, and it is dedicated to all of you.

A ROUTE TO FLAVOR

Where does flavor begin?	10
How do we sense taste?	12
How does salt bring our food to life?	14
What kind of salt is best?	16
Why do foods taste sweet?	18
Why do we crave sweetness?	20
What is bitterness?	22
How can I use bitterness in cooking?	24
What is umami?	26
How can I enhance umami?	28
What is sourness?	30
How can I cook with acids?	32
What is mouthfeel?	34
How does texture boost flavor?	36
Why do we need fat?	38
What fats should I use?	40
Why do we crave the heat of chiles?	42
Which ingredients are spicy?	44

WHERE DOES FLAVOR BEGIN?

Our journey begins within the sensory realm of the mouth, where every part has an important role to play. And your first port of call in this flavor trip is the lips.

Did you know that your lips are just as sensitive as your fingertips? The soft "vermilion" skin on your mouth is exquisitely attuned to temperature, pain, and touch. What is felt affects the flavor: when the sandpapery roughness of a French fry is first felt with the lips, its crunchy golden crust will be experienced more vividly. More dramatically, the cold hardness of chilled glass will make a drink taste refreshing, a hot cup will make the drink seem hotter than it really is, while a plastic utensil will dull the flavor of whatever morsel it holds.

PAST THE TEETH

Food that passes this first checkpoint now faces the teeth—each slicing, crushing stroke releasing plumes of aroma-carrying substances into the oral cavity, which waft backward into the throat and up into the back of the nose (pp.56–57) where they transform into flavor itself. Teeth do more than grind and mash to make food digestible; acutely sensitive nerve endings in your teeth sense the very structure of food, telling your brain how hard it is and whether it's crunchy, elastic, or gritty.

SALIVA, THE DISSOLVER

Mouthfuls of food are puréed with saliva squirted from glands in the cheeks and under the tongue, dissolving

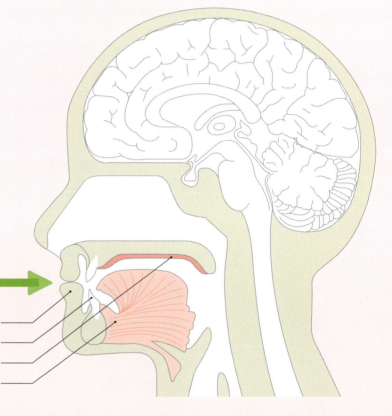

Lips
Teeth
Palate
Tongue

Food's journey

More than tasting and swallowing, each part of the mouth has an important role to play in the flavor journey. This helps us to truly appreciate food.

LIPS
Food's texture is first experienced by the lips, which are as sensitive as your fingertips.

TEETH
These release aroma and sense food's structure, guiding the brain in flavor perception.

PALATE
Texture and mouthfeel are experienced on the palate as food is pushed up against the palate by the tongue.

the flavor chemicals of taste (salts, sugars, acids), which then slide over the tongue, bringing taste buds to life. Surprisingly, it's not the food itself we taste, but saliva that has been mixed with it. Chemicals in the saliva (called enzymes) start to digest sugar and fats in the mouth, while other floating proteins temper unpleasant tastes by masking bitterness.

PALATE AND TONGUE

The entire oral cavity is lined with acutely sensitive nerves—the tongue and palate are continually touching, probing, and examining the shape, texture, and consistency of each mouthful, creating the impression of "mouthfeel" (pp.34–35) and of pungent heat, astringency, and effervescence.

As food reaches your tongue, it finally approaches the taste buds. Stick your tongue out and look in the mirror—those tiny, barely visible bumps that cover the top of the tongue are called papillae. Taste buds themselves are embedded within these papillae and are far too small to see; they are balls of 50–100 cells, bundled like tiny leaves inside a flower bud (hence the name). These send messages to your brain about the taste of the food in your mouth.

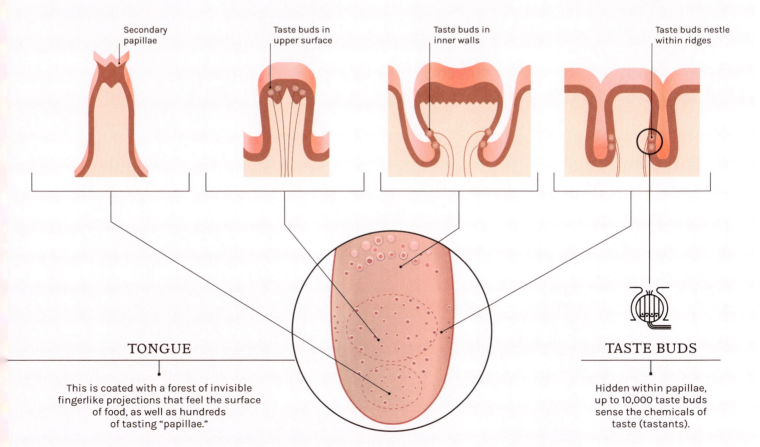

FILIFORM PAPILLAE
Cone-shaped structures on the tongue's surface. Offer grip for licking and sense texture, but lack taste buds.

FUNGIFORM PAPILLAE
These red papillae, which look like mushrooms, are responsible for most of the actual tasting.

CIRCUMVALLATE PAPILLAE
Few in number (8-12), these large papillae at the back of the tongue are attuned to bitterness.

FOLIATE PAPILLAE
Each ridge at the side of the tongue has hundreds of taste buds that are more sensitive to sourness.

TONGUE
This is coated with a forest of invisible fingerlike projections that feel the surface of food, as well as hundreds of tasting "papillae."

TASTE BUDS
Hidden within papillae, up to 10,000 taste buds sense the chemicals of taste (tastants).

HOW DO WE SENSE TASTE?

Taste is the body's way of checking whether food is safe and nutritious before swallowing. Although it contributes just a fraction of the entire flavor experience, it nevertheless serves as its essential foundation.

Although we use the words interchangeably, taste and flavor are not the same thing. Taste comes from our taste buds and is a simple sense with six dimensions: sweet, salty, sour, bitter, umami, and fat.

FLAVOR VS. TASTE

Flavor includes taste, but most of what you think you taste on your tongue comes from your nose (pp.56–57). Taste tells you that an apple is sweet and has some sourness; flavor tells you that this apple is also fruity and aromatic. Our taste evolved as a crude way to check whether a food is safe and/or nutritious. Sweetness indicates that a food contains easy-to-access energy; saltiness says it's worthwhile because it contains a mineral vital for daily life—sodium; sourness is a sign that a food is acidic, suggesting it may contain vitamin C (an acid), or is a fermented food and so likely safe to eat; bitterness is a warning sign of danger; umami—a sense of savory—is fired up by a protein fragment called glutamate, hinting that the food may be a rich source of protein, essential for growth and repair.

HOW TASTE BUDS WORK

The tip of each taste bud lies at the mouth of a tiny pore, into which saliva pools. Tiny hairs sweep up tastants (molecules that trigger the taste sensation) within the saliva and receptors catch them as they pass. Each tastant fits a specific receptor, sending a chemical and electrical impulse through the cell and along one of the threadlike nerves at the bud's base on its way to the brain. The tip of the tongue is slightly more sensitive to sugar, the back a little better at sensing bitterness, and the sides are marginally more attuned to salt and sourness. This relates to the three types of tasting papillae on the tongue: the multipurpose fungiform papillae are scattered all over the tongue, while the more bitter-attuned circumvallate papillae are at the back, and the sour-detecting foliate papillae are on the sides.

The six tastes

Traditionally we think of five main tastes, which the tongue alone can detect. Increasingly, fat is included as a sixth, although this is still an area of research.

SWEET   UMAMI   BITTER   SALTY   SOUR   FAT

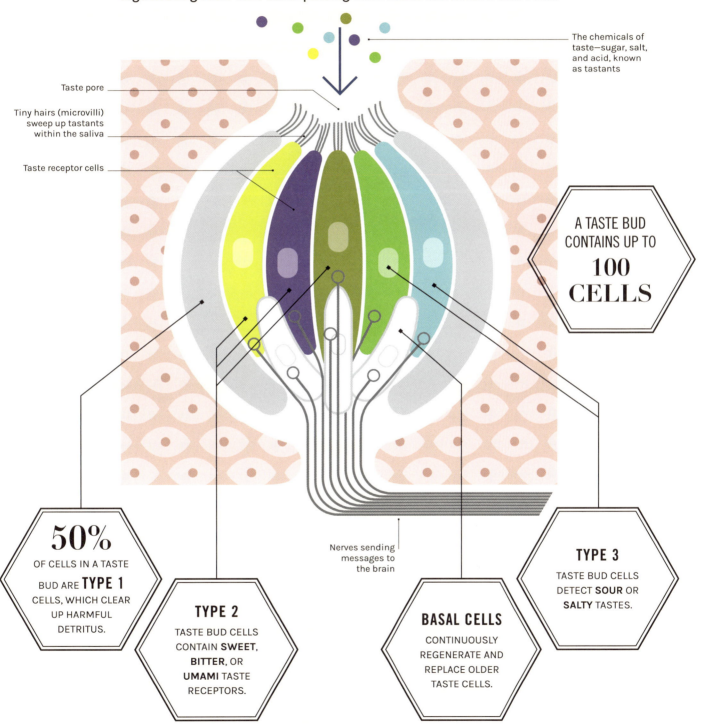

HOW DOES SALT BRING OUR FOOD TO LIFE?

For cooks, salt is probably the single most important ingredient in the kitchen. Used well, it can turn a monochrome meal into a glorious technicolor experience, awakening dormant flavors and bringing richness and complexity.

Salt (sodium chloride) preserves food and causes the proteins in meat, fish, and cheese to break down to produce new umami flavors. Without salt, we wouldn't have some of the world's greatest foods: pickled vegetables, olives, soy sauce, cheese, ham, bacon, and more. Presalting makes scrambled eggs more tender, meats firmer, and vegetables greener and softer when cooked. It draws moisture out, helping foods brown and develop a crust when roasted or fried (pp.74–75). When used to make a brine, salt adds moisture to meats, plumping them up before cooking. In baking, a little salt strengthens gluten, making dough firm and elastic and giving bread a firm, airy structure.

MASKING AND ENHANCING TASTE

Salt masks tastes, and any chemical or metallic tang. It impairs bitterness taste buds—the word "salad" comes from the Latin for salt because Romans used salt to mute the bitterness of leafy greens.

The saltiness sensor

When salt reaches a taste bud, it enters the receptor cell and triggers an electrical impulse to the brain. If salt has been used in the correct amounts, the signal is the low-salt "yum" taste, which is flavor-enhancing and pleasurable and explains why we enjoy eating salty foods.

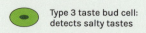

Type 3 taste bud cell: detects salty tastes

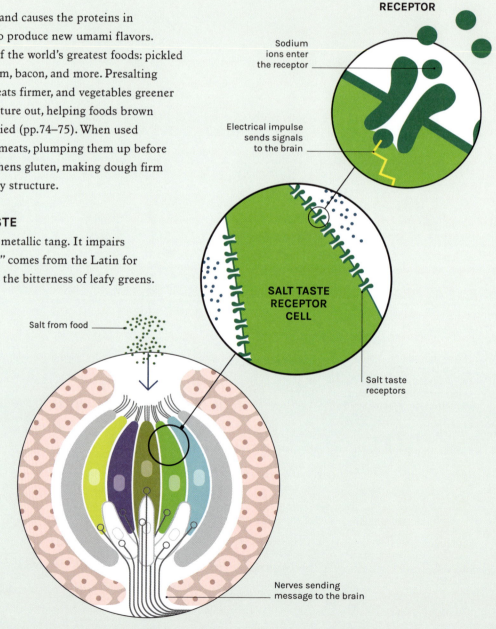

A ROUTE TO FLAVOR 15

TEXTURE
SALT IN BREAD DOUGH STRENGTHENS THE GLUTEN STRANDS SO IT HOLDS CARBON DIOXIDE, CREATING AN AIRY LOAF.

Salt makes foods taste thicker and richer, increasing their savory (umami) qualities, as well as enhancing sweetness, which is why it's often used in cake recipes and added to many processed foods.

DANGERS OF SALT

We taste and enjoy salt because it contains the life-giving mineral sodium. It keeps our fluid levels balanced, our nerves firing, and our muscles contracting. We typically need about half a gram (a small pinch) a day to keep our 9oz (250g) reserves topped off. However, too much salt is dangerous—just 8 teaspoons taken at once would be enough to send an average adult into a coma. For this reason, we have two salt tastes: a low-salt "yum" taste, and a high-salt intensely bitter and metallic taste. Tolerance of salt varies, but liquids saltier than blood (0.8 percent salt or 1.5 teaspoons per quart) usually start to taste unpleasant.

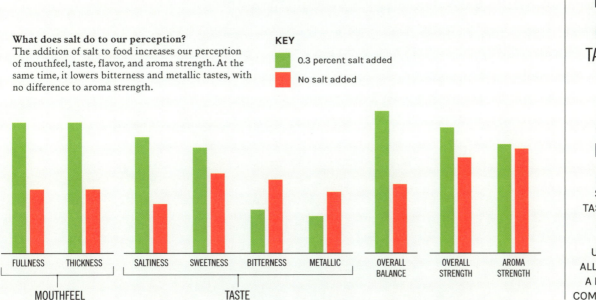

What does salt do to our perception?
The addition of salt to food increases our perception of mouthfeel, taste, flavor, and aroma strength. At the same time, it lowers bitterness and metallic tastes, with no difference to aroma strength.

KEY
- 0.3 percent salt added
- No salt added

NEWBORN BABIES

CANNOT TASTE SALT

IT TAKES

3–6

MONTHS

FOR THEIR SALTINESS TASTE BUDS TO MATURE

UNTIL THEN, ALL THE SODIUM A BABY NEEDS COMES FROM MILK

WHAT KIND OF SALT IS BEST?

Salt can bring out and intensify subtle flavors and even change the texture of food, but why is still not fully understood. The various types don't taste significantly different from each other and which one you use comes down to your preference.

Salts used for cooking can be categorized by grain size (fine and coarse) and whether they are for cooking or finishing. Most household salts are fine-grained and come from ground rock salt mined in its solid form, or from the sea, where it is produced by evaporating seawater, leaving the natural salt behind. This type of salt comes with anti-caking agents to stop clumping, which can make cooking water murky and harsh-tasting. Special pickling salts omit anti-caking additives for this reason, although the amounts are so small that you're unlikely to taste them in a cooked dish. In some regions, table salt also contains iodine or fluoride, which can impart a metallic taste.

Coarse salts have larger grains, making them a favorite with chefs for controlled seasoning as a little can be added at each stage of cooking. Like fine salts, coarse salts can be rock or sea salts. It's worth remembering that saltiness increases as food cools (pp.72–73) so caution is needed when adding it during cooking. Sprinkling coarse or kosher salt with your fingers will give much more control than pouring or using a shaker.

Finishing salts are often sea salts, or others with subtle flavors and colors. The crystals tend to form as thin flakes, and these flaked versions give a delightful crunch and dissolve rapidly on the tongue for a sudden hit of the sea. A selection of finishing salts is summarized opposite.

How to salt

Salt is used to change the texture and flavor of foods. In some foods, salt extracts water, while in others it draws it in. Curing meat and fish in salt reduces bacterial growth so that it can be kept for several months without refrigeration.

KEY

- Salt
- Water molecules

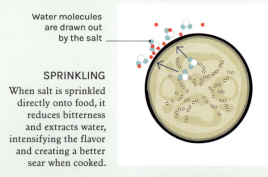

Water molecules are drawn out by the salt

SPRINKLING
When salt is sprinkled directly onto food, it reduces bitterness and extracts water, intensifying the flavor and creating a better sear when cooked.

EGGPLANT SHRINKS

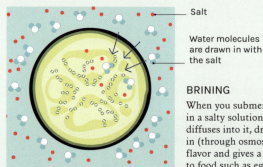

Salt

Water molecules are drawn in with the salt

BRINING
When you submerge an ingredient in a salty solution (brine), the salt diffuses into it, drawing moisture in (through osmosis). This enhances flavor and gives a succulent texture to food such as eggplants.

EGGPLANT SWELLS

Salt types
Salts with subtle flavors are best reserved for finishing, as their flavors and textures are lost in cooking. They are obtained from different sources.

FINISHING SALTS

- **Fleur de sel:** This luxurious French salt has fine, hand-harvested flakes, offering a clean, oceanic flavor. It is formed by evaporating seawater and skimming off the top crust.
- **Gros sel and sel gris:** Hand-harvested from the marshes of Brittany's western coast in France, these salts have granular textures. Gros sel ("large salt") is coarse and used for brining, while clay-colored sel gris ("gray salt") has a moist, crumbly texture. Both are prized for their complex mineral flavors.
- **Maldon sea salt:** This famous British salt is famed for its unique pyramidal crystals, which add crunch and flavor. It has a delicate texture and unique taste and is prized as a finishing salt to add both flavor and a crunchy texture to dishes.

ROCK SALTS

- **Himalayan pink salt:** Recognized for its pink color, it offers a sweet, mineral-rich taste.
- **Persian blue salt:** Harvested from rocky mountains, and unique for its blue shade due to sylvinite, Persian blue salt boasts a crisp taste.
- **Black lava salt:** Blended with edible charcoal, this salt lends an earthy taste and dramatic hue when used to finish dishes.

SMOKED SALTS

Both rock and sea salts can be smoked with a variety of woods (such as hickory, oak, applewood, and so on). These woods release smoky flavors into the salt, which then makes them particularly suitable for seasoning meats.

WHY DO FOODS TASTE SWEET?

Sugar is called a "simple carbohydrate" and works like electricity for your body, coursing through blood to deliver fuel on demand to every muscle and organ as it needs it. In nature, this pure form of energy source is hard to come by—typically being found only in ripe fruits and honey.

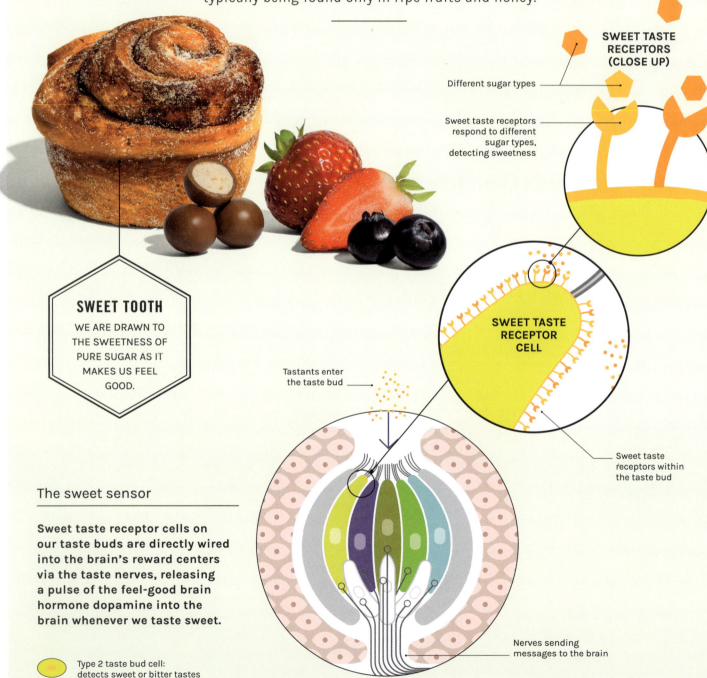

SWEET TASTE RECEPTORS (CLOSE UP)

Different sugar types

Sweet taste receptors respond to different sugar types, detecting sweetness

SWEET TASTE RECEPTOR CELL

Tastants enter the taste bud

Sweet taste receptors within the taste bud

Nerves sending messages to the brain

SWEET TOOTH

WE ARE DRAWN TO THE SWEETNESS OF PURE SUGAR AS IT MAKES US FEEL GOOD.

The sweet sensor

Sweet taste receptor cells on our taste buds are directly wired into the brain's reward centers via the taste nerves, releasing a pulse of the feel-good brain hormone dopamine into the brain whenever we taste sweet.

Type 2 taste bud cell: detects sweet or bitter tastes

A ROUTE TO FLAVOR 19

The building blocks of sugar

Sugars are actually a catalog of different molecules, such as fructose, glucose, and galactose, each activating the sweet taste receptors in a different way and having a different sweetness strength.

KEY
- Fructose
- Glucose
- Galactose

Artificial sweeteners

SYNTHETIC SWEETENERS LIKE ASPARTAME, SUCRALOSE, AND SACCHARIN TASTE 200–600 TIMES SWEETER THAN SUGAR.

They are very different in structure to natural sugar—aspartame, for example, is made up of amino acids, aspartic acid, and phenylalanine—but they still bind to sweet taste receptors, and so taste sweet.

+80% SWEETER THAN SUCROSE

FRUCTOSE

FRUCTOSE
This is the main sugar found in fruits and is in honey and some syrups. The sweetest of all the sugars, fructose is used widely in soft drinks.

MAILLARD NOTES:
Fructose can lead to faster browning (pp.74–75) at lower temperatures than some other sugars. It can produce sweeter, fruitier flavors than glucose.

BASELINE FOR SWEETNESS

SUCROSE

FRUCTOSE + GLUCOSE
Sucrose comes from sugar cane and sugar beet and is the main sugar molecule used in the kitchen. In the body, it splits into glucose and fructose.

NO MAILLARD REACTION:
Unlike other sugar molecules, sucrose does not accelerate Maillard browning.

−20%

GLUCOSE

GLUCOSE
This is the main sugar type in blood; the body converts starches and other sugar types into glucose. It is found in some fruits, vegetables, and honey.

MAILLARD NOTES:
Glucose can accelerate the Maillard reaction, and as it's slightly less sweet than some sugars, it can lead to milder caramel flavors and earthy tastes.

−50%

LACTOSE

GALACTOSE + GLUCOSE
Also called milk sugar, this is found in milk and some dairy products and is made of glucose and galactose. Some people develop intolerances to lactose.

MAILLARD NOTES:
In purified form, lactose is sometimes added to baked goods because of its power to accelerate Maillard browning.

−80% LESS SWEET THAN SUCROSE

MALTOSE

GLUCOSE + GLUCOSE
Also called malt sugar, this is produced by some germinating seeds as they break down their starches (malting). It is used in brewing and malted drinks.

MAILLARD NOTES:
Maltose introduces unique nutty and caramel-like "malty" flavors in the Maillard reaction.

WHY DO WE CRAVE SWEETNESS?

We are all born with a sweet tooth, even if not everyone likes sugary treats. Our built-in love of sweetness has been vital to our survival, first making us long for the sugar in our mother's milk and then driving us to forage for high-energy foods.

Sweet taste receptor cells in our taste buds are directly wired into the brain's reward centers via the taste nerves—but more than that, blood-sugar surges after food trigger a feel-good dopamine hit, making you want more. Age, genetics, and lifestyle are also factors that say whether or not you can easily let the chocolate box pass you by. For example, children and adolescents like their foods a third more sugary than adults. Hunger, blood-sugar levels, and hormone fluctuations during the menstrual cycle can all affect sugar cravings, too. Sweet taste receptors also vary between each person, contributing to how much pleasure sugar gives.

Irresistibly sweet

CORN SYRUP IS PRODUCED THROUGH THE BREAKDOWN OF CORN STARCH INTO SIMPLER SUGARS, PRIMARILY GLUCOSE. The resultant thick, sweet liquid can be chemically processed further, converting some of the glucose into fructose, and boosting its sweetness to create high-fructose corn syrup. There are widespread health concerns around consuming high levels of fructose as it can contribute to obesity.

WHITE SUGARS

These are refined from beet or sugar cane and are over 99 percent sucrose, offering very pure sweetness. White sugars vary in texture and grain size: granulated sugar has a medium grain (0.3–0.5 mm crystal size), suitable for general purpose cooking. Caster sugar is finer with 0.1–0.3 mm crystals, ideal for delicate cakes, meringues, and soufflés, while powdered sugar is smoother still (0.01–0.1 mm grains), containing small amounts of an anti-caking agent to prevent clumping.

BROWN SUGARS

Brown sugar is mostly sucrose crystals (85 percent or more) coated with molasses. Molasses is a thick syrup from sugar cane, known for its robust, bittersweet flavor. Refined brown sugar has molasses added back, while natural brown sugar retains its original molasses. Crystal size and flavor vary, from crunchy demerara to earthy muscovado.

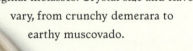

100 AROMA COMPOUNDS IN MOLASSES GIVE BROWN SUGAR ITS BITTER, CARAMEL FLAVORS.

A ROUTE TO FLAVOR 21

Syrups and natural sources of sugar

Sugars are made of different molecules, each activating the sweet taste receptor differently and with a different sweetness strength. The sweet taste of ingredients such as syrup and honey is based on the amount and types of sugars they contain.

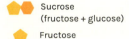

SWEETNESS KEY

- Sucrose (fructose + glucose)
- Fructose
- Glucose
- Other sugars
- Water

40–60% SWEETER TASTE

20–50% SWEETER TASTE

30% LESS SWEET TASTE

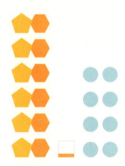

GRANULATED SUGAR
99+% SUCROSE

FLAVOR NOTES
Pure sweetness

AROMA COMPOUNDS
None

USES
Sweetening | Baking
Sauces | Dressings

HONEY
40% FRUCTOSE
30% GLUCOSE | 17% WATER
13% OTHER SUGARS, INCLUDING MALTOSE AND SUCROSE

FLAVOR NOTES
Floral, fruity, spicy, or earthy, depending on the nectar source

AROMA COMPOUNDS
Benzaldehyde and furfural (almond), isovaleraldehyde (apple), linalool (floral)

USES
Sweetening | Glazing
Baking | Sauces | Dressings

AGAVE SYRUP
56–92% FRUCTOSE, GLUCOSE, AND WATER

FLAVOR NOTES
Mild, slightly floral or vanilla-like

AROMA COMPOUNDS
Vanillin (vanilla), hydroxybutanone (buttery), linalool (floral)

USES
Sweetening beverages
Baking | Vegan cooking

MAPLE SYRUP
68% SUCROSE
31% WATER
1% OTHER SUGARS

FLAVOR NOTES
Woody, caramel, vanilla

AROMA COMPOUNDS
Pyrazines (roasty, nutty), vanillin, hydroxyacetone/acetol (caramel)

USES
Pancakes | Waffles
Glazing | Baking
Sweetening beverages

WHAT IS BITTERNESS?

Bitterness is the tongue's warning sign telling us not to swallow because what is in the mouth could be poisonous. For some food types, such as coffee, dark chocolate, and olives, many of us overcome this natural aversion to their bitterness.

Most toxic plants or berries are bitter, making our dislike of bitter tastes a life-saving screening tool. However, other bitter substances can be good for us in moderation, such as the harsh flavonoids in tea, and some bitter-tasting foods are known to aid digestion and stimulate the immune system.

Bitterness is a complex taste that interacts with other tastes in different ways; understanding these interactions can help us balance flavors. Bitterness and sweetness are natural partners, moderating one another—for example, when combined in dark chocolate desserts. The interaction between bitterness and acidity is more complicated: when adding acids (like lemon juice) to sauces in small amounts, it can enhance a bitter taste, but as you add more, it will become too sour and lose the bitter taste. Fat can also affect bitter-tasting foods. Large fat molecules trap bitter compounds, dulling their effect. This is seen in dishes using creamy dairy products such as tiramisu, in which bitter coffee is softened by high-fat mascarpone and cream.

Bitter tastes

Sweet, salty, sour, and umami tastes each come from a single taste receptor that detects one or a small handful of substances. Bitter tastes are detected by at least 25 receptors that work together to prevent possible toxins from entering the body.

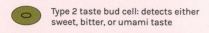

Type 2 taste bud cell: detects either sweet, bitter, or umami taste

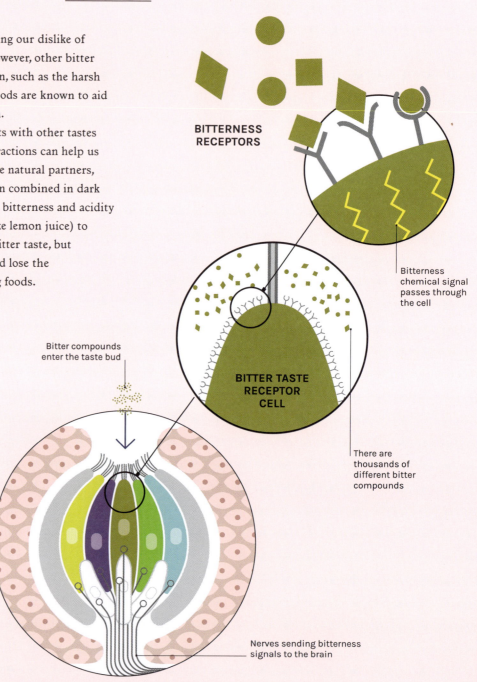

BITTERNESS RECEPTORS

Bitterness chemical signal passes through the cell

Bitter compounds enter the taste bud

BITTER TASTE RECEPTOR CELL

There are thousands of different bitter compounds

Nerves sending bitterness signals to the brain

A ROUTE TO FLAVOR **23**

COMPOUNDS
IN CACAO, INCLUDING THEOBROMINE AND FLAVONOLS, BRING BITTERNESS TO CHOCOLATE.

GINGER PEEL
CAN BE BITTER. TRIM IT OR TEMPER WITH SWEET, ACID, OR CREAMY FOODS.

BRUSSELS SPROUTS
ARE PARTICULARLY RICH IN SULFUR-CONTAINING BITTER COMPOUNDS.

BITTER
COMPOUNDS CALLED GLUCOSINATES ARE PRESENT IN RADICCHIO, ENDIVES, AND OTHER BRASSICAS.

Bitter-tasting foods derive their flavor from various chemical compounds. Many people develop a preference for these foods later in life (pp.60–61).

HOW CAN I USE BITTERNESS IN COOKING?

We don't usually want bitterness to be the dominant taste in a dish, but adding a background of bitterness works perfectly in sweet dishes as well as in rich, fatty, and highly flavored dishes. Mastering how and when to do this is key.

You are probably aware of some ways that bitterness can be used to balance flavors in food. The weighty bitterness of dark chocolate or coffee with sugar is a classic sweet-bitter marriage, and if you add sugar or cream to your coffee, then you are already familiar with the delicate art of balancing bitterness with sweet and/or fat. There are, however, many other ways of using bitter flavors when cooking.

KNOWING YOUR INGREDIENTS

While the essence of bitterness is the same in all ingredients, its duration and quality can vary significantly. Tannins, the large molecules that give a dry, puckering sensation (pp.204-205), impart a bitter taste. Those found in red wines and black tea in particular tend to linger longer than most other bitter compounds. Similarly, alcohol can create a lingering effect by both activating bitter taste receptors and producing a warming or burning sensation in the back of the throat (pp.214–215). Hops (the dried flowers of the hop plant), once added to beers for their preservative qualities, are now mainly used for flavoring. They contain intensely bitter alpha acids that often leave a lingering aftertaste. Grapefruits contain a potent bitter-tasting substance called naringin, especially in pale-colored varieties. Use these long-lasting bitter ingredients sparingly, particularly in rich dishes that also feature sweet, sour, and salty elements, to avoid the bitterness overwhelming other tastes.

TIMING AND SIZE MATTER

How and when you add bitterness to a food affects how it is experienced in the mouth: adding spices,

BEFORE COOKING
INFUSE SPICES, RED WINE, OR BAY LEAVES IN SAUCES FOR A GENTLE BITTERNESS.

DURING COOKING
CARAMELIZATION CREATES RICH, BITTER FLAVORS THAT BRING COMPLEXITY.

AFTER COOKING
ADD LEMON ZEST OR MATCHA FOR CONTRASTING BRIGHT BITTER NOTES.

When to add bitterness
You can add bitter flavors to a dish at any stage of the cooking process, with different results.

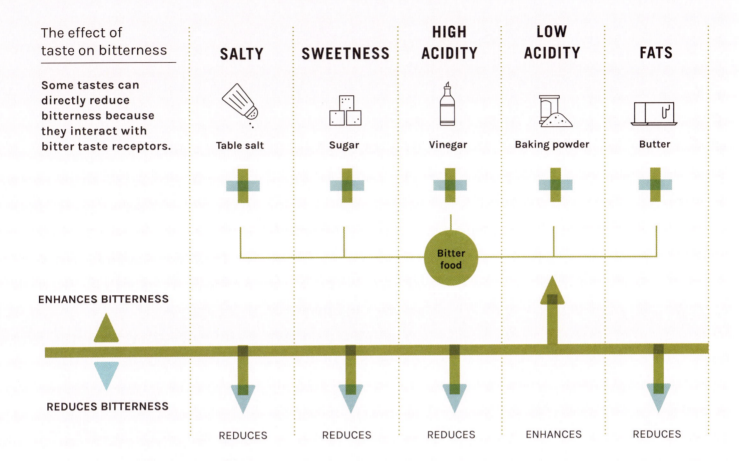

red wine, or bay leaves to sauces gently ups the bitterness throughout a dish. Coffee and cocoa rubbed on roasted red meats are delightful, adding a delicious, flavor-paired coat of bitterness. Similarly, a dusting of green tea or matcha over the surface of an ice cream gives an initial hit of intense bitterness, followed by a longer-lived, more mouth-filling experience. If these ingredients were incorporated from an early stage and worked throughout the ice cream, the effect would be different. The size of a vegetable also affects the experience of bitterness: bite-sized chunks offer a palate-cleansing burst, whereas thinly sliced (chiffonade) greens give a subtler contrast. You can also consider adding kale, bitter greens, endive, or chicory to a stew or curry for contrasting bites of bitterness, adding delightful complexity of flavor.

CREATING BITTERNESS

As well as using ingredients, we can also introduce bitterness in the cooking method. Maillard browning (pp.74–77) and the caramelization of sugars (pp.78–79) both introduce bitter undertones; the further you push these processes, the greater the bitterness. Charring the surface of food or cooking sugar down to a dark caramel can also be used to offset some sweetness, for example, by lightly charring meat or vegetables that will then be dressed with a sweet relish, or by blowtorching the sugar on top of a crème brûlée.

WHAT IS UMAMI?

Today, the word "umami" (from the Japanese for "deliciousness") is common in food writing, but it wasn't until 2002 that it was acknowledged as the fifth basic taste. However, we can trace a knowledge of umami back to antiquity.

As long ago as the fifth century BCE, ancient Romans used a fermented fish sauce, garum, as their go-to flavor-enhancing condiment. In 1825, the French food writer Jean-Anthelme Brillat-Savarin noticed something that was giving his meat broth an unmistakeable meatiness, but it was neither sweet, acid, nor bitter. He called it "osmazône." Then in 1908, Japanese scientist Kikunae Ikeda extracted pure umami from a kelp broth as tiny white crystals of glutamate (monosodium glutamate, known as MSG). However, it took nearly a century for scientists in the Western world to accept that and recognize it officially.

AN ESSENTIAL NUTRIENT

Umami flags up to our body that a food contains an essential nutrient for life—in this case, protein. Many people say they don't know what umami tastes like; this is because they were never told that it existed. Western cultures learn the names for sweet, sour, salty, and bitter but not savoriness. All babies know umami—from a very young age, they will squeal with delight if they get some on their tongue—and breast milk has a strong umami tang.

UMAMI RECEPTORS

The taste receptors for umami are on the tips of the same taste bud cell type (type 2) that senses bitter and sweet (pp.12–13). When food containing umami molecules reaches these taste receptors, they send a signal to the brain so we know we are eating protein fragments. Glutamate is one of the 20 building blocks (called amino acids) of protein and is the main driver of umami taste.

Mushrooms are a rich source of umami—the darker, the better. Adding mushrooms in any form to a dish will add an umami lift.

A ROUTE TO FLAVOR 27

Protein disintegration

Meats and some vegetables naturally contain some glutamate in varying amounts, but to liberate more, their proteins need to be broken down. Cooking is the most basic way to do this, while drying, aging, ripening, and fermenting allow time for proteins to be dismantled, sending glutamate levels soaring.

NO TASTE
PROTEIN CHAIN (20 AMINO ACID TYPES)

**RIPENING
COOKING
CURING
FERMENTING**

PROTEIN CHAIN BREAKS, RELEASING AMINO ACIDS

TASTE
AMINO ACIDS CAN ACTIVATE TASTE RECEPTORS

Catching umami

Umami molecular sensors wait for a molecule called glutamate to pass by. When the molecular sensor snaps shut around a glutamate, an electrical signal hurtles toward the brain along a nerve at the cell's base and travels with the other taste messages into the brain's flavor center (pp.48–49).

 Type 2 taste bud cell: detects sweet, bitter, and umami tastes

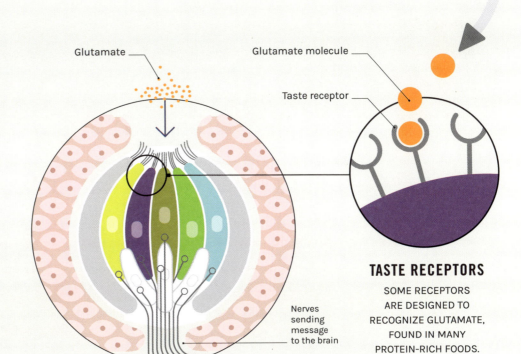

Glutamate

Glutamate molecule

Taste receptor

Nerves sending message to the brain

TASTE RECEPTORS
SOME RECEPTORS ARE DESIGNED TO RECOGNIZE GLUTAMATE, FOUND IN MANY PROTEIN-RICH FOODS.

HOW CAN I ENHANCE UMAMI?

Umami gives foods a comforting, healthy taste. As well as enhancing all the other flavors in a dish, it brings its own taste dimension, while also dialing down sourness and bitterness.

As well as glutamate-rich foods, the umami taste sensation makes us enjoy eating other nourishing foodstuffs, such as oily fish, mushrooms, and certain vegetables. The three substances that amplify umami (inosinate, IMP; guanylate, GMP; and adenylate, AMP, a less potent intensifier) are called ribonucleotides—the digested parts of a plant or animal's genetic machinery. These molecules cause the mouth of the umami taste receptor to clamp down even tighter around a captured glutamate, sending a magnified umami signal into the brain. This doesn't just increase umami, but multiplies the signal's strength manyfold, sending tastiness soaring.

From a splash of soy sauce in your stir-fry to a dollop of miso in your caramel sauce, or a dusting of Parmesan cheese over fresh fruit, it's easy to add umami. For pure umami, add monosodium glutamate (MSG). It enhances flavor like salt and can be used in a similar way. For maximum flavor, you should replace about a third of the salt you would normally add with MSG.

Umami intensifiers

NO GLUTAMATE

A taste receptor with no glutamate remains open.

TASTE RECEPTOR WITH NO GLUTAMATE HAS NOTHING TO CATCH SO THERE IS NO UMAMI

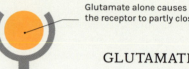

Glutamate alone causes the receptor to partly close

GLUTAMATE

FOUND IN SEAWEED, ONIONS, CARROTS, GREEN ONIONS, GINGER, AND MORE

Inosinate (IMP) amplifies umami and causes the receptor to fully close

INOSINATE + GLUTAMATE

FOUND IN MEATS LIKE BEEF AND FISH, INCLUDING TUNA AND SARDINES

Guanylate (GMP) amplifies umami and causes the receptor to fully close

GUANYLATE + GLUTAMATE

FOUND IN MUSHROOMS (SHIITAKE, PORCINI) AND PLANTS; SMALL AMOUNTS IN MEATS LIKE PORK

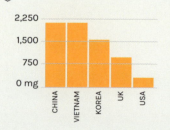

Consumption (mg) per person per day of MSG: The statistics speak for themselves—the use of MSG in cooking is significantly higher in Asian cultures than the West.

Don't fear MSG

THE GLUTAMATE IN MSG IS NO DIFFERENT FROM THAT IN CHEESE, BEEF, SEAWEED, OR ANY OTHER UMAMI-RICH INGREDIENT.
Dubbed "Chinese restaurant syndrome" after a doctor complained about symptoms experienced when he ate Chinese food in 1968, the medical world soon spread the word that MSG caused all manner of ills, including headaches and palpitations. All have since been proven untrue, yet the stigma remains.

A ROUTE TO FLAVOR 29

JAPANESE	ITALIAN	CHINESE
THIS COMBINATION CREATES DASHI STOCK/BROTH, WHICH FORMS THE BASIS OF MANY JAPANESE DISHES.	THIS CLASSIC PASSATA AND BEEF MIX FORMS THE BASIS OF POPULAR DISHES SUCH AS BOLOGNESE.	SOY SAUCE, CHICKEN, AND MUSHROOMS ARE COMBINED IN DISHES SUCH AS CHICKEN STIR-FRY.
↓	↓	↓
KOMBU SEAWEED	TOMATO PURÉE	SOY SAUCE
+	+	+
DRIED BONITO	GROUND BEEF	CHICKEN
+	+	+
SHIITAKE MUSHROOMS	PARMESAN CHEESE	CHINESE BLACK MUSHROOMS
↓	↓	↓
DASHI STOCK/BROTH	BOLOGNESE SAUCE	CHICKEN STIR-FRY

Umami-rich

DARK SOY SAUCE
(1,000–1,700mg glutamate/100g)
A staple in many cuisines for adding depth and saltiness.

PARMESAN CHEESE
(1,200–1,680mg glutamate/100g)
Grate it over pasta, salads, and some sweet dishes.

MISO PASTE
(200–700mg glutamate/100g)
Works well in sauces, soups, and marinades.

TOMATO PURÉE
(700mg glutamate/100g)
Adds richness and acid to stews, sauces, and soups.

DRIED SHIITAKE
(1,060mg glutamate/100g)
Use in soups and stews.

FISH SAUCE
(300–1,500mg glutamate/100g)
Common in Southeast Asian cooking to add depth of flavor.

ANCHOVIES
(630mg glutamate/100g)
Can be worked into sauces or used as a base for dressings.

KELP SEAWEED
(1,600–3,000mg glutamate/100g)
Use dried in stocks and soups or fresh in salads or stir-fries.

KOMBU SEAWEED
(300–3,000mg glutamate/100g)
Use in soups or salads for umami earthiness and briny tang.

NUTRITIONAL YEAST
(2,800mg glutamate/100g)
Popular among vegans, it has a cheeselike umami flavor.

DRY-CURED HAMS
(340mg glutamate/100g)
Adds a flavorful, salty umami element.

WHAT IS SOURNESS?

When we think of sour-tasting food, we imagine the mouth-puckering shock of licking a lemon. This reaction has evolved to protect us from harm because sour tastes are a warning for harmful foods, which may be spoiled or corrosive to teeth.

The sourness sensor

Acids have an abundance of tiny particles called hydrogen ions. These trigger sourness receptors inside taste buds, rushing in through the receptor channel and setting off an electrical taste signal to the brain.

- Type 3 taste bud cell: detects sour or salt tastes

- Hydrogen ions (from acid)
- Sour taste receptor
- Electric signals sent to the brain

SOUR TASTE RECEPTOR

- The taste is picked up by the type 3 taste bud cells
- Hydrogen ions from acidic food enter taste bud

SOUR TASTE RECEPTOR CELL

- Nerves sending sour messages to the brain

Sour ingredients get us salivating like no other taste, because the body tries to dilute the acid they contain to protect the enamel on our teeth. More saliva in the mouth means added flavor and taste—more flavor compounds slide over the tongue and are released into the nose. Unlike other taste receptors that stand tall with open mouths waiting for a passing taste substance, the sour taste receptors only pick up acid particles—hydrogen ions—before sending a sourness signal brainward.

Our natural reaction when we taste milk that has gone off is to involuntarily flinch and spit it out. However, when this is accompanied by the buttery aroma of lactic acid that comes from friendly bacteria that ferment milk into yogurt, we can enjoy it as a pleasant counterpoint to the sweetness of a strawberry. Similarly, we can learn to associate a nose-cleansing whiff of malt vinegar with salt and vinegar–flavored chips.

The powerful zingy refreshment of freshly squeezed lemon juice and the tang of a sour fruit sweet are a joy, but acid can also be used to bring brightness to a dish. Purified acid has no aroma compounds, hence distilled vinegar (acetic acid) is pure sourness. Other acids have flavor compounds. If these are added before serving, their flavors shine through vividly, whereas more are lost if added early. Add acids early into cooking to infuse stronger flavors throughout the dish and to use their other culinary effects. Reserve richly flavored balsamic vinegars for finishing to let them shine. Use sourness to balance sweet, bitter, and umami and cut through fattiness: a squeeze of lemon juice added just before serving can offset any oiliness; a late dusting of sumac can give brightness to grilled meats; while a dollop of yogurt added after cooking can cut through the fattiness in a heavy curry or stew. Acid can also reduce bitterness—try a couple of drops of lemon juice in a cup of coffee for a drink with a smoother finish or a drizzle of vinaigrette over bitter leaves.

How acidic?

A one-point difference in pH is a tenfold difference in acidity. Lemons are a hundred times more acidic than oranges; Granny Smith apples, ten times more acidic. Understanding acidity helps balance flavors.

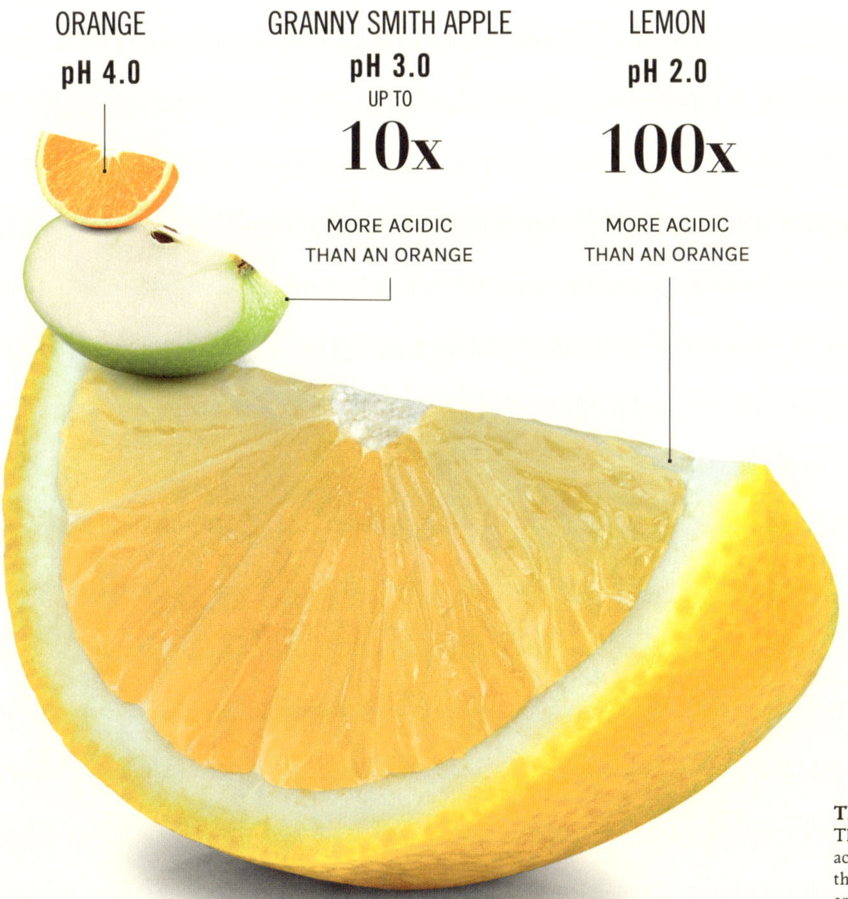

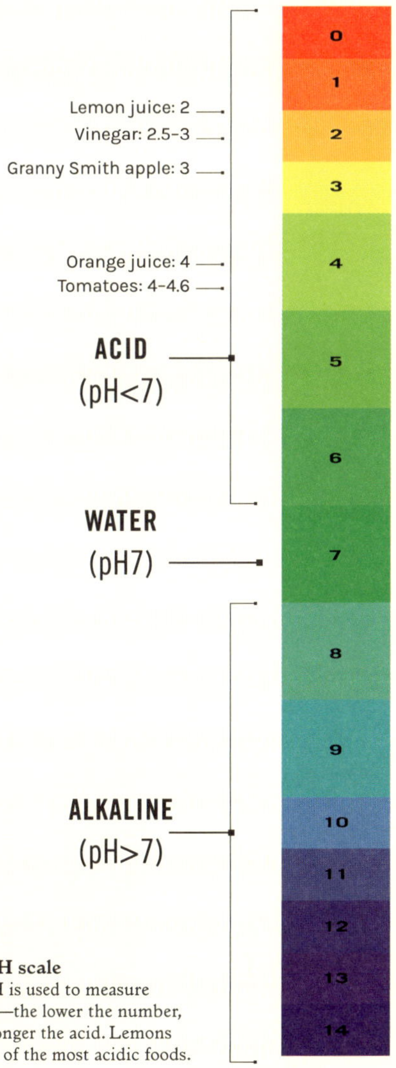

ORANGE
pH 4.0

GRANNY SMITH APPLE
pH 3.0
UP TO
10x
MORE ACIDIC
THAN AN ORANGE

LEMON
pH 2.0
100x
MORE ACIDIC
THAN AN ORANGE

Lemon juice: 2
Vinegar: 2.5-3
Granny Smith apple: 3

Orange juice: 4
Tomatoes: 4-4.6

ACID
(pH<7)

WATER
(pH7)

ALKALINE
(pH>7)

The pH scale
The pH is used to measure acidity—the lower the number, the stronger the acid. Lemons are one of the most acidic foods.

HOW CAN I COOK WITH ACIDS?

A dash of acid in the form of citrus juice or vinegar can transform a dish. Like salt, acids are potent flavor enhancers, shining a light on flavors that are blurred and bringing each component to the fore.

Acids aren't just important for flavor; they have the power to chemically tinker with almost every culinary process. Acids will "cook" meat and fish by breaking down their muscle fibers and proteins, as is seen in fish ceviche, and acidic marinades and sauces left on meat will first toughen then soften the surface as proteins are coagulated and broken down.

Acids likewise coagulate egg proteins—a glug of vinegar makes poached eggs less stringy and a few tablespoons of lemon juice when whisking makes scrambled eggs fluffier and meringues lighter and higher. They also "cook" milk proteins, curdling milk, yogurt, and cream, so add to dairy sauces just before serving to avoid this problem.

STARCHES

Acids strengthen the glue (called hemicellulose) that holds plants together, toughening vegetables cooked in acidic water and lengthening their cooking time. In jam-making, acids help another plant glue, pectin, set into a firm jelly. Acids also break down starches, making sauces thinner and helping to separate cooked pasta.

COLORS AND CARAMELIZATION

By destroying chlorophyll, acids turn green vegetables a dull color if cooked in acidic water, although they strengthen red pigments, making cherries and red cabbage bolder and more vibrant.

Acid: the multitasking ingredient

Acidic ingredients can be used in many ways, serving as powerful flavor enhancers when added in small amounts and cutting through fattiness in larger amounts. Here are some of their uses.

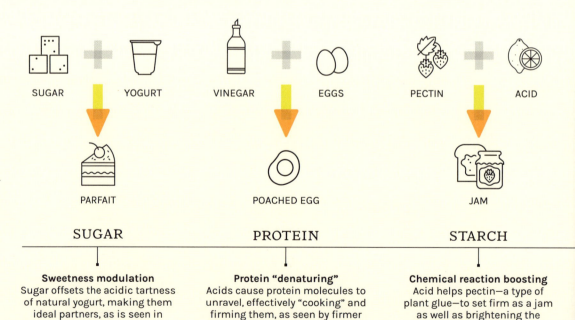

SUGAR + YOGURT → PARFAIT

VINEGAR + EGGS → POACHED EGG

PECTIN + ACID → JAM

SUGAR

Sweetness modulation
Sugar offsets the acidic tartness of natural yogurt, making them ideal partners, as is seen in fruit parfaits.

PROTEIN

Protein "denaturing"
Acids cause protein molecules to unravel, effectively "cooking" and firming them, as seen by firmer poached eggs in acidified water.

STARCH

Chemical reaction boosting
Acid helps pectin—a type of plant glue—to set firm as a jam as well as brightening the natural pigments.

A ROUTE TO FLAVOR **33**

Acid slows the Maillard reaction (pp.74–75), meaning fried and grilled foods are paler and less flavorful. Conversely, it slows sugar caramelization and prevents crystals from forming, resulting in a smoother caramel (pp.78–79).

ALKALI FOODS

Alkaline ingredients like baking powder work in the opposite way to acid. In baking, baking soda fizzes carbon dioxide gas when mixed with an acid (cream of tartar, buttermilk, or lemon juice), making the bake rise. Elsewhere, it brightens green vegetables but makes them mushy, and speeds up the Maillard reaction to make onions "caramelize" faster and meats and vegetables fry or roast a deeper brown.

ALKALIS

The anti-acids
Alkalis neutralize acids and accelerate browning. A little baking powder added to a meat rub results in a crispier finish.

VITAMIN C

HUMANS MAY LOVE ACIDIC CITRUS FRUITS BECAUSE THEY CONTAIN VITAMIN C, WHICH IS BENEFICIAL TO HEALTH.

WHAT IS MOUTHFEEL?

Our mouths contain an astonishing array of sensory equipment, primed and ready to detect texture. The sensations of food or drink in our mouth combine to create what we call the "mouthfeel"—another cornerstone of flavor.

The mouth holds a canopy of microscopic sensors, from the tip of the tongue to the back of the hard palate, all sending signals to the brain to create an experience of flavor (pp.10–11). A suite of acutely sensitive feelers allows us to experience food's texture: whether it's rough, dry toast; a smooth wheat noodle; hard, brittle candy; a soft lettuce leaf; crunchy popcorn; or mushy mashed potato. Usually, it's only if the texture seems wrong or fails to meet our expectations that we notice it: soggy bread, limp carrots, or mushy apples, for example. In fact, not liking a texture is one of the main reasons we turn our nose up at a dish. Textural preferences are extremely personal—research suggests that each of us gravitate toward one of four mouthfeel camps. So-called "chewers" often like chewing gum; "crunchers" adore chips and flaky pastry; those who delight in the creaminess of yogurt and ice cream are "smooshers"; while "suckers" are hard candy fans who enjoy savoring food for a long time.

INTO THE MOUTH

ONCE FOOD PASSES YOUR LIPS, A CONSTELLATION OF SENSORS SPRINGS INTO ACTION TO SENSE ITS TEXTURE.

Sensing texture, creating mouthfeel

No other part of our body has such a rich forest of sensitive nerves as the mouth. Small, invisible sensors line every surface and each is attuned to a different sense—all of these mouthfeel signals are sent to the brain where they converge with those of taste and aroma to create flavor.

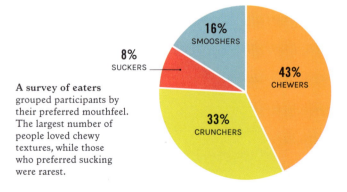

A survey of eaters grouped participants by their preferred mouthfeel. The largest number of people loved chewy textures, while those who preferred sucking were rarest.

- 43% CHEWERS
- 33% CRUNCHERS
- 16% SMOOSHERS
- 8% SUCKERS

A ROUTE TO FLAVOR 35

Just behind the teeth, the rugae palate is a hard, bumpy portion of the roof of your mouth. Crisscrossed with nerve endings, it is exquisitely sensitive, like your fingertips.

THE PALATE
LIKE THE TONGUE, THE ROOF OF THE MOUTH IS COVERED IN SENSORS, WITH NERVES TO DETECT TOUCH, VIBRATION, TEMPERATURE, AND PAIN.

Toward the rear of the palate, the smooth post rugae is less sensitive but still critical for creating an overall impression of mouthfeel, with receptors for light touch and temperature.

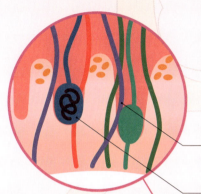

Free nerve endings sense temperature, pain, and light touch

Meissner's corpuscle detects vibrations and light touch

RUGAE (WRINKLED) PALATE

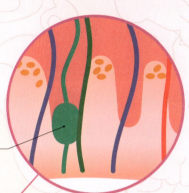

Neuronal densities detect light touch and stretch

POST RUGAE

Starburst cells surrounding taste buds are important for experiencing texture and mouthfeel

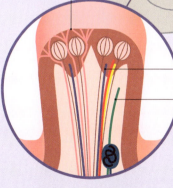

Pain-sensing free nerve ending

Temperature-sensing free nerve ending

FUNGIFORM PAPILLAE

Scattered across the tip and sides of the tongue, there are papillae (bumps) containing taste buds with receptors for taste, as well as nerve endings sensing vibration, temperature, touch, and pain.

THE TONGUE
THE TONGUE IS COVERED IN TINY BUMPS (PAPILLAE), MOST OF WHICH SENSE TEXTURE, NOT TASTE. THE TONGUE PROBES FOOD, FORMING ITS MOUTHFEEL.

Merkel cells detect the pressure, edges, and roughness of food

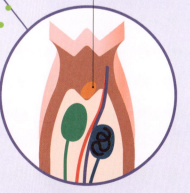

FILIFORM PAPILLAE

Covering the tongue's central surface, filiform papillae do not taste but sense texture through clusters of specialized cells, nerve endings, and receptors for touch, pain, temperature, and pressure.

HOW DOES TEXTURE BOOST FLAVOR?

Our palates are attuned to a vast array of textures—dry, juicy, sticky, creamy, oily, fibrous, stringy, gritty, crispy, crunchy, and more. Texture creates flavor not only in the physical process of eating but in associations in our imaginations, too.

If an ingredient has lost its original texture, then the flavor illusion can fracture, rendering each mouthful bland. Understanding how texture, mouthfeel, and flavor affect one another can springboard your culinary skills. For example, making a ketchup that is chunky rather than smooth will intensify its flavor. Adding vanilla to a creamy dessert will make it feel creamier, and adding cream to a hot dish will make it seem cooler. Adding roughness to a food enhances sourness (think sweets coated in rough sugar).

Adding sweetness to a thick, sticky food will make it feel thicker, while making it more sour will give it a thinner mouthfeel. Putting soft chips in the oven to restore their crunch will give them a fresh flavor. Melting a solid ingredient into a liquid will liberate more flavor compounds and intensify aroma and taste: thinning a gravy will allow more aromatic molecules to vaporize, boosting flavor. Adding fat

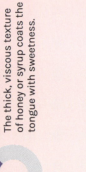

STICKINESS
The thick, viscous texture of honey or syrup coats the tongue with sweetness.

RICHNESS
Brittle chocolate gives way to creamy, bitter richness as the flakes melt.

CRUNCH
Crunching on toasted cereal clusters highlights their nutty, roasted notes.

CRISPNESS
Toasted, slivered almonds release their powerful nutty aroma compounds with each bite.

CHEWINESS
Soft, plump raisins bring a treat in every mouthful and linger on the palate.

CREAMINESS
Mouth-coating full-fat yogurt brings luxurious silkiness.

JUICINESS
The burst of sharp, sweet berry juices creates a refreshing, mouthwatering sensation.

SOFTNESS
Soaked chia seeds and grains such as oats add body to a light breakfast.

= **THE PERFECT BOWLFUL**

will increase moistness, hence why lean, fat-free meats like turkey breast taste dry despite having the same water content as other meats.

Each culture has mastered ways of manipulating the texture and mouthfeel of ingredients through techniques that include deep frying, pickling, slicing, blanching, steaming, and making confits. Learning how to combine ingredients to meet your perfect textural preferences is a mix of art and science.

CRISPNESS AND CRUNCH ARE ASSOCIATED WITH TASTINESS AROUND THE WORLD. THE JAPANESE LANGUAGE HAS

7

DIFFERENT TERMS MEANING

CRISP

Cereal science

We usually prefer foods with a number of different textures over those with a single texture, so it is important to vary textures within a dish to add interest and boost enjoyment.

WHY DO WE NEED FAT?

Anthony Bourdain once famously wrote that butter is "almost always the first and last thing a chef puts in the pan." The unglamorous secret behind the tastiest foods is often that oodles of fat, especially butter, can make most things taste sublime.

Fat on the tongue

Fat receptors on the tongue send signals to the brain, making food appealing. One receptor is a protein that can bind to fatty acids, the building blocks of fat.

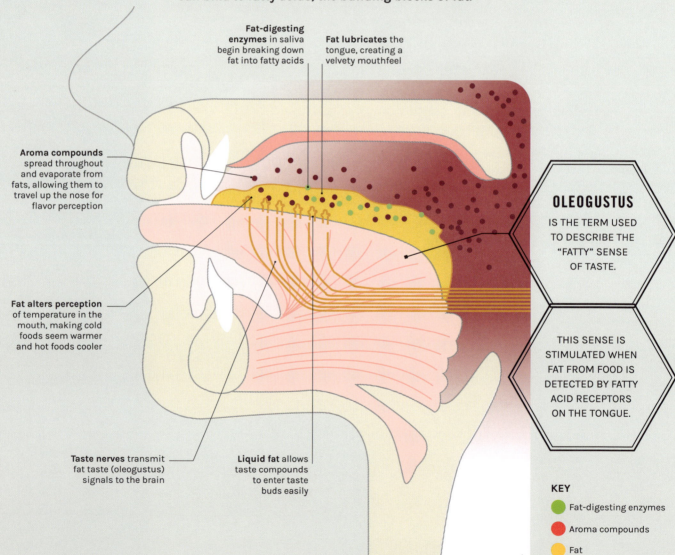

Fat-digesting enzymes in saliva begin breaking down fat into fatty acids

Fat lubricates the tongue, creating a velvety mouthfeel

Aroma compounds spread throughout and evaporate from fats, allowing them to travel up the nose for flavor perception

Fat alters perception of temperature in the mouth, making cold foods seem warmer and hot foods cooler

Taste nerves transmit fat taste (oleogustus) signals to the brain

Liquid fat allows taste compounds to enter taste buds easily

OLEOGUSTUS IS THE TERM USED TO DESCRIBE THE "FATTY" SENSE OF TASTE.

THIS SENSE IS STIMULATED WHEN FAT FROM FOOD IS DETECTED BY FATTY ACID RECEPTORS ON THE TONGUE.

KEY
- Fat-digesting enzymes
- Aroma compounds
- Fat

We are programmed to crave fat. It is the densest, most calorie-rich fuel our bodies can get; if we hadn't evolved to hanker for and gorge on fat-filled foods, then our ancestors would have perished when famine came. Fat is one arm of the unholy trinity of fat, sugar, and salt, which we are all drawn to and which junk food is brimming with.

Our taste buds can't be duped when it comes to fat. Despite food manufacturers' best efforts, low-fat versions are usually an unsatisfying replica of the real thing, no matter how much sugar, salt, and flavorings they add. Scientists now know that this is partly because there are fat receptors on the tongue, potentially making it the sixth basic taste (called oleogustus) alongside sweet, salt, bitter, sour, and umami. These molecular sensors on the tongue (especially toward the back) detect molecules called fatty acids—the building blocks of fats.

A FLAVOR ESSENTIAL

As well as a taste, fat carries flavor. Most flavor compounds dissolve and disperse in oil, but not water, making fat essential for flavors to permeate a dish. Compounds like cinnamaldehyde in cinnamon and anethole in fennel are examples of flavor compounds carried in their essential oils—tiny droplets found in plant seeds and stems. Flavors in meats like beef mainly come from the animal fat during cooking (pp.146–147).

MOUTHFEEL AND TEXTURE

Of all culinary ingredients, fats hold the most power to alter a dish's mouthfeel. Without adding fat, a luxurious, velvety mouthfeel is almost impossible. The reason that meats such as turkey can be dry once cooked isn't due to a lack of moisture but rather a lack of fat. A cake or a cookie without fat will similarly have a dry, powdery crumb. Fat also moderates how hot or cold food feels in the mouth—making cold foods, like ice cream, seem less cold, and hot dishes, such as stews, cooler.

COOKING

An oil is simply a fat that is liquid at room temperature and is often essential for cooking at the high temperatures needed for the Maillard reaction (pp.74–77). Commonly used oils are olive oil or sunflower oil. Battered food dropped into a pan of very hot oil will sizzle and puff up with trapped steam to create a voluminous crunchy, golden-brown crust. Conversely, adding watery ingredients into a hot frying pan will plunge the temperature to below 212°F (100°C)—the boiling point of water—stalling further browning.

Fat in cooking

Oils serve as a pan's "thermal interface," through which heat can evenly pass into food. Using more oil creates crunchier, tastier flavors, although it isn't the healthiest option.

WITHOUT OIL
When you add food to a hot pan without oil, heat passes into food only where it touches the pan and can scorch it.

WITH SHALLOW OIL
This method means that the heat is distributed around the pan and the food becomes evenly browned.

DEEP FRIED IN OIL
Cooking food fully submerged in oil gives a crispy exterior while keeping the moisture of the food inside.

WHAT FATS SHOULD I USE?

There are dozens of different kinds of fats that can be used in cooking. These can be divided into saturated and unsaturated fats, depending on whether they are solid or liquid at room temperature.

Your choice of fat depends on the flavor you want to achieve and your cooking method.

SMOKE POINT

Oil gets much hotter than water can, but it has a limit. At its "smoke point," acrid black fumes are given off as fat molecules are ripped apart in the heat. Rancid flavors are imparted to food and harmful chemicals, such as acrolein, are produced. Smoke point varies between 320°F (160°C) and 428°F (220°C), depending on the type and purity of the fat. Refined, flavorless oils have the highest smoke points because impurities and flavor compounds burn easily. Save flavorful oils (extra-virgin olive oils, nut oils, and so on) for finishing drizzles or in salads instead of using them for cooking.

SATURATED VS. UNSATURATED

"Saturated" fats, such as butter, lard, tallow, and coconut oil, are solid at room temperature because their fat molecules stack together tightly. They often have high smoke points but aren't always used for frying because they are harmful when eaten too often. "Unsaturated" fats are liquids and are called oils. Their fat molecules have kinked limbs, preventing them from stacking into a solid easily. For good health, enjoy them in moderation.

Liquid (unsaturated) fats

Liquid fat
Liquid fatty acids aren't straight because they contain double bonds between pairs of carbon atoms. This prevents them from packing together tightly, so they don't solidify easily.

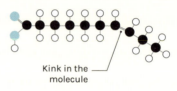

Kink in the molecule

UNSATURATED FAT MOLECULE

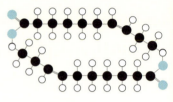

ARRANGEMENT OF MOLECULES

	OLIVE OIL	**VEGETABLE OILS**	**NUT OILS**
	EXTRA-VIRGIN VIRGIN REFINED LIGHT-TASTING	SOY | CORN | SUNFLOWER SAFFLOWER | CANOLA PEANUT/GROUNDNUT REFINED AVOCADO	WALNUT SESAME HAZELNUT
TASTE	Ranging from rich, fruity, and peppery (extra-virgin) to flavorless (refined/pure/light).	All are neutral tasting with high smoke points. Multipurpose cooking oils are often blends.	Very strongly flavored and used for finishing. Hazelnut has an unusually high smoke point.
USES	Extra-virgin oil is best for finishing/drizzling; light olive oils are ideal for frying and baking.	Good for baking, deep-frying, roasting, and searing.	Best used for finishing dishes.
SMOKE POINT	Very variable: EXTRA-VIRGIN 347–410°F (175–210°C) REFINED/PURE/LIGHT 392–464°F (200–240°C)	CANOLA 401°F (205°C) REFINED AVOCADO 518°F (270°C)	WALNUT 320°F (160°C) SESAME 350°F (177°C) HAZELNUT 430°F (221°C)

A ROUTE TO FLAVOR 41

ROOM TEMPERATURE

THESE FATS ARE SOLID AT ROOM TEMPERATURE

Solid (saturated) fats

Solid fat
Molecules of hard or solid fats are straight in structure. The fatty acids pack together more closely so are denser than unsaturated fats. Therefore, they have a higher melting point and are solid at room temperature.

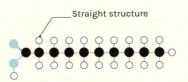

SATURATED FAT MOLECULE

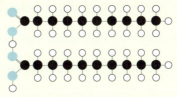

ARRANGEMENT OF MOLECULES

KEY
○ Hydrogen
● Oxygen
● Carbon

COCONUT OIL

UNREFINED
VIRGIN

BUTTER

UNSALTED
SALTED
CULTURED

GHEE

CLARIFIED BUTTER

LARD

ANIMAL FAT

TASTE	Melting at 75°F (24°C), it is solid at room temperature and imparts a distinct coconutty flavor to dishes.	Adds richness and sweetness to dishes. European butters are normally cultured (partly fermented), giving them more acidity, taste, and aroma.	Milk solids are removed to give pure butterfat with a high smoke point ideal for high-temperature cooking. It has a nutty, buttery flavor.	Derived from pigs, lard's unique, slightly meaty flavor is useful for baking, sautéing, or frying. It has a higher melting point than butter.
USES	Useful for all cooking and baking purposes, and for adding coconut flavor.	Very flavorful and a chef's favorite. Great for spreading and finishing as well as shallow frying.	High-temperature cooking; used a lot in Indian cuisine.	Refined lard is suitable for sweet bakes. It makes excellent flaky pastry.
SMOKE POINT	356°F (180°C)	APPROX. 300°F (150°C)	485°F (252°C)	356°F (180°C)

WHY DO WE CRAVE THE HEAT OF CHILES?

Chiles contain the same eye-watering, face-burning chemical that law enforcement officers use in pepper spray. The nasty chemical, called capsaicin, evolved in chile plants to stop microbes, insects, and mammals (like us) from eating their fruits.

Spicy heat (pungency) isn't a taste or flavor—it's a pain identical to being burned. Although tolerance levels differ, pungency turns all the flavors in a dish up a notch and adds an exciting dimension, sparking the brain's emotion circuits and increasing activity in its flavor center (pp.48–49), as well as firing up the salivary glands.

Whatever you're cooking—sweet or savory—it's worth asking yourself whether a dash of heat could make it even better. Acting on the taste buds, a little bit of intense spiciness gives saltiness a lift and tones down bitterness. Pungency also counteracts sourness, taking the edge off very tart ingredients, although adding too much will overpower the dish.

ENDORPHINS AND DOPAMINE

Humans seem to be unique in their love for fiery pain when we eat; most animals are repulsed. For us, the pain comes with a wave of the body's natural opium-like painkillers—endorphins—that give a little buzz when the burning fades, like the natural high felt after intense exercise. This lift also comes with a feel-good hit of the brain hormone dopamine—the reward substance that is released after a roller-coaster ride or a scary movie (possibly explaining why thrill-seekers prefer spicy food). After we learn to tolerate the discomfort, we find ourselves being drawn to spicy foods like moths to a flame.

Capsaicin binding with burning-pain nerves

After mixing with saliva, pungent compounds seep into the upper layers of the tongue, binding with molecular temperature sensors (TRPV1 receptors) on the pain fibers that detect burning, causing them to fire.

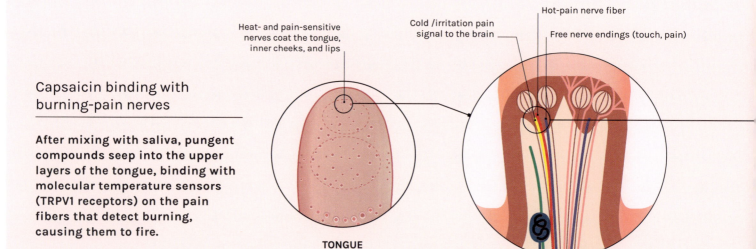

TONGUE

FUNGIFORM PAPILLAE

A ROUTE TO FLAVOR 43

THE BURNING POWER OF CHILES

Chiles create a spicy heat because capsaicin, the active compound they contain, "hot-wires" the same pain fibers that send burning messages to the brain when you are scalded. These normally turn on only at above 110°F (43°C). Your brain simply cannot tell the difference between heat from a vindaloo and the agony of a mouthful of just-boiled tea—the signal is the same. The scorch lingers until the chemical has been degraded by the body, typically after about 15 minutes. Drinking water doesn't speed this up, and the sparkle of carbonated drinks makes the heat worse.

Milk, yogurt, and sour cream will take the edge off it, thanks to the dairy protein they contain, casein, clinging to the capsaicin molecule.

TRPV1 receptors (on hot-pain nerve fibers) are found in different parts of the body. Capsaicin binds to these receptors on the tongue, sending an alert to the brain. Other pungent chemicals contained in mustard, garlic, and onions disrupt a pain nerve called TRPA1, which sends a painfully cold or irritating message to the brain. Pungent compounds dissolve in fats/oils, but poorly in water, so need to be cooked or mixed in oils to suffuse a dish.

NATURAL HIGH
THE PAIN FROM EATING CHILES RELEASES ENDORPHINS, WHICH CAN CREATE A FEEL-GOOD EFFECT.

COLD
TRPA1 ARE COLD/IRRITATION RECEPTORS TRIGGERED BY COMPOUNDS LIKE ISOTHIOCYANATES IN MUSTARD.

Isothiocyanates from mustard

Capsaicin from chiles

HOT
TRPV1 ARE BURNING-PAIN RECEPTORS, NORMALLY ACTIVE ABOVE 110°F (43°C), BUT TRIGGERED BY CAPSAICIN.

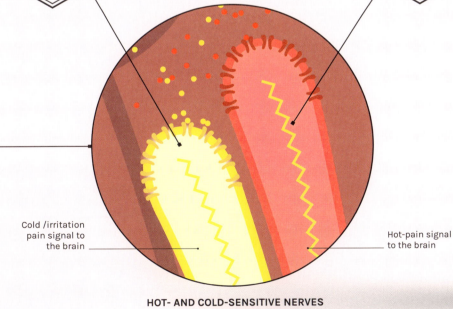

Cold/irritation pain signal to the brain

Hot-pain signal to the brain

HOT- AND COLD-SENSITIVE NERVES

WHICH INGREDIENTS ARE SPICY?

Although capsaicin is a pungent compound, it's not the only option on the menu. Other compounds give unique sensations and behave differently in cooking.

GARLIC AND ONIONS: ALLICIN

Allicin forms in garlic and onions only when they are damaged and has a different heat from capsaicin. It breaks down over time and is destroyed at around 158°F (70°C). Cooking softens the pungency of garlic and onions, allowing milder flavors to emerge (pp.94–97). Allicin triggers both TRPV1 and TRPA1 receptors, contributing to its unique, somewhat cooling heat.

WASABI AND MUSTARD: ISOTHIOCYANATES

Found in wasabi and mustard, isothiocyanates trigger pain nerves that have the TRPA1 receptor, which is also sensitive to cold temperatures and irritants like smoke. They vaporize easily in the mouth, providing a nasal-clearing sensation. Whole mustard seeds need to be broken and wetted; isothiocyanates form only when a defensive enzyme called myrosinase breaks out of damaged cells, mixes with water, and reacts with specific molecules, forming sinalbin in white mustard and singrin in black and brown mustard, known as isothiocyanates.

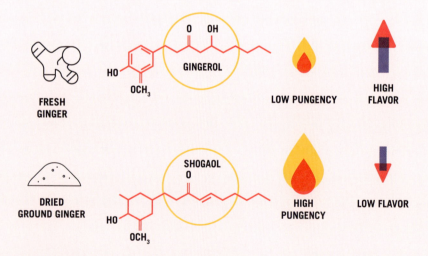

Fresh vs. ground ginger: When fresh ginger is dried and powdered, its pungency increases, as hot gingerol converts to fiery shogaol. However, 20 percent of flavor compounds are lost in the process.

Mustard seeds

HERE'S HOW TO RELEASE THE FULL FLAVOR AND HEAT OF MUSTARD SEEDS:

1. DAMAGE

FIRST, CRACK OR GRIND THE MUSTARD SEEDS TO RELEASE THE MYROSINASE ENZYME. THIS WILL START THE CHEMICAL PROCESS TO PRODUCE SPICY COMPOUNDS.

2. SOAK

FOR FULL FIERINESS, SOAK THE CRUSHED SEEDS IN WATER, VINEGAR, OR BEER TO ALLOW THE ENZYME TO ACT ON THE MOLECULES CALLED GLUCOSINOLATES, TRANSFORMING THEM INTO SPICY ISOTHIOCYANATES.

3. TOAST

TOAST DRAINED MUSTARD SEEDS IN A DRY PAN OVER MEDIUM HEAT TO BRING OUT THE NUTTY PYRAZINE FLAVOR COMPOUNDS FROM THE MAILLARD REACTION (PP.74–77). HEAT ABOVE 140°F (60°C) DEACTIVATES MYROSINASE, LOWERING PUNGENCY.

GINGER: GINGEROL
Like capsaicin, gingerol, which is found in ginger, interacts with TRPV1 receptors but at a different binding site, resulting in a less intense heat. When dried, gingerol is converted into shogaol, which is twice as hot, giving ground ginger a harsher heat.

CINNAMON: CINNAMALDEHYDE
Cinnamaldehyde, found in cinnamon, activates the TRPA1 receptor, leading to a gentle warming, tingling sensation (p.186).

PEPPERCORNS: PIPERINE
As well as piperine, peppercorns contain 19 other pungent compounds, all less potent than capsaicin. These withstand cooking temperatures well, collectively binding to both TRPV1 and TRPA1 receptors, giving them a mild, unique warmth.

CHILE PEPPERS: CAPSAICIN
It is the white pith of the chile pepper, rather than the seeds, that is the hottest part of the chile. Scrape this out to remove at least half of the capsaicin, along with the bitter seeds. Cooking chiles early will infuse capsaicin into the oil, melding it into the dish, allowing flavors from the chiles to develop (pp.180–181).

PUNGENT
ISOTHIOCYANATES ARE FOUND IN MUSTARD SEEDS AS WELL AS HORSERADISH AND BROCCOLI.

GINGEROL
IS THE COMPOUND IN FRESH GINGER THAT GIVES IT SPICY HEAT.

FLAVOR AND THE BRAIN

How does the brain experience flavor?	**48**
How does food's appearance change its flavor?	**50**
How does anticipation influence flavor?	**52**
Does food taste better arranged neatly?	**54**
How does smell affect flavor?	**56**
Why do we have such different tastes?	**58**
Does taste change with age?	**60**
How are sound and flavor connected?	**62**

HOW DOES THE BRAIN EXPERIENCE FLAVOR?

Flavor is actually an illusion conjured in the brain. Eating involves not only all our senses but every part of what makes us human.

Imagine biting into a fresh tomato just picked from the vine. In less than a second of the flesh touching the tongue's surface, sweet, sour, and umami taste signals crackle along nerves into the very base of the brain (the brain stem). Here, electrical impulses have reached into the brain's most primitive areas, the thalamus and amygdala, and are soon met by the fruity aroma signals sent from the back of the nose (p.56).

Taste and smell weave their way along tiny biological wires toward the brain's "flavor center," mingling and merging into one sweet, tangy, fruity message. The flavor center is in the orbitofrontal cortex, a small region directly above the eyes. It has been primed to receive a tomatoey sensation, having seen the fruit's red skin sent from the visual cortex at the back of the brain a few moments earlier,

The flavor journey

Taste from the tongue and aroma from the nose blur as they make their way to the flavor center. Visual information and memories also play a key role in our perception of flavor.

FRONTAL LOBE
WHERE THOUGHTS, DECISIONS, AND CONSCIOUS CHOICES ABOUT FOOD ARE MADE.

FLAVOR CENTER
THIS IS WHERE WE PROCESS TASTE TO CREATE A FLAVOR EXPERIENCE.

Smell
Mouthfeel
Taste

KEY
- Smell
- Taste
- Mouthfeel
- Sight
- Thoughts, expectations
- Touch

FLAVOR AND THE BRAIN 49

PARIETAL LOBE
THE PART OF THE BRAIN THAT PROCESSES THE TEXTURE AND TEMPERATURE OF FOOD.

VISUAL CORTEX
WHERE THE BRAIN PROCESSES INFORMATION ABOUT THE APPEARANCE OF FOOD.

as well as the anticipatory signals flooding in from the neighboring thinking regions, heightening the experience. As flavor forms, the emotional circuits whirl into life and memories are invoked with chatter between the flavor and memory centers. Squelching sounds from the ears and juicy mouthfeel coming from the mouth and tongue are similarly relayed into the mix, imparting succulence, rounding off the joy of eating a ripe tomato.

HOW IT FITS TOGETHER

Scientists using new scanning technologies have found that the richness of the flavor experience is mirrored by an equally complex web of connections within the brain. The aroma and flavor of food is experienced like a face: freshly baked bread is recognized as instantly as a familiar friend. We used to think that each sense—taste, aroma, and mouthfeel—made its own path through the brain. We now know that the senses merge almost as soon as their messages enter the brain.

Sense of touch

OTHER SENSES, LIKE THE SENSE OF TOUCH, MELD TOGETHER ON THEIR JOURNEY TO THE FLAVOR CENTER.

Picking up your food before eating it makes flavors more vivid than when eaten with a utensil. Food seems to have a smoother texture when you're sitting in a soft chair and with our fingers resting on smooth linen, compared to sitting on a hard chair touching a piece of sandpaper.

Symphony

LIKE THE DIFFERENT INSTRUMENTS PLAYING IN A SYMPHONY, EACH PLAYER IN THE FLAVOR EXPERIENCE CAN BE DIRECTED:

VISION
BRIGHTER-COLORED FOODS TASTE MORE INTENSE (PP.50–51)

SOUND
CRUNCHIER FOODS TASTE FRESHER

TOUCH/ MOUTHFEEL
THICKER FOODS SEEM RICHER

THOUGHTS
INCREASED EXPECTATIONS ENHANCE FLAVOR (PP.52–53)

EMOTIONS
ANTICIPATION AND EXPECTATION ARE IMPORTANT, AND POSITIVE MOODS ENHANCE SWEETNESS (PP.52–53)

HOW DOES FOOD'S APPEARANCE CHANGE ITS FLAVOR?

Almost everyone has heard the phrase "you eat first with your eyes"—the most overused cliché in the culinary world. It was apparently first uttered by the famous first-century CE Roman foodie Marcus Gavius Apicius, although he never wrote it down.

The phrase captures the idea that how a food looks holds huge sway over how it tastes. In reality, the flavor experience begins long before you have set eyes on it (pp.52–53). Nevertheless, the brain's flavor center greedily sucks up information from our visual processing areas, meaning food's appearance influences whether it tastes delicious.

THE IMPORTANCE OF COLOR

Human vision is among the best in the animal kingdom, and we see more colors than most mammals. Our ancient forebears evolved eyesight so they could pick out the safest and most nutritious fruits and leaves—which have a subtle reddish hue—from the dense forest greenery. Today, drinks colored red or pink also taste sweeter, as does Coke drunk or served from a red can or bottle. We quickly learn what colors taste like: strawberry yogurts taste fruitier when they are colored red; mint ice cream tastes more minty when dyed green. Following this science, manufacturers usually dye canned peas green to give them a fresher flavor. Miscoloring food reveals how powerful vision is: a glass of orange juice colored bright red will more likely taste like cherry, strawberry, or cranberry, depending on which you are most familiar with.

COOKING WITH COLOR

As a cook, you can accentuate the flavors of your ingredients by heightening their natural hues or create confusion by recoloring them. Colors are particularly important when preparing fruits and vegetables:
- Preserve the natural color of those that brown after cutting by putting them in a bowl of water with a few drops of lemon juice.
- Brighten pigments by blanching vegetables before freezing, sautéing, or roasting. Plunge them in boiling water for 1–2 minutes then chill—this will destroy the plant's self-destructive enzymes that degrade its pigments when slowly heated.

BROWN
Earthy, roasted

COMMON PIGMENTS:
Melanoidins from Maillard reaction (roasted meats, coffee)

GREEN
Fresh, herbal

COMMON PIGMENTS:
Chlorophyll (spinach, green beans)

WHITE
Mild, neutral

COMMON PIGMENTS:
No pigment or anthoxanthins (potatoes, cauliflower)

BLUE
Deep, rich, sometimes tart

COMMON PIGMENTS:
Anthocyanins (blueberries, eggplants)

FLAVOR AND THE BRAIN 51

Flavors are a fusion of all the senses and color plays a key role. For example, more orangey foods taste sweeter, greener leaves are fresher, and red makes spicy food more fiery.

PINK
Sweet, fruity

COMMON PIGMENTS:
Anthocyanins (pink grapefruit); astaxanthin (shrimp, salmon)

BLACK
Strong, intense

COMMON PIGMENTS:
Melanins (black garlic); anthocyanins (black rice)

ORANGE
Sweet, citrusy

COMMON PIGMENTS:
Beta-carotene (carrots, sweet potatoes); beta-cryptoxanthin (oranges)

RED
Sweet, ripe

COMMON PIGMENTS:
Lycopene (tomatoes); anthocyanins (cherries, strawberries)

YELLOW
Tart, refreshing

COMMON PIGMENTS:
Carotenoids (bananas, corn); curcumins (turmeric, saffron)

HOW DOES ANTICIPATION INFLUENCE FLAVOR?

Food's appearance affects how it tastes, but the entire flavor experience begins much earlier, before an aroma even reaches your nostrils. Understanding anticipation, which powerfully shapes flavor, will take your dining experience to the next level.

The frontal, thinking regions of the brain greatly influence flavor in the neighboring flavor center (pp.48–49) and the appetite center. Positive emotions also heighten flavor and our overall satisfaction with food.

Make the room's ambiance and setting in keeping with the style of the meal: the decor, music, and layout of a room can have a major bearing on the meal experience, heightening expectation. Research shows that diners being seated too close to each other worsens their experience, especially in Western cultures. Foster a social environment: great food and drink are nearly always pleasures better shared, lifting mood and heightening the flavor experience.

When you serve food, tell your guests more about it: how you discovered it and why you chose it. As well as building anticipation and expectation, this will infuse each element of the meal with emotion and meaning, heightening its flavor and helping diners forge a lasting memory of the meal.

Humans and other animals desire novelty and have their appetites supercharged when many different tidbits are offered. Embrace this by including as many different aromas, flavors, textures, and tastes as possible on the plate.

Social elements and cultural context
The presence of others and the general social setting can have a considerable impact on how much one enjoys a meal. Cultural expectations of dining etiquette and food presentation can also shape one's eating experience.

Cool color scheme
Cooler colors, like blue, may suppress your appetite.

Controlled lighting
Avoid having the lighting turned up.

AMBIENT AROMAS CAN INFLUENCE HOW FOOD TASTES AND HOW MUCH IS CONSUMED.

Scent
Allowing diners the chance to smell the food before it arrives at the table builds anticipation.

Social interaction
In this room, the diners do not seem to be engaging with each other, which may affect their dining experience.

FLAVOR AND THE BRAIN 53

Music
The tempo and genre of background music can affect the pace of eating as well as mood.

Warm color scheme
Warmer colors, like red and yellow, are believed to stimulate appetite.

DIMMER LIGHTING CAN CREATE A RELAXED AMBIANCE, LEADING TO LONGER DINING TIMES.

MEAL PLANNING AND TIMING

Hunger is the strongest biological impulse we have, altering mood, behavior, and thoughts. Hunger hormones fire up the appetite center of the brain, in a region called the hypothalamus, and heighten smell and taste, causing thoughts to pivot uncontrollably toward food. Harness these natural impulses by allowing the smell of your cooking to waft into the dining area. The aroma of food has an unparalleled ability to fire up our appetite and passes into the animalistic amygdala part of the brain, stirring emotions. Tease diners further by letting them see the food a few minutes before serving!

Serve a small starter before the main event: chewing and eating boosts the appetite center and stimulates digestion, magnifying the flavor experience when the main course arrives. When preparing several courses or a meal with a starter, avoid serving too many protein-rich elements (meats, pulses, fish) early on because these hard-to-digest foods suppress the appetite, knocking the edge off the enjoyment of what is to come. They cause the hunger hormone to plunge, and "full up" hormones (such as GLP-1 and PYY) to wash through the blood.

Finally, don't rush dessert: a longer interval between the main course and dessert will aid appetite by allowing a full stomach to empty, so the meal's conclusion can be properly savored.

Furniture and spacing
Comfortable seating and adequate spacing can improve the dining experience by increasing comfort and reducing stress.

Extra touches
Flowers and pictures help create a comfortable atmosphere for eating.

DOES FOOD TASTE BETTER ARRANGED NEATLY?

Fads and styles come and go: miniature portions, minimalist dining, deconstructed dishes, ingredients stacked high. Now science is starting to pin down how we can put food on the plate so that the dish tastes its best.

Food images catch and keep our attention like nothing else, and brain scanning experiments suggest looking at food triggers a surge of blood flow in the brain, setting off a release of appetite-driving hormones. Artists have always painted bowls of fruit and opulent banquets, and today 70 percent of young to middle-aged adults say they take pictures or videos of their food. Not only have experiments proved that we will pay more than double for a dish if it has been plated beautifully, but they have also proved that it tastes better. Elegant plating will never make a mediocre meal taste great, but it will make a great dish taste better.

CONTRASTING BACKGROUNDS

If food is an art, then the plate is the canvas, and its color, size, and shape can make a difference to a food's flavor. In Western dining, nearly every meal is served on a round, white porcelain plate, while in Japanese culture, "harmony" is prized, and bowls and plates are colored and shaped to suit each dish. By contrast, a shared eating plate or bowl is the norm in many other cultures. Research shows that the color of a plate should provide a contrast with the food so that it stands out from its backdrop. White, round plates seem to intensify sweet flavors, whereas dark, angular plates bring out more savory flavors.

NEAT PLATES VS. MESSY PLATES

The most consistent finding in research is that neatness matters. A similarly robust finding is the importance of balance on a plate, where all components are arranged around a central point, rather than off to one side. Chefs have long been taught the rule of three, which is always to plate odd numbers of items: three, five, or seven scallops, shrimp, or ravioli are more appetizing. But research flips this on its head, showing the theory doesn't hold up. We're drawn to more elements, as long as the plate isn't crowded and there's plenty of clear space near the rim.

PLACEMENT

Allow for a clear buffer of 1/2in (13mm) from the plate's edge, taking care not to overfill the plate by leaving at least a third empty.

APPETIZING PLATEFUL WITH SPACE AROUND

OVERCROWDED

FLAVOR AND THE BRAIN 55

Vegetables — Protein — Carbohydrate

Traditional plating
A traditional meal. A large piece of protein, usually meat or fish, plus a carbohydrate and a vegetable. None of the ingredients are touching; the diner can choose how to combine flavors for every forkful.

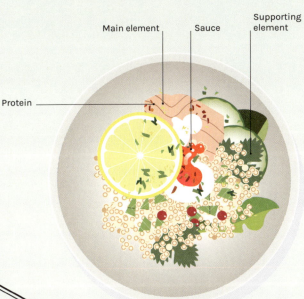

Main element — Sauce — Supporting element
Protein

An elegant plate
A pleasing arrangement. Sauces are drizzled to bring the elements together and garnishes add color and pops of flavor. The chef has chosen the combination of flavors.

PROTEIN IS OFTEN THE MAIN ELEMENT ON A PLATE, WITH SUPPORTING ELEMENTS LIKE VEGETABLES AND GARNISHES.

Shapes on the plate

Placing your food in different shapes on the plate can affect how you enjoy your food. Different elements can be placed in ways that can increase your appetite.

ARCS, SWIRLS, AND SWIPES
Making these shapes with sauces introduces an element of movement and fluidity, leading the eye across the plate.

TRIO PLATING
This method is often used to present the same ingredient prepared in three different ways.

OFF-CENTER MAIN ELEMENT
If the main element is off-center, it should be placed nearest the diner.

TRIANGLES
If placing ingredients in a triangular shape, research consistently shows that diners prefer it to be pointing away from them.

SINGLE LINE
Research shows that diners find food with a straight element most appetizing when it is pointing away from them and to the right.

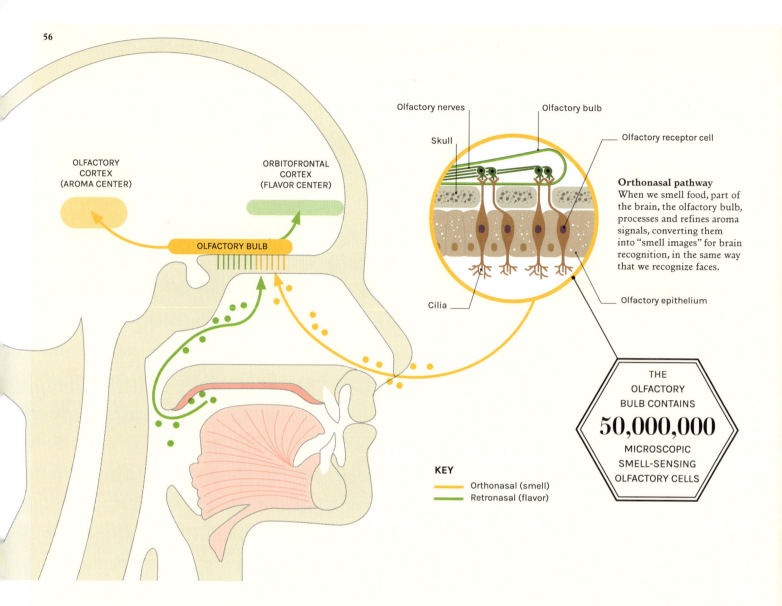

HOW DOES SMELL AFFECT FLAVOR?

Surveys show that smell is the sense we value least and would be most happy to lose. To do so, however, would be to confine ourselves to a world of bland food: scientists agree that between 75 and 95 percent of food's flavor comes from the sense of smell.

Human noses are large compared to those of our primate relatives. They grew bigger over the course of several millennia to spin, clean, heat, and humidify the air we breathe. Although our ability to detect odors is not as strong as that of other mammals, we are able to discern around one trillion odors. Unlike most animals, we smell our food "retronasally" as we eat, meaning that when it comes to experiencing flavor, our nose's true powers really start to shine.

SMELL AND FLAVOR

As anyone with a blocked nose will tell you, without a sense of smell, food becomes flavorless and bland. Flavor seems to come from the tongue, but this is a hallucination—our brain "paints" the food's aromas onto the surface of the tongue, convincing us that this is where the flavor comes from.

HOW SMELL WORKS

In the roof of the nasal cavity inside the nose is a small patch called the olfactory epithelium where odor detection takes place. Jammed in here are 50 million microscopic smell-sensing olfactory cells, each dangling tentacle-like cilia covered in mucus. These are peppered with molecular receptors, which can snag a particular part of a passing aroma compound: airborne substances that give food its aroma and flavor (pp.66–67). When ensnared in the mucus, these compounds are sensed by one or more of the 300 to 400 different types of smell cells, causing an electrical signal to be fired into the brain. The combination of cell types activated is imprinted on the brain as an "image" that is unique to that odor. It is like having a keyboard with 400 different keys being played in a chord, each one a unique aroma.

AROMA ROUTES

There are two routes for aroma perception to reach your brain. The orthonasal route, where aroma compounds enter your nasal cavity through your nostrils, is experienced as smell. When the same aromas come from food in your mouth, they are translated into flavor. This second whiff takes a different, retronasal, route into the brain, where the yeasty, toasted, malty aromas are translated into bread's uniquely delicious flavor, for example.

AROMA COMPOUND TASTE NOTES

THE CHEMICALS IN FOODS AND DRINKS THAT GIVE THE SMELLS WE EXPERIENCE (PP.66–67) FALL INTO DIFFERENT CATEGORIES:

Rose
ALCOHOLS

Fruity
ESTERS

Vanilla
ALDEHYDES

Butter
KETONES

Citrus
TERPENES

Cloves
PHENOLS

Roasted
PYRAZINES

Onion/Garlic
SULFIDES

Aroma cells
The unique flavor of a food comes from activated aroma receptors combined with the basic tastes. Dragon fruit has a more complex aroma, with sweet and sour tastes, than the more bitter cabbage.

EACH PERSON HAS A SET OF
300–400
AROMA RECEPTORS

DIFFERENT TYPES OF AROMA RECEPTORS ARE ACTIVATED BY AROMA COMPOUNDS TO CREATE FLAVOR.

ACTIVATED NOTES FOR
DRAGON FRUIT

ACTIVATED NOTES FOR
RED CABBAGE

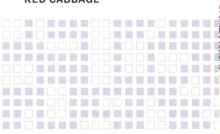

WHY DO WE HAVE SUCH DIFFERENT TASTES?

If you've ever been amazed that someone else loathes a food you adore, or vice versa, then you'll know that everyone's experience of flavor is different, and often these differences can be profound. Understanding this helps you create food for all palates.

Our genetics mean we are not all born with equal tasting powers. It is estimated that adults have between 2,000 and 8,000 taste buds, and those of us with a larger number are blessed with a more acute sense of taste.

Researchers are continually discovering new genes that gift humans with exceptional tasting powers, but around a quarter of people are "supertasters" who have inherited one supercharged bitterness receptor (TAS2R38), which equips them to better pick out subtle changes in ingredients. Supertasters may or may not have extra taste buds. For them, sweet things are sweeter, salty things saltier, and umami more intense. This is a mixed blessing: the bitterness of Brussels sprouts and other leafy greens is usually repulsive to them, and coffee and alcohol are both bitter pills to swallow. Chile heat and the effervescence of bubbles are more pronounced. Salty and fatty foods also lack the allure they have for those without the "superpower." Baby supertasters are harder to wean and have a tendency to turn out as picky eaters.

Science of the supertasters

Whether you were born with a higher-than-average complement of taste buds or a turbocharged bitterness receptor is down to a roll of the genetic dice. You may or may not be either type of supertaster. Shown right is research from 2020 illustrating both often go together.

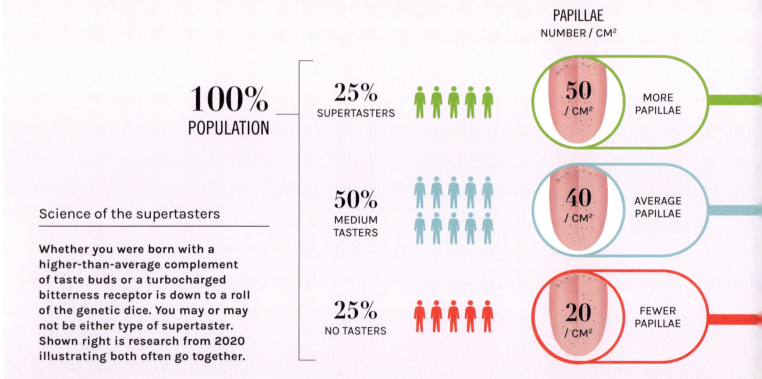

FLAVOR AND THE BRAIN 59

AROMA

The largest slice of the flavor experience comes from the aroma of food, as it passes from the mouth up into the back of the nose (pp.56–57). None of us are born with a full complement of aroma receptors; some will be missing or will not work fully. It is as if we have each been given a piano with a unique set of missing keys and a handful of faulty keys that play inferior notes. A flavor can, therefore, be symphonic for some but jarring for others.

One aroma receptor in our 400-key aroma scale is called OR6A2, which, when not working normally (as happens in up to 17 percent of people of European descent and 21 percent of East Asians), causes the pleasant herby and slightly citrusy flavor of cilantro to mutate into an unpleasant soapy flavor (pp.188–189). Similarly, people who find that pork meat smells sweaty or like urine probably have an overly sensitive "OR7D4" aroma receptor.

ALL FLAVORS ARE ENHANCED → **PICKY EATERS** DON'T LIKE BITTER TASTES.

TASTES ARE MODERATE → **NORMAL EATERS**

TASTES ARE DIALED DOWN → **ADVENTUROUS EATERS** WILL EAT ANYTHING, LOVE HOT AND SPICY.

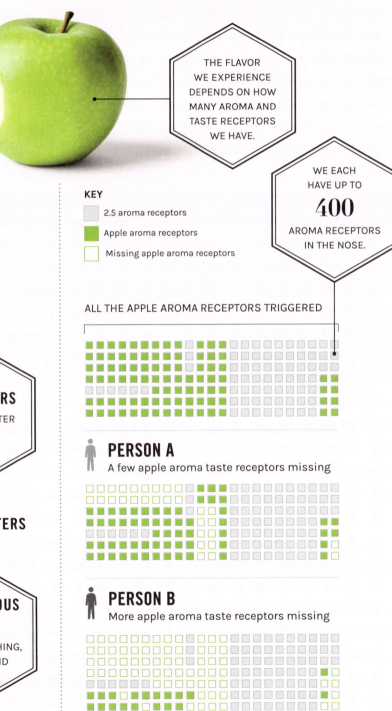

Apple flavor

If you bite into an apple, your aroma receptors detect its different aromas and send messages to your brain. People missing more receptors may perceive fewer of the apple's flavors.

THE FLAVOR WE EXPERIENCE DEPENDS ON HOW MANY AROMA AND TASTE RECEPTORS WE HAVE.

WE EACH HAVE UP TO **400** AROMA RECEPTORS IN THE NOSE.

KEY
- 2.5 aroma receptors
- Apple aroma receptors
- Missing apple aroma receptors

ALL THE APPLE AROMA RECEPTORS TRIGGERED

PERSON A
A few apple aroma taste receptors missing

PERSON B
More apple aroma taste receptors missing

DOES TASTE CHANGE WITH AGE?

Taste bud cells recycle every week or two, but their total number withers as we age. By the time we are adults, we have lost around a third of our taste buds—one reason foods seem much more vivid when we are young, and older people often salt their food.

As well as a reduction in taste buds, the number of smell receptor cells in the roof of our nasal cavities also plummets after our late sixties, further deadening our flavor perception.

Our taste can also be affected by its strong links with emotional memory centers in the brain. One bad experience can be enough to cause a lasting revulsion to a particular taste. This can be particularly affecting if the experience happens when we are young. Anyone who has had a bad seafood experience or been sick after overindulging in a certain alcohol in their youth will avoid those tastes in the future. It takes longer to learn to love a strong flavor, although we can do this more quickly if our mothers ate those things during pregnancy or while breastfeeding.

We are all born hardwired to like sweet things and dislike bitter ones, but practically every other flavor preference has been learned at some point in our past, although we may not remember it—especially if it happened in the womb.

During pregnancy, some flavor compounds are passed to the baby via the placenta and through breast milk, imprinting in the brain that this food is safe. Research shows that expectant mothers who have a diet rich in spiced foods and strong-flavored foods are less likely to have a picky eater for a child.

Aroma perception through life

Over time, the tastes we experience change and develop. This is linked to the number of taste buds we have and our sense of smell, which declines dramatically with age. Women have more aroma receptors than men so can generally identify more flavors.

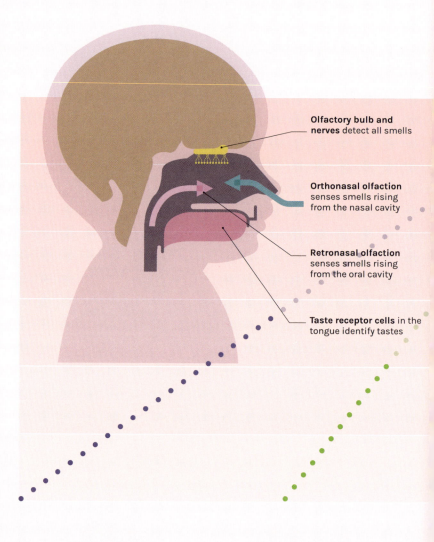

Olfactory bulb and nerves detect all smells

Orthonasal olfaction senses smells rising from the nasal cavity

Retronasal olfaction senses smells rising from the oral cavity

Taste receptor cells in the tongue identify tastes

AT BIRTH

Babies are born with more taste buds than adults and are sensitive to taste. Babies are biologically inclined to prefer sweet tastes and detest bitter ones.

EARLY YEARS

As young children move on to solid foods, they remain sensitive to taste and prefer salty and sweet flavors.

HOW ARE SOUND AND FLAVOR CONNECTED?

Whether it fizzes, squelches, crunches, or pops in your mouth, the sound of your food (and where you're eating) holds huge sway over how it tastes.

As strange as it sounds, if you can't hear fully then neither can you taste fully—research shows that deaf people don't taste foods as vividly as those with full hearing. Given that flavor is an illusion created in the brain (p.48), sound powerfully primes our mind for what it is about to experience, heightening the anticipation of flavor. A rustling potato chip packet and loud crunch when a chip is eaten induces a fresh taste, regardless of the quality of the fried potato slice. Chocolate tastes more chocolaty if it cracks loudly; we believe a beer is of premium quality if the bottle opens with a high-

TREBLE = SWEET AND SOUR
HIGH-PITCHED SOUNDS AMPLIFY SWEET AND SOUR TASTES.

BASS = BITTERNESS
LOW-PITCHED OR JARRING SOUNDS INCREASE BITTERNESS.

STACCATO = CRUNCH
OUR PERCEPTION OF FRESHNESS OR CRISPNESS IS BOOSTED BY AMPLIFYING CRUNCHING.

Pitch the taste
Sound converges with vision, taste, and aroma in the brain's flavor center, and research has revealed some surprising ways that auditory cues can tip the balance. Some academics think it hints at a primal food language, as babies the world over squeal with joy at sweet tastes and grumble a "yuck" at bitter foods.

pitched hiss; and we associate a gentle tinkling fizz of sparkling wine with high-quality Champagne rather than cheaper Prosecco.

As any expert chef will know, we don't just eat with our ears; we cook with them too: from the spluttering sizzle of a fish placed into a hot-enough skillet to the bubbling pasta pot's reassuring burble, the sounds of the kitchen are like the spoken directions of a cook's GPS. Distinctive sounds can make flavors more striking—pitch it all just right and the ingredients of a good meal will sing together in harmony.

It's not just the snap and crackle of what's in your bowl that matters—ambient noise profoundly affects flavor and may even subvert our food choices. Static, humming, or hissing "white" noise, like that on an airplane, deadens our tastes, partly explaining why in-flight food tastes so bland (extra salt is often added to offset this). The graph below shows the results of an experiment that tested the effects of background noise on taste perception.

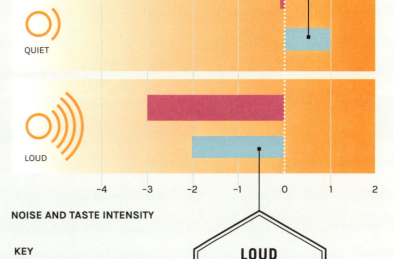

QUIET
IN QUIETER SURROUNDINGS, FOOD TASTED MORE SALTY BUT SLIGHTLY LESS SWEET.

NOISE AND TASTE INTENSITY

KEY
- Perception of sweetness
- Perception of saltiness

LOUD
LOUDER BACKGROUND NOISE MADE FOOD TASTE LESS SWEET AND LESS SALTY.

SMOOTH = CREAMINESS
SMOOTH, FLOWING SOUNDS ENHANCE THE TEXTURAL SENSE OF CREAMINESS.

Eating to the beat

ELECTRICAL ACTIVITY IN THE BRAIN PULSES TO THE RHYTHM OF ANY MUSIC or beat that we hear, so the speed we eat also tends to keep pace with the tempo of music. Slower music makes us linger, savoring food and conversation, whereas upbeat tunes prompt diners to eat and move on quickly. Musical genre matters as well—experiments have repeatedly shown that classical music can enhance the apparent quality of the food we are eating.

ACTIVATING FLAVOR

What are flavor compounds?	66
What is the science behind food combinations?	68
How can I bridge the flavor gap?	70
How important is serving temperature?	72
What is the Maillard reaction?	74
How can I control the Maillard reaction?	76
What is caramelization?	78
What else influences the flavor experience?	80
How can I preserve flavor?	82
How does fermentation affect flavor?	84

WHAT ARE FLAVOR COMPOUNDS?

For humans, aroma is flavor. We are unique among mammals in that we smell our food while it is in our mouths, in a process called retronasal smelling. Many other animals, such as dogs, do not smell their food as they chew—they merely sniff it, chew it, and swallow.

Airborne chemicals, called "compounds," in food convey the aromas (smells) that are critical to flavor. When the aroma compound cocktail of a familiar food floods the nasal cavity, we instantly recognize it, unconsciously and automatically. The skill of a wine sommelier or professional taster is to tease out individual aromas and notes. Each hint of wood smoke, note of green grass, and scent of peach comes from an aroma compound.

PROFILING AROMA COMPOUNDS

Scientists can use devices that sample the air coming from a person's nostrils as they eat, to precisely capture the profile of aroma compounds that circulate in the nose as food is chewed and swallowed. Their befuddling chemical names mask their evocative power—the sweet scent of banana comes from isoamyl acetate, and the meaty depth of roasted meat is from 4-Mercapto-3-methyl-2-butanol. This is prized information for food manufacturers, who can bottle these up and use them as food flavorings. Aroma compounds are one type of flavor compound—the molecules that are the actual essence of a food's flavor. Chocolate, for example, is a mixture of about 300 flavor compounds. There are well over 25,000 known types of flavor compound molecules, some of which are called "tastants" and act on the tongue (such as sugar and salt) to create the basic tastes.

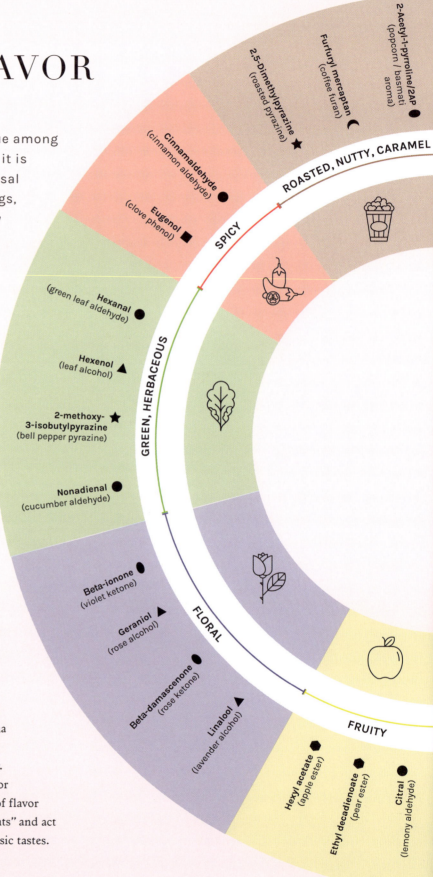

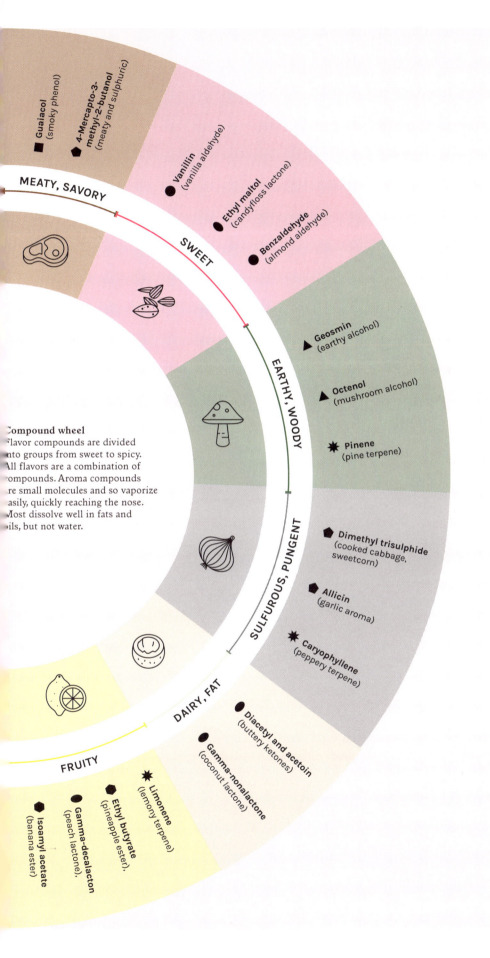

Aroma compound families

ALDEHYDES
Responsible for nutty, fruity, and grassy flavors.

KETONES AND LACTONES
Buttery, creamy, fruity notes, adding richness to aromas.

ALCOHOLS
Unlike ethanol (pp.213–214), these add to complexity of flavor and can be sweet, spicy, or even medicinal in aroma.

PHENOLS
Often found in smoked or charred foods, they give bitter and astringent flavors.

SULFUR COMPOUNDS
Pungent, savory, or sulfurous notes, adding depth to roasted or umami-rich foods.

ESTERS
Responsible for fruity flavors.

PYRAZINES
Contribute to roasted, nutty, and chocolaty flavors, produced in the Maillard reaction (pp.74–77).

TERPENES
Found in many plants and produce woody, spicy, and citrus flavors.

FURANS
Roasted, nutty, and caramelized notes, key to grills and bakes.

WHAT IS THE SCIENCE BEHIND FOOD COMBINATIONS?

Some foods are just made for one another, from the comforting cuddle of mozzarella, tomato, and basil atop a pizza to the tantalizing trinity of ginger, garlic, and soy sauce. But what about those that clash? There is a way to create harmony there, too.

Take a step back, and most food pairings are utterly bizarre. Why would a cooked fruit (tomato) taste better when slathered in a fermented dairy product (mozzarella) and be further heightened with a simple sprinkling of chopped green leaves (basil)? Each region has its own peculiar pairings, and this mystery has long confounded foodies and scientists alike.

In the 1990s, British chef Heston Blumenthal and master flavorist François Benzi hit the labs to try to unpick this culinary riddle. They eventually happened upon "flavor pairing" theory, concluding that foods that taste good together also share many flavor compounds (pp. 66–67).

IMPACT OF FLAVOR PAIRING

When scientists confirmed flavor pairing theory in 2011 by analyzing 56,498 recipes from different international cuisines alongside the flavor compounds they contain, the culinary world was wowed. Books, websites, and food pairing business start-ups sprang up, claiming that flavor compound data would let cooks and chefs make improbable and delicious food combinations. And yet for every flavor pairing fan, there is a critic in both academic and cheffing circles. The theory stands up well in Western cuisines—in lasagna recipes, for example, every ingredient pairs strongly with another—but it doesn't always work elsewhere. Some also rightly point out that the theory says nothing about an ingredient's texture and mouthfeel, relative saltiness, sweetness, sourness, savoriness, or the amounts of the different flavor compounds each one has.

INGREDIENTS VARY

Individual ingredients vary hugely. Beef from grass-fed cows has a subtly different blend of flavor compounds from beef from grain-fed cows. Each fruit has its own flavor compounds based on the soil it was grown in, how ripe it is, the variety, as well as whether it grew on a sunnier part of the plant (making it sweeter). Nevertheless, flavor pairing theory can be a powerful tool for creating new dishes. Use the common and uncommon pairings in chapter four as a springboard for your creativity.

CHOCOLATE AND BLUE CHEESE SHARE AT LEAST **73** FLAVOR COMPOUNDS.

ACTIVATING FLAVOR 69

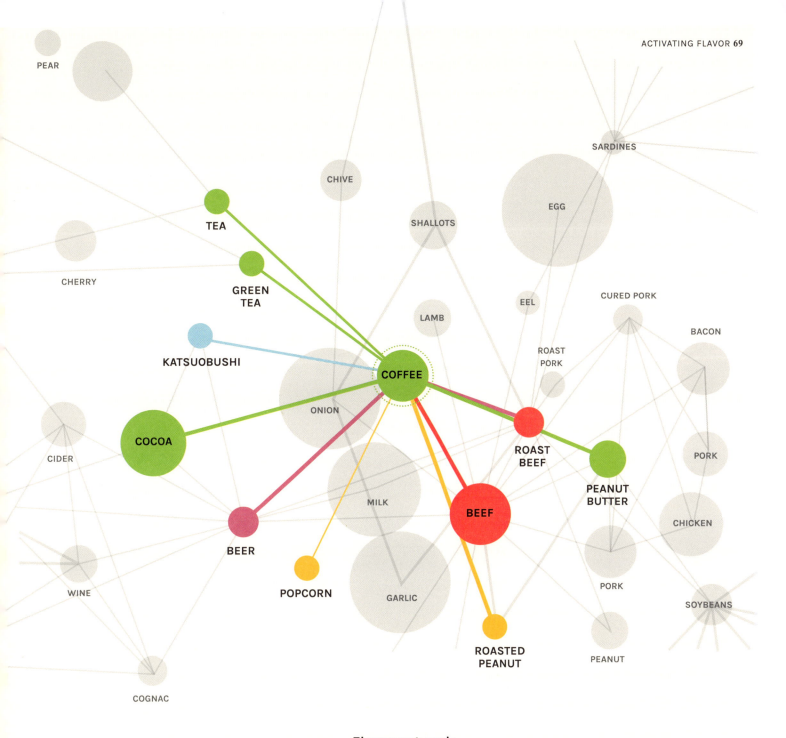

Flavor network

This is a small portion of the original 2011 flavor pairing network, which connects ingredients that share a significant number of flavor compounds. The thickness of the line indicates the number of shared compounds, and the ingredients' size reflects how often they are used in recipes. Similar ingredients, such as meats, cluster together, while some unexpected new connections are revealed.

KEY
- Meats
- Plants
- Nuts/seeds/pulses
- Alcoholic drinks
- Fish

HOW CAN I BRIDGE THE FLAVOR GAP?

Although books, websites, and many chefs swear by flavor pairing theory, it is far from watertight, and the idea started to run aground when researchers discovered that the theory works only for Western cooking. The solution to this riddle came from the most unlikely of places.

For all flavor pairing theory's successes, Southeast Asian, Indian, West African, and some South European cuisines often do the complete opposite, actually combining ingredients that are least likely to share flavor compounds. These are foods that should clash and be jarring eaten together but turn out to be truly delectable.

The answer to the reverse pairing puzzle came about when telecommunications multinational Telefonica tasked an academic with decoding the vast sprawling network of flavor connections seen in the world's cuisines. They hoped their computing network expertise could create them a tool that top chefs could use to reach new gastronomic highs.

CREATING A FLAVOR BRIDGE

Lead researcher Tiago Simas ran the numbers and, teaming up with legendary Spanish chef Ferran Adrià, discovered that two incompatible ingredients can be blended harmoniously when a third ingredient "bridges" the two. This third ingredient pairs with each of the unmatched ingredients, tethering them together (see opposite). In flavor pairing theory, ingredients like cocoa,

> **GLOBAL DIFFERENCES**
> CUISINES AROUND THE WORLD USE DIFFERENT ELEMENTS OF FOOD BRIDGING AND FOOD PAIRING.

APRICOT

TOMATO

WHISKEY

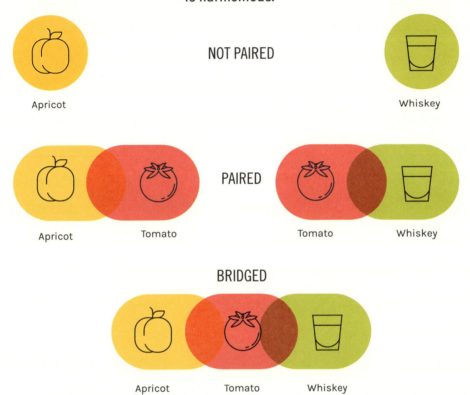

Paired or bridged

Apricot and whiskey share few flavor compounds, so taste bad when eaten together. But both apricot and whiskey share flavor compounds with tomato, so when tomato is added, the flavor is harmonious.

coffee, and cheeses are the most important, but with flavor bridging, teas, wines, tomatoes, and a plethora of less familiar ingredients are the key players. Suddenly, this confusing galaxy of international food combinations crystallized into a logical whole.

Tiago also created an online tool for fusing ingredients to create ever more imaginative recipes. To discover your own food bridges, consult online databases that focus on flavor compounds. These often suggest food pairings, allowing you to identify an ingredient that can harmonize two otherwise incompatible elements. Once you have your main components, think about texture and richness. You can introduce different textures by using various cooking techniques such as frying or baking.

You can also experiment with proportions, and incorporate other flavors. For example, you may introduce sourness with an acid like lemon juice, sweetness with sugar, or seasoning with salt. For a finishing touch, consider creating a complementary sauce or garnish.

Although much research has been done, we still don't have all the answers. Traditional Japanese and South Korean dishes often break both flavor pairing and food bridging rules, somehow bringing together ingredients that ought not to partner well at all!

HOW IMPORTANT IS SERVING TEMPERATURE?

Few restaurants would ever send out a main course that wasn't piping hot, or dream of pouring red wine straight from the chiller. Serving temperature might not be the hottest of topics, but it really does affect whether flavors fly or flop.

If you've ever noticed that ice cream tastes sickly sweet when it melts or that coffee becomes unpleasantly bitter when left to cool, then you'll appreciate how the temperature of food affects how it tastes. Many foods taste better when not too hot or too cold. Our taste buds are most active in temperatures closest to human body temperature. This is why, for example, dark chocolate, tomatoes, and cheese are best eaten at room temperature. For each degree above or below 99°F (37°C), each of the basic tastes is deadened (see graph).

FIRING UP FLAVOR

If science says taste buds work best when tasting tepid food, why do we insist on having food served hot? This is largely for the same reason that a hot loaf of bread fills a kitchen with delicious aroma, but a cold one does not. The hotter a food is, the more aroma compounds evaporate and suffuse the air, enticing the senses. When hot food is in the mouth, these airborne substances flood the nasal cavity, intensifying flavor (pp.56–57). The loss of taste when serving hot is usually outweighed by the enhanced flavor that these aromas bring.

Some foods also fundamentally change when they are heated: gravies and custards thin, chocolate melts, and fat softens, releasing more aroma compounds and letting more of the molecules of taste slide over the tongue, drenching taste buds. The result is a richer, more succulent mouthfeel.

BODY TEMPERATURE
OUR TASTE BUDS WORK BEST AT AROUND 99°F/37°C.

Hot foods will also degrade if left to cool before eating, making them less appealing. Gravies and custards develop unappetizing skins. Foods with a crispy coat, such as fries and roast vegetables, turn limp. Cooked starches also firm up, rendering cold or refrigerated rice, pasta, pizza dough, and flatbreads hard and chewy.

HOT OR COLD?

Psychology and expectations matter when it comes to the "correct" serving temperature. Warm foods conjure comforting memories of home-cooked meals and security. Soft drinks are often served chilled because we experience them as more refreshing and thirst-quenching. However, this may be true only for some—people in North America like iced drinks while eating, whereas Europeans prefer room temperature drinks, and Asian people tend toward hot water or tea, surveys show.

Red wine is served at room temperature and white wine chilled because experts say room temperature enhances a red's aroma and complexity while softening its tannins (pp.210–211), whereas white wines have their acidity and fresh fruit flavors highlighted by the coolness. Research, however, says this is an illusion. Warmer serving temperatures do improve aroma for all wines, but there is very little difference in tasting notes across wine serving temperatures (39–73°F/4–23°C).

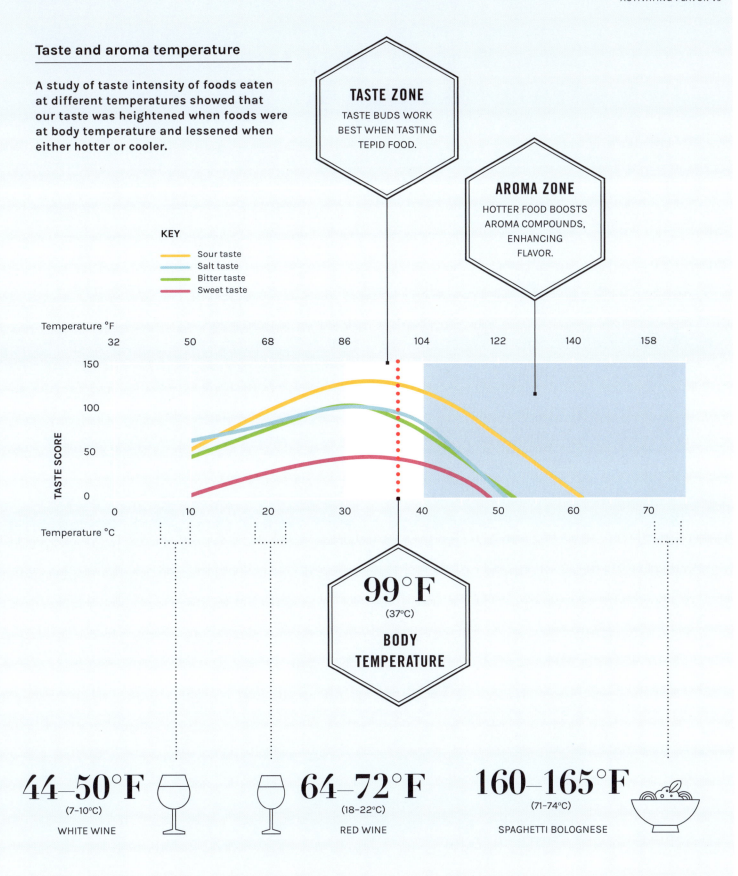

WHAT IS THE MAILLARD REACTION?

In 1911, French scientist Louis-Camille Maillard noticed droplets of brown liquid at the bottom of his flask. He had uncovered what would become the cornerstone of flavor chemistry, now called the Maillard reaction—the alchemy that makes all our favorite foods taste so good.

Every seared steak, crispy fish skin, aromatic bread crust, and roasted coffee bean owes its deliciousness to the Maillard (pronounced "may-ard") process, sometimes called the "browning reaction."

CHEMICAL REACTIONS

A cascade of chemical reactions are at play in the reaction. Hundreds of flavor compounds flood out: pyrazines with their nutty, roasted flavors; lactones with creamy and coconut notes; and meaty-tasting sulfur compounds (thiols), to name but a few.

OPTIMAL CONDITIONS

Crucially, the Maillard magic happens only when the surface of food gets hotter than the temperature of boiling water (212°F/100°C): you will never get the meaty crust on a meat roast or the crunch of a roasted potato by boiling or steaming. It also means that the outer layer needs to dry out before it will brown. Dabbing dry and salting the surface of food can get the reactions off to a flying start.

OIL ACCELERANT

Oil accelerates the Maillard reaction as well as the cooking speed, because it forms a super-hot slippery liquid bridge (thermal interface) between the food and the cooking surface, which lets heat rush in rapidly and evenly. If the food gets too hot (above 356°F/180°C), it will quickly scorch and burn, and in an oilless pan, only the edges of the food's underside will touch the hot surface, causing patches to scorch and blacken.

DRY PAN
HEAT ONLY PASSES INTO FOODS THAT ARE IN DIRECT CONTACT WITH THE PAN, CAUSING CHARRING.

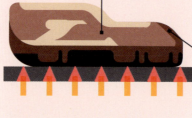

PLUS OIL
OIL ENSURES THAT HEAT EVENLY SPREADS ACROSS THE UNDERSIDE OF FOOD.

ADDING SALT
DRYING THE FOOD'S SURFACE AND ADDING SALT CAN SPEED UP THE PROCESS.

ACTIVATING FLAVOR 75

TO MAKE COFFEE
START WITH

GREEN COFFEE BEANS

PROCESS:
ROASTING

START AT:
284°F
(140°C)

Amino acids (the building blocks of protein) react with sugar to give birth to many different flavor compounds

Amino acids + sugars = pyrazines, furans, etc.

FLAVOR MOLECULES
Pyrazines: roasted, toasted
Furans: meaty, caramel-like

COFFEE
A cup of coffee with complex aroma and taste
(pp.206–207)

Adding heat

At around 284°F (140°C) and above, fragments of protein and traces of sugar on the surface of the food momentarily fuse before shattering into dozens of new chemicals. The resulting flavor compounds make our favorite foods and drinks, including coffee and beer, taste good. At 356°F (180°C), molecules break apart, and food burns (pyrolysis), producing acrid, bitter compounds.

PROTEIN

284°F
(140°C)

SUGAR

356°F
(180°C)

REACTION BETWEEN PROTEIN AND SUGAR

Thiophene: smoky, roasted flavors
Thiols: meaty, roasted flavors
Pyrazines: roasted flavors

Glucose and fructose react with amino acids

Furanone: sweet caramel flavors
Furan: meaty, burnt flavors

356°F (180°C) + BURNING (PYROLYSIS)

TO MAKE BEER
START WITH

GERMINATED BARLEY

PROCESS:
KILNING

START AT:
284°F
(140°C)

Amino acids + sugars = pyrazines, pyrroles, and melanoidins

FLAVOR MOLECULES
Pyrroles: cereal-like, nutty
Melanoidins: malty, toasted

BEER
Beer with a toasted, malty aroma and flavor
(pp.212–213)

HOW CAN I CONTROL THE MAILLARD REACTION?

With a bit of chemical trickery, you can accelerate or slow the Maillard reaction. By adding extra fuel to the fire, you can amplify the tantalizing earthy and nutty Maillard aromas.

Mix honey into a marinade to speed up reactions and enhance flavor; pour cream into simmering sugar to provide milk proteins and sugar (lactose) for the Maillard reaction, creating caramel and toffee flavors; brush pastry or bread with egg to add protein for a thick crust.

ACID AND ALKALI

The Maillard reaction is also sensitive to acid levels (pp.32–33). Adding lemon juice or vinegar puts the brakes on the entire process, so be wary of adding acids to marinades. Reversely, adding an alkali, such as baking soda, speeds up Maillard flavor creation. Protein-rich egg whites are also slightly alkaline, so are doubly effective for browning.

To make your roast potatoes extra tasty, add half a teaspoon of baking soda to the cooking water when par boiling so that their surfaces become alkaline. Similarly, when you are salting meat, adding a little baking soda to the salt before roasting (a ratio of 3:1 salt to baking soda) will accelerate the Maillard reaction.

Sugars that accelerate the browning reaction

Not all sugars join in with the Maillard reaction—only those that chemists term "reducing sugars." We tend to think of all sugar being the same, but on a chemical level, there are many different types. The sugar molecules that create a browning effect are fructose, glucose, lactose, and maltose (p.19).

WHAT TO USE

THESE REDUCING SUGARS ARE NECESSARY FOR THE MAILLARD REACTION TO TAKE PLACE. THEY ARE FOUND IN DIFFERENT NATURAL INGREDIENTS.

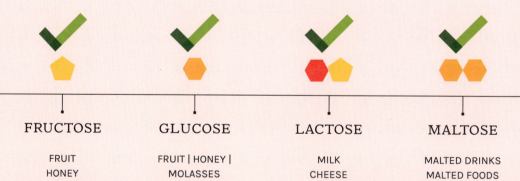

FRUCTOSE
FRUIT
HONEY
BROWN SUGAR
AGAVE NECTAR
ROOT VEGETABLES

GLUCOSE
FRUIT | HONEY | MOLASSES
BROWN SUGAR
MAPLE SYRUP
CORN SYRUP

LACTOSE
MILK
CHEESE
YOGURT
CREAM
BUTTER

MALTOSE
MALTED DRINKS
MALTED FOODS
MALTED BARLEY SYRUP

ACTIVATING FLAVOR 77

SUCROSE AND THE MAILLARD REACTION

Sucrose is a disaccharide, meaning it is made of two smaller single sugar molecules (fructose and glucose) bound together.

FRUCTOSE + GLUCOSE =
SUCROSE

This union conceals the chemical "hooks" or "reducing sites" where amino acids can react, preventing the Maillard reaction from taking place. However, when heated beyond 338°F (170°C), the union breaks apart, revealing these reactive sites, allowing them to participate in the Maillard reaction.

FRUCTOSE   GLUCOSE

WHAT NOT TO USE

THESE SUGARS DO NOT TAKE PART IN THE MAILLARD REACTION.

SUCROSE

WHITE GRANULAR SUGAR (CANE)
BROWN GRANULAR SUGAR (CANE)
CASTER SUGAR (CANE)
POWDERED SUGAR (CANE)
BEET SUGAR

HONEY
THIS DEEP BROWN COLOR HAS BEEN CREATED BY THE SUGAR IN THE HONEY.

BUTTER
THE SMALL AMOUNTS OF PROTEIN AND LACTOSE IN THE BUTTER HELP TO PRODUCE A SLIGHT BROWN EFFECT.

EGG
A WASH OF EGG HAS ACCELERATED BROWNING THROUGH ITS PROTEIN CONTENT.

Maillard-boosting glazes
A range of different glazes have been used to create varied finishes on these baked bread rolls.

NO GLAZE
THE SURFACE OF THE BREAD WITHOUT ANY GLAZE HAS LESS BROWNING.

WHAT IS CARAMELIZATION?

Caramelization is the breakdown of sugar by heat. Although sugar is a one-dimensional, odorless powder, when heated it can be transformed into a variety of richly flavored delights—from sweet, amber syrups to deep, earthy brittles.

Refined sugars are identically sized crystals made of one basic chemical (for example, sucrose, pp.18–21). Sugars are resilient little molecules, able to withstand temperatures far above those at which fats, starches, and proteins disintegrate. But even sugars have their limits, temperatures at which the chemical bonds that leash them together are shaken apart, fracturing them into hundreds of differently shaped fragments and shards, many with aromas, color, and taste. This breaking point temperature varies between sugars (sucrose, glucose, fructose, and so on), but the process is broadly the same: flavorful pieces gradually rearrange into new molecules, adding complexity and depth of flavor with each passing minute until eventually sugary remnants merge into large, dark brown, bitter-tasting compounds. If heating continues, acrid blackness follows as the compounds are torn into unpleasant, carbonized, and potentially harmful chemicals.

CARAMELIZATION TEMPERATURES

As sucrose reaches high temperatures, it breaks down, creating a range of different flavors and colors. The process can be controlled and used to make products from butterscotch to caramel.

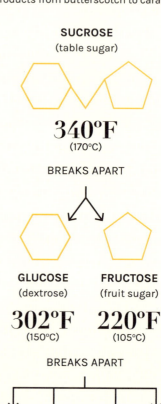

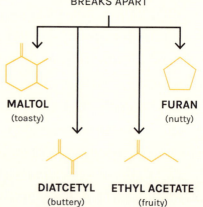

Caramelization and the Maillard reaction

BY ADDING MILK, CREAM, OR BUTTER TO SIMMERING SUGAR (266–338°F/130–170°C), the protein in the dairy products reacts with the sugar molecules to fire up the Maillard reaction, liberating an avalanche of toffee, fudgy, butterscotch aroma compounds.

	MILK	CREAM	BUTTER
Fat content	0.1–3.5%	18–48%	80–82%
Protein content	3.2–3.4%	2–3%	0.5–1%
Uses	Thin caramel sauce, dulce de leche (cooked slowly into a thick sauce/jam)	Thick caramel sauce, butterscotch sauce (with brown sugar)	Toffee, thick caramel sauce, fudge (with cream)

Caramelization cheat sheet

If you don't have a thermometer, drop a little syrup into cold water and it will turn it into a blob with a consistency that indicates the different caramel stages. After the hard crack stage, color is the best guide.

KEY FLAVOR COMPOUNDS	COLD-WATER TEST	SYRUP BOILING POINT	SUGAR CONCENTRATION	USED TO MAKE
ACRYLAMIDE Strong burnt aroma, pronounced bitterness with a charred taste	hard/solid	401°F (205°C)	>99% (BURNT SUGARS)	BLACK CARAMEL
ALDEHYDES Deep burnt sugar aroma, bittersweet taste with smoky notes	hard/solid	370–374°F (188-190°C)	>99%	DARK CARAMEL
HIGH 5-METHYLFUFURAL Intense caramel aroma balanced sweet and bitter taste with nutty undertones	hard/solid	356–360°F (180-182°C)	>99%	MEDIUM CARAMEL: SPUN SUGAR, SUGAR CAGES
CYCLOPROPANONES Rich caramel aroma, sweet with complex flavor notes, including slight acidity	hard/solid	340°F (170°C)	>99%	TOFFEE
HIGH FUFURAL Caramelized sugar aroma with rich, sweet, and slightly bitter taste	hard/solid	320–335°F (160-168°C)	>99%	BRITTLE, BUTTERSCOTCH
2-METHYL-3-FURANTHIOL Meaty, brothy	hard crack	300–310°F (149-154°C)	98–99%	HARD CANDIES, HONEYCOMB
PYRAZINES Roasted, with a hint of toasted nuts	soft crack	270–290°F (132-143°C)	95–98%	TAFFY (CHEWS), NOUGAT
DIACETYL Sweet, buttery, with marshmallow aroma, hints of vanilla	hard ball	250–266°F (121-130°C)	91–95%	CARAMEL, CANDIES
ISO-MALTOL Sweet, cotton candy aroma	firm ball	245–250°F (118-121°C)	88–91%	FONDANT, SWISS MERINGUE, MARSHMALLOWS
MALTOL, 5-METHYLFURFURAL Sweet, roasted, fruity, toasted aromas with vanilla notes	soft ball	235–240°F (113-116°C)	85–88%	FUDGE, SYRUPS, PRESERVES
FURFURAL Mild sweetness, light floral aroma	thread	215–235°F (102-113°C)	80–85%	LIGHT CARAMEL FOR SYRUPS, COLOR, AND FLAVOR

WHAT ELSE INFLUENCES THE FLAVOR EXPERIENCE?

While we often focus on the five basic tastes and the inescapable heat of spiciness, our sensory experience of food is far more nuanced. Other factors affect how we experience each mouthful of food and drink.

Consider the refreshing cooling sensation of menthol, or the back-of-the-mouth dryness of an oversteeped cup of tea, for instance. There is also the energizing fizz of bubbles from sparkling water and the throat-burning bite of spirits. These are all important facets of the flavor experience and bring new dimensions to a dish.

ASTRINGENCY

Tannins found in red wine and black tea are thought to make proteins in saliva clump together, making saliva feel rough. New research, however, shows that there seem to be tannin receptors in the mouth that give this cloying sensation. Sugar and acids both work to reduce astringency, so adding sugar to tea would have this effect.

COOLING SENSATIONS

Toothpaste and chewing gums are mint flavored because menthol is a chemical that creates a refreshing cooling feeling (coolth) in the mouth. Menthol activates "TRPM8" cold-sensitive nerves in the mouth, which normally turn on only below 79°F (26°C), tricking your brain into feeling coldness. Other TRPM8 stimulants include geraniol (from geraniums, rose oil, and lemongrass) and linalool (from lavender and basil).

EFFERVESCENCE

The sparkling sensation from carbonated drinks comes from popping bubbles tickling the touch sensors in the mouth. A carbon dioxide sensing system on the tongue also rapidly turns dissolved carbon dioxide into sour-tasting carbonic acid.

COOLING
Compounds like menthol and eugenol (pp.198–199) give a cooling effect.

EFFERVESCENCE
Carbon dioxide and other gas bubbles give a fizzing mouth sensation.

METALLIC
Heme, the iron-containing molecule in blood and rare meat, gives a distinct metallic tang.

NUMBING
The sanshools in Sichuan peppercorns give an effervescence-like numbing sensation (pp.176–177).

ACTIVATING FLAVOR **81**

ASTRINGENCY
Tannins found in wine lead to mouth "dryness" (pp.210–211).

ETHANOL
Alcohol interacts with flavor compounds and saliva to change mouthfeel, taste, and aroma (pp.210–215).

MINERALS
Magnesium, copper, and calcium are among the minerals that can add a metallic or chalky taste to tea.

HOT, PUNGENT COMPOUNDS
These include capsaicin, found in chiles (pp.180–181).

METALLIC
The distinctive metallic tang from rare red meat seems to come from the iron it contains, although scientists aren't sure whether there is a metal taste receptor.

ALCOHOL WARMTH
The throat-burning sting of strong spirits takes place because concentrated alcohol (ethanol) fires up the high-temperature "TRPV1" pain nerves (p.43) to create a burning illusion. It also directly irritates the soft lining of the mouth and throat, causing reddening, and strips away the lining's thin, protective fatty coat.

KOKUMI
Some taste researchers claim that there is a taste called kokumi, which features alongside umami in Japanese cuisine. Coming from umami-rich ingredients, it is a rich "mouth fullness" from dishes that have been cooked for a long time.

HOW CAN I PRESERVE FLAVOR?

Flavor and flavor compounds can be preserved in many ways, ancient and modern. While these methods work differently, they all aim to preserve the quality and flavor of food.

To keep food flavorful and safe, we restrict the growth of microbes that spoil its taste and appearance. Preserving aroma compounds and preventing reactions with air (oxidation) are also crucial, as these can cause rancid flavors, browning, and staleness. Most preservation methods work by reducing the water content in food, halting these chemical and biological processes.

DRYING

Drying is one of the oldest methods because of its simplicity. The sun and a breeze are enough to dry food. As the food is left in a dry area with airflow and heat, the water it contains begins to slowly evaporate, dehydrating it. The drier the food, the longer it lasts—most bacteria, mold, and chemical reactions stop when moisture falls below 15 percent. This concentrates sugars, salts, and acids, intensifying the flavor. Some aroma compounds evaporate during drying, slightly altering the flavor profile.

OIL

Oil is often used to preserve foods like herbs and vegetables. Many flavor compounds are fat-soluble so they are able to enter the oil directly—producing an oil with these flavors locked in.

SUGAR

Sugar preservation reduces the available water in food, preventing bacteria and mold from growing. High sugar levels, as in jams, jellies, and candied fruits, create an environment hostile to microbes while enhancing the food's sweetness and flavor.

SALT CURING

Salt-cured food is either rubbed with or soaked in brine until the salt fully penetrates and cures the

Dried fish flakes

Creating this Japanese delicacy takes several months and uses several different processes to preserve the fish.

FILLETED

The bonito fish is filleted and cut into pieces.

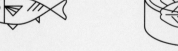

COOKED

It is cooked for several hours, to remove excess fat.

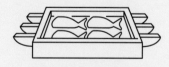

SMOKED

Fish is smoked and dried until it is hard. The scales, skin, and brine are removed.

ACTIVATING FLAVOR 83

SUN-DRYING

When food reaches around 15 percent moisture, most microbes can't grow and spoilage reactions stop.

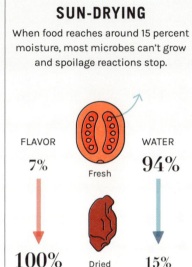

OIL

Oil creates a barrier around the food, preventing moisture and oxygen from entering.

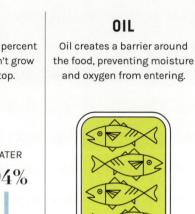

SUGAR

Sugar binds with water, preventing bacteria and mold from growing.

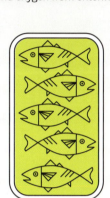

SALT

Salt draws water out, reducing moisture and preventing microbe growth.

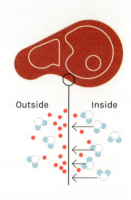

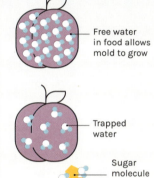

food. Salting enhances flavor by drawing out moisture and triggering chemical reactions that break down compounds to form new ones. Salted food may also be smoked, further aiding preservation and creating additional flavor compounds, such as cheesy notes from aldehydes, meaty and earthy tones from sulfur compounds, and buttery or creamy notes from ketones.

FISH FLAKES

KATSUOBUSHI (BONITO FISH FLAKES) HAVE A UMAMI TASTE FROM THEIR HIGH IMP (INOSINATE) LEVELS (P.28).

DRIED

The fish is dried to remove further moisture.

FERMENTED

The fillets are sprayed with a mold culture to break down protein and enhance the flavor.

AGED

The fish may be left for months to allow flavor compounds to develop.

FLAKED

The smoked, dried, and fermented fish is shaved into flakes ready for use.

HOW DOES FERMENTATION AFFECT FLAVOR?

Fermentation is perhaps the oldest form of preservation used by humans, with evidence of it being used for thousands of years. This makes food safe to eat and also adds a variety of mouthwatering flavors.

Fermentation, usually without oxygen, encourages beneficial microbes and discourages harmful ones. Microbes like lactic acid bacteria thrive in low-oxygen environments, breaking down sugars into acids, gases, or alcohol. Some fermentations, such as vinegar or kombucha, require oxygen at certain stages.

FERMENTATION FLAVORS

There are several methods of fermentation, including acetic acid fermentation and lactofermentation.

Acetic acid bacteria preserve flavor compounds while also bringing some nuanced compounds of their own, including a sweet and slightly solvent-like note from ethyl acetate, apple notes from acetaldehyde, and a tang from acetic acid.

During lactofermentation, lactic acid is produced as well as a number of unique flavor compounds, including cream and butter notes from acetoin and diacetyl, honey notes from phenethyl hexanoate, and medical notes from p-cresol.

ACETIC ACID

Acetic acid bacteria (AAB) and oxygen convert alcohol into acetic acid. Used for vinegar, kombucha, and other pickled foods.

ALCOHOL + OXYGEN + ACETIC ACID BACTERIA (AAB) → ACETIC ACID

KEY
- Hydrogen
- Oxygen
- Carbon

LACTOFERMENTATION

Lactic acid bacteria (LAB) break down sugars into lactic acid, which preserves food. Used for vegetables, including dill pickles, sauerkraut, and kimchi.

GLUCOSE + LACTIC ACID BACTERIA (LAB) → LACTIC ACID

MOLD FERMENTATION

Mold spores are spread onto the food to be fermented and left to grow in a controlled environment. Used for miso and tempeh.

PROTEIN CHAIN + MOLD → INOSINATE (IMP) (p.28), GLUTAMATE (p.28), GUANYLATE (GMP) (p.28)

THE USE OF MOLD

Camembert, tempeh, miso, and soy sauce all involve mold fermentation, which creates some of the world's favorite flavors. Although the types of mold differ—such as *Penicillium* in cheese and *Aspergillus* in miso—the process is similar. As mold spores grow, they extend hyphae (rootlike fibers) into the food and release enzymes. These enzymes break down proteins into amino acids, giving umami, and starches into sugars, adding sweetness. This makes the food more digestible for the mold and delicious for us.

ALCOHOL FERMENTATION

Yeast, a type of fungus, is responsible for converting sugar into alcohol and carbon dioxide. This process, used to create sourdough, wine, and beer, produces a wealth of flavor compounds. Different strains and mixtures of yeast act like specialists, creating unique bouquets of a huge range of flavor compounds, including grassy notes from acetaldehyde, smoky notes from 4-vinyl guaiaco, cacoa notes from 2,3-dimethylpyrazine, almond notes from benzaldehyde, and rose notes from phenethyl alcohol.

> AFTER CONSUMING ALL THE ALCOHOL, AAB MAY START TO CONSUME THE ACETIC ACID IT MADE, REDUCING VINEGAR'S SOURNESS.

> MISO PRODUCTION INCLUDES THE USE OF MOLDS, ENZYMES, LACTIC ACID BACTERIA, YEASTS, AND ACETIC ACID BACTERIA.

> FLAVOR COMPOUNDS IN FERMENTED TOFU INCLUDE MUSHROOM NOTES FROM 1-OCTEN-3-ONE (MUSHROOM KETONE).

FLAVOR DIRECTORY

Tomatoes	88	Citrus	120
Bell peppers	90	Apples and pears	122
Eggplants	92	Stone fruits	124
Onions	94	Berries	126
Garlic	96	Tropical fruits	128
Leafy green vegetables	98	Rice	130
Carrots	100	Corn	132
Salad science	102	Bread	134
Potatoes	104	Sandwich science	138
Root vegetables	108	Pasta and noodles	140
Broccoli and cauliflower	110	Mushrooms and truffles	142
Cabbages and Brussels sprouts	112	Seaweed	144
Legumes	114	Beef	146
Soybeans	116	Lasagna science	148
Stir-fry science	118	Poultry	150

Pork	**152**	Allspice	**187**
Lamb, mutton, and goat	**154**	Cilantro/Coriander	**188**
Game meat	**156**	Fennel	**190**
Offal	**157**	Parsley	**191**
Fish	**158**	Dill	**192**
Crustaceans	**160**	Basil	**193**
Mollusks	**162**	Oregano and thyme	**194**
Milk and cream	**164**	Sage	**196**
Butter	**166**	Rosemary	**197**
Yogurt, kefir, and cheese	**168**	Mint	**198**
Eggs	**170**	Saffron	**200**
Nuts	**172**	Vanilla	**201**
Olive oil	**174**	Bay leaves	**202**
Black pepper, ginger, and mustard	**176**	Curry leaves	**203**
Nutmeg and mace	**178**	Tea	**204**
Cloves	**179**	Coffee	**206**
Chiles	**180**	Chocolate	**208**
Curry science	**182**	Wine	**210**
Turmeric	**184**	Beer	**212**
Cumin	**185**	Spirits	**214**
Cinnamon and cassia	**186**		

TOMATOES

The tomato, now the world's most popular fruit, was first cultivated by the Aztecs, who bred this once small, bitter berry into sweeter, plumper varieties. These made their way to European shores in the 1500s and from there around the world and into today's more than 400 varieties.

Ripe tomatoes owe their appeal to high levels of savory glutamate (pp.26–27), and with a sugar content of 3 percent—lower than most fruits—they are primarily a savory ingredient. Citric acid gives tomatoes their tartness. Of the 400+ aroma compounds in tomatoes, just 13 give them their characteristic flavor profile. Sulfur-containing compounds bring a meaty quality, and when cooked, dried, or puréed, tomatoes' umami, aroma, and sweetness are intensified.

Growing large, long-lasting tomatoes for the mass market has come at the cost of flavor, with most commercial varieties having less sugar and acid than traditional ("heirloom") varieties, and fewer key flavor compounds, including sweetness-enhancing "apocarotenoid" aroma compounds, citrus-fruity sulcatone, and geranylacetone, which has a strong rosy and fruity flavor.

COOKING WITH TOMATOES

Cooked and canned tomatoes are invaluable bridging ingredients (pp.70–71) for bringing together disparate savory foods, having shared compounds with potatoes (methional), mushrooms (1-octen-3-one), and green vegetables (hexenal), as well as cheeses, roasted foods, and most herbs and spices.

Cooked tomatoes synergize with meats and give depth to vegetarian dishes because they are both rich in glutamate (umami) and release sulfur-containing flavor compounds similar to those

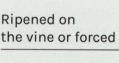

Ripened on the vine or forced

Most supermarket tomatoes are picked and shipped while still green and force-ripened in warehouses with ethylene gas. This denies them the sugars and flavor compounds that accumulate when matured on the vine.

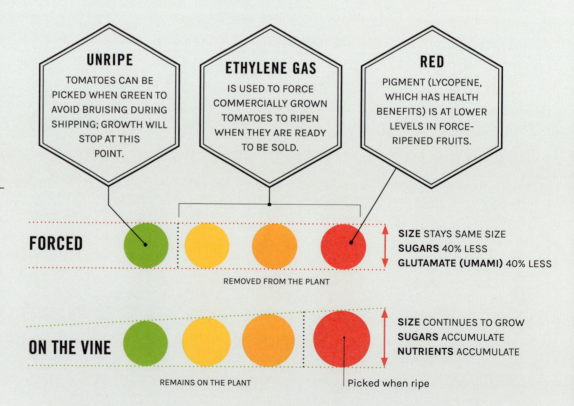

FLAVOR DIRECTORY 89

Common pairings
Apple, mango, basil, oregano, olive oil, and mozzarella.

Uncommon pairings
Dark chocolate, coffee, guava, grape, melon, and strawberry.

Apple — Tomato — Mango   Coffee — Tomato — Chocolate

found in meats. Cooking tomatoes down to make a thick sauce introduces new flavors, including floral aroma compounds from the breakdown of pigments. Avoid canned tomatoes that contain calcium salts, which are a firming agent and will prevent this. When cooking tomatoes with beans, pulses, and other vegetables, allow extra time as the acidity of tomatoes slows vegetable cooking (pp.32–33).

Tomato varieties

HEIRLOOM

BRANDYWINE Known for its sweet, complex flavor and meaty texture.

CHEROKEE PURPLE Offers a rich, smoky flavor.

GREEN ZEBRA Tangy and zesty, with green and yellow stripes.

SAN MARZANO A plum tomato, ideal for sauces due to its low water content.

BLACK KRIM Dark, almost black in color, with a salty, rich flavor.

YELLOW PEAR Small, pear-shaped, and sweet.

PINK PONDEROSA Large and juicy, with a sweet, mild flavor.

MASS-PRODUCED

GLOBE OR ROUND The standard supermarket tomato, versatile but often less flavorful.

ROMA OR PLUM Elongated shape, often used in sauces and paste.

CHERRY Small, round, and sweet, often used in salads.

BEEFSTEAK Large and meaty.

CAMPARI Slightly larger than cherry tomatoes; sweet and juicy.

VINE-RIPENED Picked in a riper state than most commercial varieties, but not fully ripened on the vine.

CLUSTER OR TRUSS Sold on the vine; offer a more aromatic profile compared to other commercial varieties.

STORAGE
REFRIGERATION SLOWS RIPENING, SO TOMATOES WON'T TASTE GOOD STRAIGHT FROM THE FRIDGE.

Green to red

As bell peppers ripen, their flavor aromas develop and change from the slightly bitter, sharp, and grassy flavor of the unripened green peppers to the sweeter, fruity, and floral aromas of the riper red pepper.

PICKED WHEN GREEN

PICKED WHEN RED

Chlorophyll is dominant

Carotenoids are less prominent

Chlorophyll pigment breaks down

Carotenoid pigment revealed, leading to red peppers

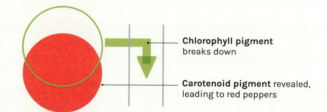

FLAVOR COMPOUND
Bell pepper pyrazine (2-methoxy-3-isobutylpyrazine)

FLAVOR COMPOUNDS
Beta-ionone (sweet, fruity)

SUGAR LEVEL
LOW

SUGAR LEVEL
+100%

BITTERNESS
HIGH

BITTERNESS
LOW

ALSO FOUND IN CABERNET SAUVIGNON, CILANTRO, AND PEAS.

ALSO FOUND IN TOMATOES, BLACK CURRANTS, CARROTS, AND RASPBERRIES.

BELL PEPPERS

The bell peppers we see today emerged sometime during a 7,000-year history of growing, when mutant strains of chile pepper (capsicum), unable to produce mouth-burning capsaicin, were selected.

Christopher Columbus brought capsicum plants to Europe from South America, where they have been bred into the sweet, nonspicy varieties we enjoy today. Coming in a vibrant palette—green, yellow, orange, chocolate brown, and red—each hue has a subtly different taste.

All start life as an unripe green before maturing into a particular color. Supermarket green peppers are typically picked before they ripen, although a "Permagreen" variety does exist. Unlike fruits that continue ripening after picking, such as tomatoes, bananas, avocados, and pears, bell peppers stop ripening the moment they are picked.

FLAVOR COMPOUNDS

Delightfully crisp and fresh tasting when raw, peppers turn soft, fruity, and richly flavored when cooked, as new flavor compounds emerge, with hints of caramel and cacao. The unique fresh, "green" flavor from a green pepper comes from a powerful flavor compound called "bell pepper pyrazine" (2-methoxy-3-isobutylpyrazine), which is also found in some Cabernet Sauvignon wines.

As greenness fades with maturity and the leafy green chlorophyll pigment is replaced with brighter, healthy ones, sugar levels double, bitterness fades, and fruity and almondy flavors come to the fore as levels of grassy aroma compounds hexanol and hexanal fall. Red are the sweetest and fruitiest, with yellow, brown, and orange usually slightly less so, with bitterness sometimes dominating in green.

Bell pepper varieties

The astonishingly diverse pepper fruits are a continuum from fruity to fiery. Those listed below are all under 500 Scoville Heat Units (pp.180–181).

CORNO DI TORO ("HORN OF THE BULL") PEPPERS
Slender, curved, yellow, orange, or red peppers that are thick fleshed, sweet, and very fruity. Ideal for roasting and stuffing.

SHEPHERD PEPPERS (POIVRONS MARCONI)
Large and substantial, these thick-fleshed, sweet red peppers are similarly well suited to roasting and stuffing.

PIMENTO (CHERRY PEPPERS)
Small and sweet, their soft texture lends them well to blending for sauce-making and for stuffing olives. Low levels of capsaicin mean they are often termed mild chile peppers.

LIPSTICK PEPPERS
Thicker-skinned types of pimentos that grow quickly in colder climates, making them popular in the United Kingdom and other Northern European countries.

BANANA PEPPERS (POIVRONS BANANE DOUX)
Sweet, tangy, and sometimes a little spicy, these large, cheerful yellow peppers can have mild heat when picked at their most ripe.

Common uncooked pairings
Olives and olive oil are ideal with uncooked pepper. Pepper also works with lettuce, cucumber, green beans, and tomato.

Olive **Pepper** Lettuce

Tomato **Pepper** Onion

Common cooked pairings
Roasted and stewed red pepper works with tomato, onions, cured meat and sausage, chocolate, hazelnut, citrus, honey, pork, and bacon.

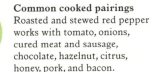

EGGPLANTS

Termed "eggplants" due to their original small, egglike form, eggplants were first farmed in China 1,500 years ago, then spread westward by Arab traders. Following this, they were bred into various colored varieties and are now a key ingredient in many Asian, African, and European cuisines.

Eggplants are mildly sweet and slightly nutty, with bitterness that fades with cooking. In contrast to their fruity South American relatives (tomatoes and peppers), eggplants have a very mild aroma profile that has not been well studied by scientists. They are instead prized for their meaty or creamy texture and as a vehicle for other flavors. Among the aroma compounds, leaf aldehyde (hexenal) contributes to its green and grassy notes; hexanone carries hints of sweet rum and grape; while propionaldehyde contributes to earthy and nutty qualities. When grilled, roasted, or fried, eggplants take on complex smoky and caramelized flavors through pyrazines and furans (compounds produced in the Maillard process, pp.74–77). Cooked in sauces, such as ratatouille, eggplants take on the flavor of the

Adding salt

The spongy texture of an eggplant soaks up oil in a pan, making a dish overly rich and heavy. Salting before cooking can reduce the amount of oil that is absorbed. Once cooked, the texture becomes smooth and silky.

Phenolic compounds | Air pocket

LARGE AIR POCKETS

The spongy interior of an eggplant is due to millions of tiny air gaps between plant cells, into which cooking oil is rapidly absorbed.

ADD SALT

Salting dehydrates the cells, crumpling this architecture and pulling the flesh tighter. Precooking has a similar effect and can be done in a microwave.

BITTER COMPOUNDS

As water is drawn out by salting, so are bitter compounds, chief among which is chlorogenic acid: up to 50 percent of the acid can be extracted this way and with rinsing.

DEFLATED AIR POCKETS

As the salt draws the water out of the cells, the air pockets become deflated and shrink.

BROWN WHEN CUT

Chlorogenic acid is among various phenolic compounds that aggregate into large, brown-colored chainlike molecules (called polymers) when cut.

FLAVOR DIRECTORY 93

Common pairings
Pepper and chile, particularly chipotle chile, share many compounds with roasted, grilled, or fried eggplant.

Chile — Eggplant — Pepper

Cheddar cheese — Eggplant — Pork

Uncommon pairings
Pork loin shares the most flavor compounds among meats, while Cheddar cheese is the most compatible dairy choice.

---

herbs, tomatoes, garlic, and spices. They're also used to give a sweet, buttery flavor in Mediterranean dishes like moussaka.

One way to avoid eggplants turning brown is to salt them before cooking. To do this, slice, salt, then rinse them to lessen bitterness and astringency, and firm up flesh. Salt draws out moisture from within its cells (a process called osmosis), collapsing the millions of spongy air pockets. Bitter, astringent phenolic compounds, which accelerate browning when cut, also move out with the water, resulting in tastier, brighter flesh. Salting also helps reduce the amount of oil that is soaked into the eggplant as it cooks. Modern varieties have been developed to have fewer bitter compounds and so salting is optional, although it still helps in absorbing less oil.

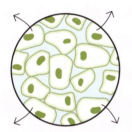

ACID ESCAPES

BITTER-TASTING CHLOROGENIC ACID HAS HEALTH-GIVING PROPERTIES, INCLUDING LOWERING CHOLESTEROL.

AIR POCKETS DEFLATE

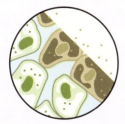

CELLS TURN BROWN

AS A KNIFE'S BLADE EXPLODES PLANT CELLS, DEFENSIVE ENZYMES ESCAPE, TRIGGERING THE PROCESS OF BROWNING.

Eggplant varieties

ASIAN

CHINESE EGGPLANTS
Long, slender, vibrant purple. Tender texture, sweet, mild flavor.

JAPANESE EGGPLANTS
Similar to Chinese but thinner, with a delicate texture and subtly sweet taste.

THAI EGGPLANTS
Small and round, green to white in color. They can be slightly bitter and are often used in curries.

INDIAN EGGPLANTS (brinjal)
Varied shapes/sizes, deep purple. Rich flavor, slightly meaty texture.

WHITE EGGPLANTS
Milder, less earthy than purple, delicate texture, smaller size. European varieties also exist.

EUROPEAN

GLOBE EGGPLANTS (AKA AMERICAN EGGPLANT)
Large, bulbous, little bitterness, dense texture. Grill or roast.

ITALIAN EGGPLANTS
Smaller, sweeter than globe. Creamy texture, mild flavor, ideal for eggplant parmigiana.

GRAFFITI (striped) EGGPLANTS
Purple and white stripes, mild taste, spongy texture.

ROSA BIANCA
Italian heirloom, pinkish-purple with white stripes. Creamy texture with a delicate flavor.

BLACK BEAUTY
Deep purple to black in color with a rich, mildly sweet flavor that is popular among home gardeners.

ONIONS

Onions—the bulbs of the *Allium cepa* species—are the second most used vegetable in cooking. As the plant's underground storage organ, they hold a hearty stockpile of sugars.

The characteristic flavor and aroma of onions comes from a suite of defensive sulfur-containing compounds. Evolved to deter predators, raw onions have a sharp quality, owing to vapors released when onion cells are crushed. When these vapors reach the moisture of our eyes and nose, they turn into painful sulfenic acid. When cooked, the harshest triple-sulfur molecules (trisulfides) disintegrate into milder single and double sulfur-carrying molecules (sulfides and

LESS PAIN

CHILLING ONIONS BEFORE CUTTING THEM SLOWS THE REACTION THAT RELEASES THE EYE-WATERING COMPOUND.

| GREEN ONION | LEEK | CHIVES | RED ONION | WHITE ONION | BROWN ONION |

FLAVOR DIRECTORY 95

Common pairings
Other *Allium* species contain a similar palate of compounds so are natural partners with onion. Together, pepper, onion, and celery are the "holy trinity" in Creole cooking.

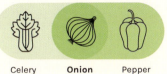

Celery   Onion   Pepper

Chocolate   Onion   Peanut

Uncommon pairings
Chocolate and peanuts have as many flavor crossovers as garlic. Try adding onion powder to a chocolate cake or dark chocolate to onion soup.

---

disulfides). This unveils a natural sweetness, bringing a more complex savory flavor, and allowing other flavors to come to the fore, which form the basis of many dishes.

CARAMELIZING

Slowly cooking onions in oil or butter is incorrectly known as caramelizing (pp.78–79). Gently cooked onions sweeten because pungent sulfides are lost and water evaporates, intensifying the onion's natural sugars. The Maillard reaction (pp.74–77) also imbues them with caramel-like flavors.

COOKING WITH ONIONS

Like the "holy trinity" of peppers, onion, and celery, which is widely used in Cajun and Creole cuisine, the classic French combination of onion, celery, and carrot (mirepoix) is used as the basis of many recipes, as the combination creates strong, savory flavors. Cooked meats contain sulfur compounds, so pair well with onions.

To make an onion seasoning with a deep, savory aroma, you can dry the skins in an oven on the lowest setting until brittle, then blend to create a powder.

Onion varieties

GREEN ONIONS and SCALLIONS (SPRING ONIONS)

Immature onions with a mild, grassy flavor and peppery kick. A scallion bulb has straight sides and is milder than a green onion. Slice thinly as a garnish.

Contain isothiocyanates, but in low concentrations, giving a mild taste.

LEEKS

Mild, sweet, and buttery when cooked.

Low sulfur compounds allow the buttery diacetyl to become prominent. Hints of apple, pineapple, and banana from ethyl butyrate.

CHIVES

Green herb used as a garnish. Delivers a fresh onion-garlic flavor with less pungency.

Low in sulfur, with unique flavor compounds such as thymol (thyme) and tiglic aldehyde (aniseed).

RED ONIONS

Sweet and mild. Ideal raw, for adding sweetness to a cooked dish, or color to a salad.

Red from anthocyanins. Low sulfur content reveals caramel notes from furanone flavor compounds.

WHITE ONIONS

Firm with a crisp flavor. Ideal raw in salads and sautéed in hot dishes.

Low sulfur and acid content gives a mild flavor, revealing natural sweetness.

YELLOW/BROWN ONIONS

Strong flavor with a balance of astringency and sweetness when caramelized.

High in thiosulfinates, giving a pungent, spicy flavor. Unpleasant eaten raw.

SHALLOTS

Small, ancient variety used in cooking, pairing well with meaty dishes.

Low sulfur and acid content give a mild flavor. Contains 1-penten-3-ol, which is buttery with hints of horseradish.

SWEET
SHALLOTS HAVE A MILD, SWEET QUALITY THAT COMBINES ELEMENTS OF BOTH GARLIC AND ONION FLAVORS.

SHALLOT

GARLIC

Perhaps the most celebrated ingredient in all history, garlic has the power to transform a dish, and has many health benefits. Its heady, complex flavor is rooted in a sulfur-carrying compound called allicin: a pungent substance that erupts from cells only when they are cut or damaged through cutting, crushing, or chewing.

Allicin docks onto TRPA1 receptors on pain fibers (p.43) to evoke a mustard-like warmth; its aroma has a pleasant savoriness reminiscent of roasted meat because of its similarity to sulfur-containing flavor compounds in meats and in the Maillard reaction (pp.74–77). With time and cooking, allicin breaks down and into a series of different flavor compounds in a chemical cascade, each with its own character: sharp and lingering flavors when raw turn mellow and sweet with sautéing, hearty with umami-rich depth upon roasting, and develop into complex notes of molasses, balsamic vinegar, and tamarind when aged until black.

AVOID COOKING GARLIC ABOVE **356°F** (180°C) TO PREVENT BITTERNESS.

Garlic intensity

The more a garlic clove is damaged or crushed, the more allicin is made through the work of its defensive enzyme, alliinase.

WHOLE
Whole garlic has a milder flavor and subtle aroma. It can be roasted for a sweeter flavor or baked whole and spread on toast.

CHOPPED
Chopping garlic coarsely with a knife causes minimal damage, with little juice released.

PRESSED
Using a garlic press results in shredded cloves that produce a strong, sweet flavor. Be careful not to scorch when cooking.

GROUND
Pounding garlic in a pestle and mortar damages more cells than in pressing, resulting in a higher flavor intensity.

PURÉED
Puréeing garlic causes maximum damage, making this the most pungent-tasting garlic. Cooking lowers the intensity dramatically.

FLAVOR DIRECTORY 97

Creating allicin
The flavor of garlic comes from allicin, which is released when the cloves are damaged. To get maximum flavor, after chopping the garlic, wait for a few minutes before cooking it.

KEY
- Alliin
- Enzyme
- Allicin + enzyme
- Allicin

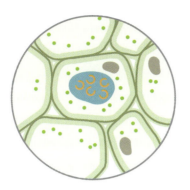

ALLIIN AND ENZYMES KEPT APART
When the garlic clove is whole and undamaged, it contains alliin, a flavorless amino acid that converts into allicin.

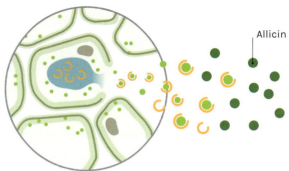

ALLIIN AND ENZYMES JOIN
When garlic is chopped or crushed, the alliin is converted into allicin by the enzyme alliinase.

ALLICIN CREATED
The allicin is released, sending out the powerful aroma of garlic.

Rest garlic after crushing—fiery allicin peaks at 60 seconds before mellowing into complex flavors, degrading into compounds like spicy diallyl disulfide and garlicky ajoene, adding rich savory notes. High-heat cooking, such as blanching above 140°F (60°C), deactivates the allicin-generating enzymes, ideal for milder dishes.

BANISHING BITTERNESS
With a lower water content than most vegetables, small garlic pieces quickly char and burn, producing acrid, bitter-tasting compounds that linger on the palate and can ruin a dish. To avoid this, cook garlic slowly in plenty of oil or butter and don't add diced or minced pieces too early, especially if you are cooking at high temperatures.

Garlic's tight cluster of six or more small, single-layered bulbs (cloves) each house a tiny green plant embryo, ready to sprout. If left to germinate, the growing shoot drains the clove of its nutrients, causing it to shrivel, while amassing bitter-tasting defensive compounds. Reduce bitterness by removing the green germ and avoid cloves that have sprouted.

Garlic varieties

SOFTNECK
Grown in warmer climates and with soft central stems, these mild-tasting varieties have a long shelf life owing to tighter and more numerous layers of papery skin. They are the ones you'll see most often in supermarkets.

HARDNECK
Grown in colder climates, with woody central stems and fewer, larger cloves. They stockpile more defensive sulfur and so have a bolder, more varied and stronger garlicky flavor.

ELEPHANT GARLIC
Actually a type of bulbous leek with garliclike flavor that can be eaten raw in salads. Large and with a milder flavor than true garlic, it is ideal for roasting or where subtle garlic taste is called for.

WILD GARLIC
A general term for various leafy plants related to traditional garlic, each with large green leaves that impart a subtle, garliclike flavor.

Common pairings
Rich in glutamate, garlic works well with other umami-rich ingredients, such as mushroom and tomato, and is popular in Italian recipes.

Mushroom — Garlic — Tomato

Honey — Garlic — Strawberry

Uncommon pairings
Garlic pairs unexpectedly well with some sweet ingredients, including honey, strawberry, apple, and pineapple. Try it in salsas and salad dressings.

LEAFY GREEN VEGETABLES

Like the food our foraging ancestors gathered in woodland, today's leafy greens are typically bitter and lack the bulky, sweet appeal of most modern produce. Brimming with vitamins, each culture's greenery offers complex bitter undertones and earthiness to the plate.

Despite the world's leafy greens coming from different plant families and climates, most are dominated by oniony, cabbagelike sulfur-containing aroma compounds alongside bitter and astringent taste compounds. These become more muted with cooking but can return with overcooking as other unpleasant compounds, such as eggy hydrogen sulfide, form. Many are edible raw.

IRON

ALTHOUGH SPINACH HAS A HIGHER IRON CONTENT THAN OTHER VEGETABLES, IT IS NOT AS EASILY ABSORBED IN THE BODY AS THE IRON IN STEAK.

20% ABSORBED

SIRLOIN STEAK
IRON/100G
2.5MG

1.7% ABSORBED

SPINACH
IRON/100G
2.6MG

SWISS CHARD'S BITTERNESS MELLOWS WHEN IT IS COOKED. THE COLORFUL STEMS HAVE A STRONGER FLAVOR.

KALE'S BITTER TASTE COMES FROM GLUCOSINATES AND ISOTHIOCYANATES (P.111), WHICH CAN ADD PUNGENT FLAVORS.

SWISS CHARD **BOK CHOY** **KALE**

FLAVOR DIRECTORY 99

Common pairings
Balance spinach's natural bitterness by pairing with cheeses and flat fish.

Cheese · Spinach · Flat fish

Common pairings
Try kale with garlic, lemon, nuts, seeds, and white fish like turbot, as well as whole grains like quinoa.

Garlic · Kale · Turbot

Amaranth varieties

The amaranth group of leafy green vegetables includes chard, sugar beets, and spinach.

SPINACH
Once known as the "Persian vegetable" and now popular on both Western and international plates, spinach's raw green and grassy flavors are joined by new potato-like flavor compounds with hints of popcorn and hay with cooking. If cooked for too long, these degrade into sulfurous compounds, and its texture turns to sludge.

SWISS (GREEN) CHARD
Related to spinach, chard has a more robust flavor, featuring peppery caryophyllene, and has a tougher texture.

AMARANTH GREENS
These are popular in India, China, and East Asia. They share spinach's texture but taste more peppery.

BEET GREENS
These have a mild, sweet, and earthy flavor.

WATER SPINACH
Unrelated to spinach, this has less earthiness and contains sweet-smelling stigmasterol.

Brassica varieties

The brassica group includes some leafy green plants as well as others like cabbage and cauliflower (pp.110–113).

KALE
The evolutionary grandfather of the brassica family (pp.110–113), this ancient Mediterranean vegetable has seen a resurgence because of its nutritional benefits. Tough, crinkly leaves are overloaded with bitter and sulfurous compounds, chiefly glucosinolates (p.111). Cooking breaks these down, along with inedible fibrous cellulose, softening the kale and releasing roasted, sweet, sulfurlike, and green aroma compounds.

COLLARD GREENS
These are popular in the American South and have a less bitter but similar flavor profile to kale. Young leaves are pleasant eaten raw.

BOK CHOY/CHINESE CABBAGE
These varieties have soft leaves and broad stems with different flavors that evolve with cooking. Subtle fruity flavors in raw leaves turn progressively green and almondy with stir-frying and new nutty and roasted pyrazine flavors from the Maillard reaction (pp.74–77) are released.

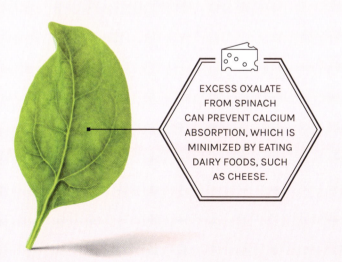

EXCESS OXALATE FROM SPINACH CAN PREVENT CALCIUM ABSORPTION, WHICH IS MINIMIZED BY EATING DAIRY FOODS, SUCH AS CHEESE.

SPINACH

Kale: massaging out the bitterness

Massaging kale by squeezing it and crushing the leaves, then cutting and washing, is a good way to soften leathery leaves and improve flavor.

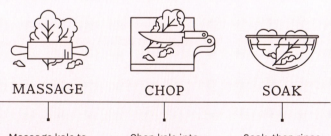

MASSAGE — Massage kale to break down cell walls, releasing myrosinase enzyme (pp.110–111).

CHOP — Chop kale into pieces to lessen bitterness.

SOAK — Soak, then rinse the chopped leaves to remove bitter compounds.

Carrot varieties

SMALL VARIETIES
Smaller variety carrots (for example, Chantenay) tend to be sweeter, unlike baby carrots, which are simply harvested before fully grown and lack the sugar and taste of a mature root. "Baby-cut" are whole carrots cut into small, babylike portions.

ORANGE
Orange carrots have the most intense flavor. While they may all look the same, there are dozens of orange carrot varieties with varying flavors and tastes and a differing repertoires of aroma compounds. "Tornado," "Nottingham," and "Bolero" are among the sweetest.

PURPLE/BLACK
Purple carrots have little bitterness or unpleasant aftertaste, and have a pleasant nutty aroma, but can be sickeningly sweet.

YELLOW/WHITE
Yellow and white carrots have the least sugar and flavor compounds, making them the blandest and least bitter.

RED
With little sugar, and a strong, green aroma, red carrots lack a full carroty flavor and are more bitter than most. Their hue is from tomatoes' pigment, lycopene (pp.88–89).

Orange carrots' bright color comes from beta-carotene (vitamin A)

Purple carrots contain high levels of the pigment anthocyanin and have a sweet flavor

White varieties contain no pigment but still provide nutrients and fiber

Yellow carrots contain lutein, which is important for eye health

COLOR MYTH
PATRIOTIC DUTCH FOLK CLAIM TO HAVE BRED THE FIRST ORANGE CARROT.

IT WAS APPARENTLY BRED TO HONOR WILLIAM OF ORANGE. ORANGE CARROTS ARE TOLERANT OF WET NORTHERN EUROPEAN WEATHER.

A SWEET TREAT
WARTIME BRITAIN WAS PLENTIFUL WITH CARROTS, AND CARROT LOLLIPOPS WERE FAMOUSLY SOLD AS A SUBSTITUTE FOR ICE CREAM.

Common pairings
Carrots pair well with many ingredients, particularly those that bring out their sweet flavors. Try with butter, honey, ginger, cumin, and orange.

Ginger   Carrot   Orange

Cardamom   Carrot   Peanut butter

Uncommon pairings
Try with miso for an unexpected flavor combination. Carrots also work with cardamom in carrot cakes and smoothies and with peanut butter in stir-fries.

CARROTS

The world's favorite orange vegetable came from the Fertile Crescent—modern-day Iran/Afghanistan—and is featured in many cuisines. Once pale and scrawny and eaten just for their feathery leaves, today's orange varieties are hardy and fat-rooted.

Nutritious, sweet, and delightfully crunchy, carrots have more sugar (4–5 percent, mostly sucrose) than even tomatoes (2–3 percent) and have long been used to sweeten foods. Natural sweetness is counterbalanced by a faint bitterness from phenolic compounds, known for their health benefits; one of which (eugenin) gives bitterness to whole cloves.

The humble root vegetable's familiar flavor comes from a remarkably rich palette of more than 100 flavor compounds. Distinct musty and earthy undertones come from a pyrazine flavor compound, 2-methoxy-3-sec-butylpyrazine, which is so potent you could sniff one drop of its vapor in an Olympic swimming pool-sized room. This comes on a background of green, piney, fruity, and peppery flavor compounds. Most significant are woody terpinolene and peppery myrcene, both of which happen to be prominent in cannabis's aroma.

CARROT CARE

Although not in the ground, the carrots you buy are alive until they are cooked, meaning the difference between a sweet, delicious carrot and a bland, bitter root can come down to how it has been treated before and after harvest. Factors include the soil, weather, how it was stored, and even whether it was machine washed (which increases bitterness). Carrots sold with their leaves have a shorter shelf life and so are more likely to be fresher and tastier when you buy them.

SEE IN THE DARK

Common wisdom that eating carrots helps you see in the dark is a myth. Orange carrots are rich in beta-carotene (vitamin A), which is essential for night vision, although most people have plenty already and eating more makes vision no better.

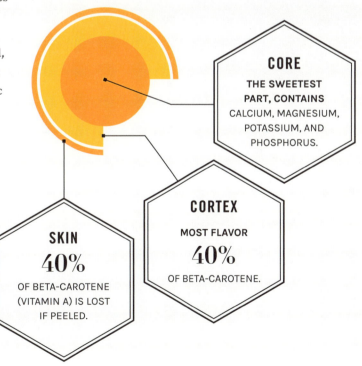

CORE
THE SWEETEST PART, CONTAINS CALCIUM, MAGNESIUM, POTASSIUM, AND PHOSPHORUS.

SKIN
40%
OF BETA-CAROTENE (VITAMIN A) IS LOST IF PEELED.

CORTEX
MOST FLAVOR
40%
OF BETA-CAROTENE.

SALAD SCIENCE

An assortment of fresh ingredients, typically leaves, in a seasoned dressing, salads have been eaten since at least the 14th century. The word "salad" comes from the Latin sal, meaning salt, a nod to their well-seasoned nature and appetite-boosting appeal.

Originally, salads were made with fresh herbs and leaves and were valued for their medicinal properties as well as their taste. Nowadays, they are often a varied mix of ingredients chosen for their complementary flavors and textures, and tossed with a piquant dressing.

THE ESSENTIAL QUALITIES OF SALAD

- **Multiple ingredients:** usually at least three ingredients that have varied but complementary characteristics.
- **Small piece size:** ingredients are carefully cut into bite-sized or smaller pieces so that each forkful contains different tastes and textures.
- **Textural contrast:** a range of textures, such as crisp, chewy, crunchy, and soft, makes salads satisfying to eat.
- **Flavor contrast:** a range of flavor profiles to create contrast between sweet, salty, sour, bitter, and umami.
- **Dressing:** ingredients are mixed, or tossed, in a highly seasoned dressing based on oil and vinegar to impart rich mouthfeel and acidity, along with salt to bring all the different flavors into focus.

FATTOUSH
THIS SALAD DERIVES ITS NAME FROM THE ARABIC WORD FATTEH, MEANING "CRUMBS."

SWEETNESS
A sprinkling of pomegranate seeds brings bursts of acidity and sweetness, and pops of color.

SHARPNESS AND SALTINESS
An emulsified dressing of lemon juice, extra-virgin olive oil, pomegranate molasses, and salt balances the salad ingredients in harmony.

CRUNCH
Add fried flatbread or pita bread for crunchy texture.

AROMA
Chopped fresh mint and flat-leaf parsley introduce refreshing aromas with grassy hexanal and cooling menthol compounds.

SALAD DRESSINGS

Most salad dressings are composed of oil, vinegar or lemon juice, an emulsifier, and other flavorings chosen to complement the ingredients. Dressing is best added just before serving so that the acid and salt in the dressing doesn't break down the leaves' cell structure and draw out liquid. Salads made with cooked ingredients like lentils, pasta, potatoes, or rice are best dressed while they are still warm, to allow the softened starches to absorb the flavors of the dressing.

EMULSIFICATION

Oil and vinegar do not naturally combine, so they need an emulsifier like mustard, yogurt, egg yolk, or honey. These contain molecules with water-soluble and fat-soluble parts, which hold tiny droplets of oil within the vinegar. This creates an emulsion: a thickened liquid that does not separate. Whisking the emulsifier into the oil and vinegar helps disperse the droplets evenly for a smooth dressing.

The perfect salad

Fattoush, from the Middle East, has a simple dressing of extra-virgin olive oil and lemon juice, often with a little pomegranate molasses, which brings sweet-and-sour flavor as well as acting as an emulsifier.

THE PERFECT SALAD

SOURNESS
Sumac comes from dried berries of plants in the cashew family. Its tangy, sour flavor, thanks to malic acid, adds a balance of subtle sweetness and citrusy sharpness to the dressing.

FRESHNESS
Fruits and vegetables bring freshness with the cooling crunch of cucumber, sweet-and-sour brightness of tomatoes, and the crisp peppery bite of radishes.

CRISPNESS
A bed of crisp green lettuce such as romaine or Little Gem, along with soft, peppery, and bitter purslane or watercress.

POTATOES

Farmed for 10,000 years, potatoes were one of the earliest cultivated vegetables. They were first brought from their native South America to Europe by the Spanish in the 1500s. Poisoning fears, however, meant it took more than two centuries for them to become a popular staple.

Like other root vegetables, potatoes grow underground and produce little aroma. Uncooked, they therefore have little flavor. Boiling or steaming releases trapped aroma compounds and creates dozens more through chemical reactions. Baking, roasting, and frying elevates flavors to new heights—more than doubling the number of aroma compound types, largely through the Maillard reaction (pp.74–77) but also from sugars caramelizing and fats "oxidizing" at high temperatures into malty, buttery flavors.

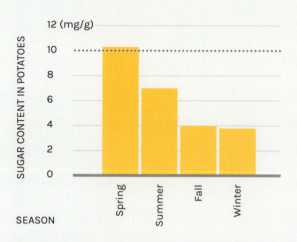

Sugar content
Potatoes harvested early in the year contain more sugar. These high sugars cause excessive Maillard browning, resulting in fried potatoes and fries that are muddy dark brown in color.

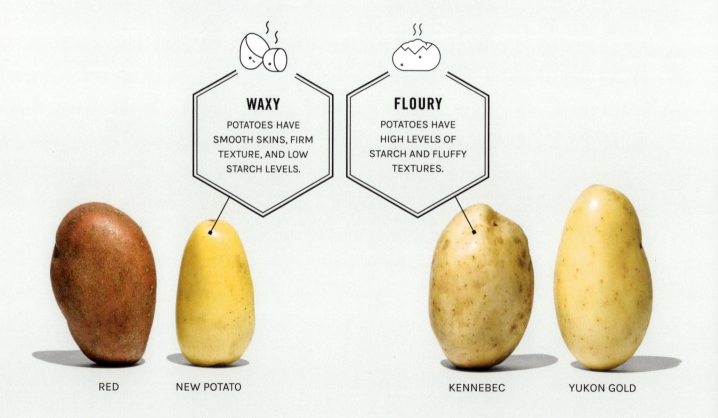

WAXY POTATOES HAVE SMOOTH SKINS, FIRM TEXTURE, AND LOW STARCH LEVELS.

FLOURY POTATOES HAVE HIGH LEVELS OF STARCH AND FLUFFY TEXTURES.

RED — NEW POTATO — KENNEBEC — YUKON GOLD

COOKING POTATOES

Crafting the perfect French fry is a science; it begins with a high-starch potato. The same care should also be applied to making perfect mashed or roasted potatoes, from choosing the right varieties to cooking them properly.

Wherever they grow around the world, potato plants dedicate their lives to preparing for the harsh winters of their native Peru. Every spare calorie of summer sunlight is stowed as starch in their underground fuel stores (called tubers), which are the vegetables we eat. This makes "new potatoes," harvested in spring and summer, sweeter than later crops, as they haven't fully converted their sugars into starch (see opposite).

When potatoes are cooked, the microscopic granules of starch concealed within each cell swell as they absorb water, softening their texture (termed gelatinization) and making the potato more palatable. Starchier potatoes break down more during cooking.

TOP MASH

Making smooth, airy mash needs floury potatoes, a potato ricer, and lots of fat. Cooked potato chunks are passed through a ricer instead of being vigorously smashed, to avoid releasing excess starch that can cause glueyness, and to incorporate air. For silky-smooth mashed potatoes, waxy potatoes are riced then worked heavily to release and bind starch, before being enriched with plenty of butter and cream. For chunky mash, or if using unpeeled potatoes, use a masher. Add soft butter with a plastic spatula to coat the starches, before gradually mixing in milk or cream. Too much mixing binds starches into a paste, while excess liquid turns it soupy.

Science of making mash

Before cooking, raw potatoes contain starch that is stable. This is changed when boiling water is added and the granules swell and burst, releasing the starch, changing the texture of the potato.

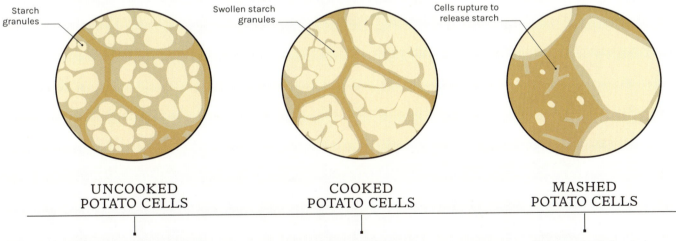

UNCOOKED POTATO CELLS	COOKED POTATO CELLS	MASHED POTATO CELLS
Starch granules are packed tightly in raw potato cells. They remain stable as long as the potato is uncooked.	**When boiling water** is added, the starch granules begin to absorb water and swell (gelatinization).	**The granules take on** more water and the starch gelatinization continues, leading to softer, fluffier potatoes.

Pairings and number of aroma compounds by cooking method

Boiled potatoes have the fewest compounds and mild flavors. Baked potatoes have more complex and intense aromas with nutty, caramel flavors, while fried potatoes have the most aroma compounds, with caramel and roasted flavors.

Common pairings
Olive oil, bacon, mushroom, white truffle, and green tea.

Olive oil — Boiled — Mushroom

MILD FLAVOR

Uncommon pairings
Cranberry, toasted walnut, and mustard seeds.

Cranberry — Boiled — Walnut

180 COMPOUNDS

Common pairings
Beef, tomato, chipotle chile pepper, and Korean miso (Doenjang).

Beef — Baked — Tomato

COMPLEX FLAVOR

Uncommon pairings
Dark chocolate, chili flakes, and goat cheese.

Dark chocolate — Baked — Goat cheese

380 COMPOUNDS

Common pairings
Beef, bacon, white truffle, honey.

Bacon — Fried — Honey

RICHEST FLAVOR

Uncommon pairings
Hazelnut, peanut, and white chocolate.

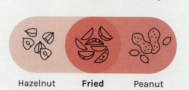

Hazelnut — Fried — Peanut

520 COMPOUNDS

THE PERFECT FRENCH FRY

North America's favorite vegetable, the potato, owes its popularity to the beloved French fry. Crafting the perfect fry is serious science: too much moisture leads to soggy fries, while high sugar levels cause brown fries. To ensure a golden, crunchy exterior and fluffy interior, top restaurants meticulously test for starch and sugar. Hence, high-starch potatoes like the Russet, harvested in fall, are ideal. Blanching in acidified hot water activates enzymes that strengthen pectin, the plant's natural glue, while deactivating softening enzymes. The acid further solidifies pectin and frying twice creates the perfect golden fry.

THE BEST ROASTED POTATOES

Like fries, a great roasted potato is all about a crispy coat. For irresistible results, start with floury, higher-starch varieties like Kennebec, Yukon Gold, or Russet. Peel, cut into large pieces, and cook until soft enough to eat, adding a pinch of baking soda to the cooking water for extra crumbliness. Drain, then roughen their surfaces by gently shaking in the pan with the lid on. Roast in preheated oil at 392°F (200°C), maximizing the Maillard reaction (pp.74–77) for crispy perfection, shaking or turning halfway through cooking. Roasted potatoes take on the flavors of seasoning, herbs, and fats such as olive oil and butter, used while cooking.

FLAVOR DIRECTORY 107

Potato varieties

WAXY

RED
Starch: Medium (16 percent).
Cooked texture: Waxy, firm.
Flavor: Sweet, subtly earthy.
Best for: Salads, boiling, roasting.

FINGERLING
Starch: High (20 percent).
Cooked texture: Waxy, firm.
Flavor: Nutty, buttery.
Best for: Roasting, salads, pan-frying.

NEW POTATO
Starch: Low (13–14 percent).
Cooked texture: Waxy, firm.
Flavor: Light, nutty.
Best for: salads, boiling, steaming, roasting, gratins.

FLOURY

YUKON GOLD
Starch: Medium (16–18 percent).
Cooked texture: Velvety.
Flavor: Sweet, buttery.
Best for: Roasting, mashing, frying/fries.

KENNEBEC
Starch: Medium (15–19 percent).
Cooked texture: Soft, fluffy.
Flavor: Rich, earthy, slightly nutty.
Best for: Mashing, roasting, baking.

RUSSET
Starch: High (over 20 percent).
Cooked texture: Dry, fluffy.
Flavor: Earthy, mild.
Best for: Baking, roasting, mashing, frying/fries.

Potato-like tropical roots and tubers

These vegetables are popular around the world and often cooked and eaten in similar ways to potatoes, sharing some of their flavor characteristics.

CASSAVA (YUCA, MANIOC)
This tuberous starchy root is poisonous uncooked but develops an earthy, slightly sweet, and nutty flavor when cooked. Guaiacol gives cassava warm, smoky, vanilla flavors.

TARO (EDDO, DASHEEN)
This high-starch root vegetable is a staple in Caribbean, African, and Southeast Asian cuisine. Subtly sweet, it tastes like a cross between a potato and a chestnut.

SWEET POTATOES
Maltol, a key aroma compound, imparts caramel-like flavors, while orange carotenoid pigments break into pumpkin-like flavor compounds when cooked.

YAM (PUNA, UBE)
Popular in Africa and the Pacific, yams have a barklike skin and hard flesh. Boiled, fried, or roasted, they release popcorn and cocoa/almond flavor compounds.

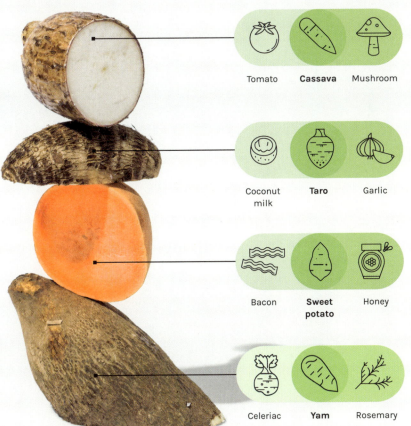

Common pairings

Tomato — **Cassava** — Mushroom

Coconut milk — **Taro** — Garlic

Bacon — **Sweet potato** — Honey

Celeriac — **Yam** — Rosemary

ROOT VEGETABLES

Old World root vegetables have historically formed the basis of many people's diet. They contain a rich combination of flavors and textures.

PARSNIPS

Parsnips are known for their sweetness. Their high sugar content causes quick Maillard browning (pp.74–77), leading to rich, caramelized flavors when roasted or fried. Boiling or adding to stews, soups, and casseroles brings out sweetness and almond hints. An almondy taste comes from myristicin (found in nutmeg) and piney notes from terpinolene (in cumin and apples). Raw parsnips are crisp, earthy, and slightly bitter, ideal for salads or garnishes.

TURNIPS

Raw turnips are bitter and pungent due to glucosinolates (p.111), similar to other brassicas. Slow cooking destroys these to bring out sweetness, earthiness, and nuttiness. Their greens are peppery and can be used like other leafy greens (pp.98–99). Sliced raw turnip adds a bitter, spicy crunch to salads; baby turnips are great with dips. Boiled, roasted, mashed, and added to soups/stews in Western cuisine, when cooked they become porous and absorb flavors, as seen in Asian pickles and spiced stir-fries.

Mediterranean origins Beets were cultivated by ancient Romans and Greeks for their leaves. By 1500, large-rooted varieties were popular.

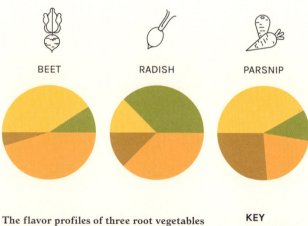

The flavor profiles of three root vegetables are compared here. These ratings can be used to help cooks select the best vegetable for their dish. Beets and parsnips are sweetest, while radishes are the most bitter.

KEY
- Sweetness
- Bitterness
- Earthiness
- Nuttiness

Common pairings							Uncommon pairings
Thyme, rosemary, carrot, potato, and apple.	Apple	**Parsnip**	Rosemary	Salami	**Parsnip**	Lime	Shichimi togarashi spice mix, lime peel, and salami.
Common pairings Onion, garlic, green beans, lettuce, cucumber, carrot, and oats.	Onion	**Turnip**	Cucumber	Cherry	**Turnip**	Lapsang souchong tea	**Uncommon pairings** Cherry, borage flowers, sauerkraut, and oolong/lapsang souchong tea.
Common pairings Cabbage, garlic, onion, horseradish, meat, fried dishes, green beans, and tea.	Cabbage	**Radish**	Garlic	Melon	**Radish**	Pineapple	**Uncommon pairings** Pineapple, watermelon, feta, apple, melon, and citrus fruits.
Common pairings Apple, pear, lemon, mustard, and blue cheese.	Pear	**Celeriac**	Blue cheese	Star anise	**Celeriac**	Cilantro	**Uncommon pairings** Marjoram, juniper berry, star anise, cardamom, and cilantro.
Common pairings Coffee, feta, and nuts.	Coffee	**Beet**	Nuts	Eggplant	**Beet**	Chocolate	**Uncommon pairings** Eggplant, bell pepper, pomegranate, chocolate, apricot brandy, and chimichurri sauce.

RADISHES

Radishes all contain peppery, sulfur-based compounds typical of the cabbage/mustard family of vegetables. They are most often eaten raw and sliced. Their peppery pungency elevates a simple green salad.

CELERIAC

Celeriac's ivory flesh offers an intense celery taste with earthy, nutty undertones. Its flavor comes from compounds called phthalides, alongside limonene (citrusy notes) and caryophyllene (woody spiciness). Crunchy and fennel-like, raw celeriac works in salads or as rémoulade (dressed in lemon juice and served with mustard mayonnaise). With low starch and high moisture, celeriac is often boiled or braised rather than roasted. When cooked, it turns sweet with hints of hazelnut and fennel.

BEETS

Beets are sweet with earthiness from geosmin (the compound in the air after summer rainfall). They can be simmered, boiled, pickled, roasted, or cooked as chips. Grated, they add crunch and sweetness to salads. Their bitterness complements greens, nuts, and tangy cheeses like feta. Cooking reduces bitterness by breaking down bitter compounds. Boiling dilutes flavor, while roasting intensifies it, introducing Maillard flavors and a meatiness that pairs with umami-rich ingredients.

BROCCOLI AND CAULIFLOWER

The brassicas include many familiar vegetables such as broccoli and cauliflower. They're all members of the same plant species (*Brassica oleracea*) that has been bred over centuries to have either gargantuan leaves, misshapen flower or leaf buds, or a swollen lower stem.

BROCCOLI
The frilly broccoli head is a mass of unopened flower buds that are green, dense, and infertile. They store sugar, bitter glucosinolates, and flavor compounds. The head's large surface area lends itself to charring, battering, and drenching in oils, vinaigrettes, and sauces. Its raw bitterness is unveiled when chewed, which activates myrosinase to form pungent radishlike sulforaphane out of its parent glucosinolate. Gentle cooking, like steaming or light boiling, also damages the cell structure to introduce bitter, cut-radish nuances. It mellows raw harshness—its 33 different raw aroma compounds dissipate to just nine. Raw, pungent, garlicky flavors from sulfur compounds fade and are eclipsed by others, as well as a ketone flavor compound that carries the aroma of geranium, accompanied by earthy and "green pea" pyrazines.

CAULIFLOWER
Cauliflower's sweet, cabbagelike, nutty aroma comes from one of its sulfur flavor compounds, dimethyl sulfide. This is complemented by a trio of fresh green, grassy aroma compounds—decadienal, and 2-octenal and hexanal, the last of which is plentiful in the leaves. Leaves and stalks roast well and make for tasty stir-fries, fritters, salads, soups, and stocks. Purple and green varieties typically have fewer bitter compounds and offer a nuttier flavor.

Common pairings
Choose from other brassicas as well as foods such as bacon, peanuts, bell pepper, morel, melon, and peach.

Bacon — Broccoli — Peanuts

Pineapple — Broccoli — Coconut

Uncommon pairings
Broccoli can also work with the sweeter flavors of pineapple and coconut.

Flavor Directory

Flavor mosaic

Each brassica's flavor profile can be thought of as a mosaic of flavor compounds, of which the most important tiles contain sulfur. These aromatic sulfur compounds don't exist in the raw vegetable but are carved out of their raw materials—odorless chemicals called glucosinolates (GTCs)—when the vegetable is chopped, crushed, gently cooked, or damaged in some way.

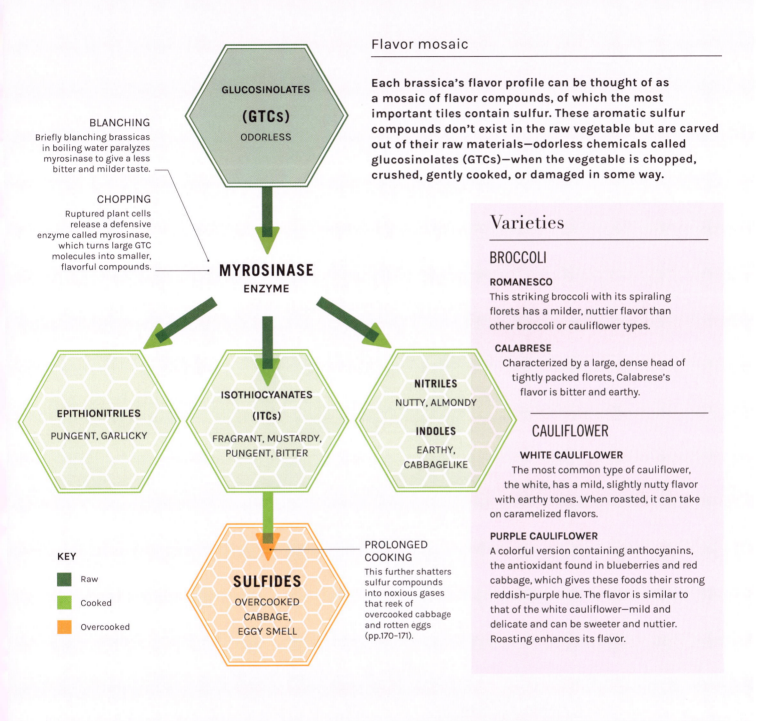

BLANCHING
Briefly blanching brassicas in boiling water paralyzes myrosinase to give a less bitter and milder taste.

CHOPPING
Ruptured plant cells release a defensive enzyme called myrosinase, which turns large GTC molecules into smaller, flavorful compounds.

GLUCOSINOLATES (GTCs) — ODORLESS

MYROSINASE ENZYME

EPITHIONITRILES — PUNGENT, GARLICKY

ISOTHIOCYANATES (ITCs) — FRAGRANT, MUSTARDY, PUNGENT, BITTER

NITRILES — NUTTY, ALMONDY

INDOLES — EARTHY, CABBAGELIKE

PROLONGED COOKING
This further shatters sulfur compounds into noxious gases that reek of overcooked cabbage and rotten eggs (pp.170–171).

SULFIDES — OVERCOOKED CABBAGE, EGGY SMELL

KEY
- Raw
- Cooked
- Overcooked

Varieties

BROCCOLI

ROMANESCO
This striking broccoli with its spiraling florets has a milder, nuttier flavor than other broccoli or cauliflower types.

CALABRESE
Characterized by a large, dense head of tightly packed florets, Calabrese's flavor is bitter and earthy.

CAULIFLOWER

WHITE CAULIFLOWER
The most common type of cauliflower, the white, has a mild, slightly nutty flavor with earthy tones. When roasted, it can take on caramelized flavors.

PURPLE CAULIFLOWER
A colorful version containing anthocyanins, the antioxidant found in blueberries and red cabbage, which gives these foods their strong reddish-purple hue. The flavor is similar to that of the white cauliflower—mild and delicate and can be sweeter and nuttier. Roasting enhances its flavor.

Common pairings
Cheese, nuts, garlic, onion, mustard, horseradish, tomato, and lemon all pair deliciously with cauliflower's nutty aroma.

Cheese · Cauliflower · Lemon

Clam · Cauliflower · Fig

Uncommon pairings
Cointreau liqueur, clam, black rice, fig, and coconut water.

CABBAGES AND BRUSSELS SPROUTS

Cabbages and Brussels sprouts are both members of the brassica family but are different in appearance, texture, and flavor. However, both are rich in nutrients and can be cooked in a variety of ways to improve their naturally bitter flavors.

CABBAGE

Farmed for more than 2,500 years, European cabbages are among the oldest cultivated brassica varieties. All types are versatile, their flavors shining when steamed, roasted, and cooked in butter. Natural acids and sugars make cabbages easy to ferment. Cabbage plant cell walls collapse with heat, quickly producing myrosinase flavors and softening to become absorbent of other flavors.

Research shows that 24 flavor compounds give cabbages their unique flavor profile, which has qualities that are green, pungent, fruity, fatty, floral, and roasted in a balance unique to each variety. The isothiocyanates that give cabbage its primary aroma are not as dominating as those in Brussels sprouts and are balanced by "leafy-green" aroma compounds as well as sweet and ethereal aromas from dimethyl ether, a gas once used as a surgical anaesthetic. Red and purple cabbages are laden with red anthocyanin pigments and have a more varied and fruity flavor profile, lending them well to pairing with sweeter ingredients, such as dried fruits. Asian and some white European cabbages have lemony notes from limonene, while mild-tasting savoy and hispi are perfect for stuffing, roasting, grilling, and braising.

BRUSSELS SPROUTS

Resembling tiny cabbages, Brussels sprouts are dense leaf buds rich in sulfur compounds, at levels higher than any other brassica. For people who are genetically sensitive to bitterness (pp.22–23), they are repulsively intense. As Brussels sprouts' raw glucosinolates and cooked isothiocyanates are both bitter, cooking can worsen the situation, especially if boiled for too long. Cooking methods such as frying or roasting can induce Maillard reactions, creating a nutty flavor that balances and complements bitterness. Enhancing with acids, salt, and sweetness can further elevate their flavor.

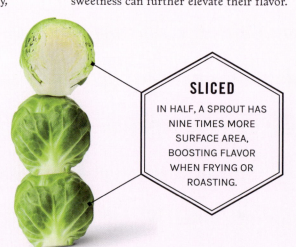

SLICED
IN HALF, A SPROUT HAS NINE TIMES MORE SURFACE AREA, BOOSTING FLAVOR WHEN FRYING OR ROASTING.

Common pairings
Alliums, other brassicas, soy sauce, meat, potato, bean, apple, and cider.

Alliums Cabbage Apple

Coffee Cabbage Cherry

Uncommon pairings
Anchovy, cherry, hibiscus flower, coffee, Swiss cheese, and mozzarella.

FLAVOR DIRECTORY 113

PEPPERY
RED CABBAGE HAS MORE BITTER AND SULFUR COMPOUNDS CREATING ITS PUNGENT FLAVORS.

Varieties

CABBAGES

GREEN CABBAGE
Grown around the world, green cabbage has a mild, slightly sweet flavor. Tangy, complex flavors can be introduced through fermentation (pp.84–85).

RED CABBAGE
The flavor of the red cabbage is slightly sweeter than the green variety and its color comes from anthocyanins. Braising, salting, and sautéing intensify sweetness.

SAVOY CABBAGE
Subtle, earthy, sweet flavors characterize the Savoy cabbage, and it is less pungent than the green cabbage.

NAPA CABBAGE
Popular in Asian dishes for its crunchy texture and sweet flavor.

POINTED CABBAGE
With a conical shape, the pointed cabbage has a mild, sweet flavor and is often used in salads.

BRUSSELS SPROUTS

STANDARD
The most common variety has a nutty, earthy flavor.

RED RUBINE
A purple-red variety with a nutty flavor.

LONG ISLAND IMPROVED
Sweet with mild, nutty flavor.

DIABLO
A sweet-tasting variety that becomes even more sweet when touched by frost.

Common pairings
Maple syrup, smoked almonds, chile, sesame seeds, lemon, pecorino, apple, and whiskey.

Apple · Brussels sprout · Lemon

Pear · Brussels sprout · Jam

Uncommon pairings
Pear, curry powder, jam, and hazelnut.

LEGUMES

SOYBEANS
LIKE MOST BEANS, THESE MUST BE COOKED BEFORE EATING TO DESTROY THEIR NATURAL TOXINS.

A selection of common legumes including fava beans, soybeans, peas, black beans, butter beans, kidney beans, and pinto beans.

RAW KIDNEY BEANS CONTAIN **PHYTOHEMAGGLUTININ**, A POISON CAUSING VOMITING AND DIARRHEA.

Beans are part of the legume family—vegetables with edible seeds that grow inside pods. This group includes beans, peas, chickpeas, and lentils, and they are also known as "pulses."

It is no exaggeration to say that human civilization was built on legumes. Not only do they provide the life-essential protein that cereals and other vegetables lack, but they're fast growing, native to every habitable continent, and they add nitrogen to the soil, letting farmers grow them indefinitely on land without fertilizer or manure. Their unique and familiar flavor comes mainly from grassy aroma compounds hexanol and hexanal—also in tomatoes, rhubarb, kiwi fruits, and apples—alongside bell pepper pyrazines (pp.90–91) and mushroomy octenol (pp.142–143). These aromas are strongest when beans are damaged, activating an enzyme called lipoxygenase that breaks fat molecules into small molecules. Cooked beans also emit sweet notes from compounds called lactones and furans. When stored for too long,

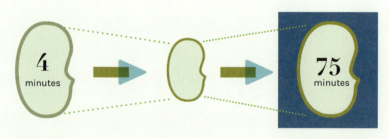

Cooking beans

Plant glues (like pectin) within the seed coat can be damaged or strengthened by various factors such as soaking in salt water or baking soda. Cooking times are given for fava beans.

FRESH — Fresh beans contain more water than dried beans and are more tender, so they cook quickly and have a "greener" flavor.

DRIED — When dried, beans have hardened seed coats and no moisture so take time to rehydrate and soften.

SOAKED IN WATER — Soaking dried beans in water (for up to 12 hours) reduces cooking time and indigestible sugars, helping digestibility.

FLAVOR DIRECTORY 115

Common pairings
Garlic, onion, corn, and sweet potato.

Uncommon pairings
Chocolate, ginger, mango, apple, or coconut.

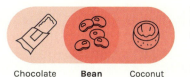

however, flavors become muddy and stale as fats, sugars, and proteins degrade into less appetizing aromas and bitter compounds.

LENTILS, PEAS, AND CHICKPEAS

Lentils are probably the oldest cultivated legume. They are small seeds that cook quickly and are a staple on the Indian subcontinent. Available in many colors (green, brown, black, orange, and red), the darker varieties have earthy, roasted pyrazines, and musty flavors, while orange and red have butterscotch and floral notes.

Peas have a uniquely sweet flavor that degrades quickly after picking. They are high in "green" flavor compounds, such as hexanal and green pea pyrazine.

The most common types of chickpeas are large, yellow garbanzo beans, which have a nutty and creamy flavor, thanks to the aroma compound hexanoic acid. Smaller, darker desi chickpeas are earthier and a staple in India, where they are ground to make gram flour.

Bean varieties

FAVA BEANS
Large, flat beans whose tough outer hull must be peeled to release tender seeds that have a distinct, brothlike, slightly sweet flavor.

BLACK-EYED PEAS
Farmed in West Africa for 6,000 years and now ingrained in US cuisine, they are known for their earthy flavor. Hints of almond and cherry come from a compound called methylethyl benzaldehyde.

PINTO BEANS
Slightly larger, thinner-skinned, mottled brown beans, whose mild, slightly nutty flavor and soft texture suits them to Mexican frijoles refritos (refried beans).

KIDNEY BEANS
Have a hearty, slightly sweet flavor and meaty texture, which makes them a global favorite for chili con carne outside Texas. Popular in North India (for example, Rajma curry). Methional gives meaty, oniony qualities.

CANNELLINI BEANS
Large, white, firmly textured beans with a nutty flavor, which are highly versatile and integral to many Italian dishes like minestrone and ribollita stew.

HARICOT BEANS
A small, softer white bean with a very mild flavor traditionally popular with the US Navy and used in Boston beans, and a sweet pork stew. Forerunner of baked beans.

BUTTER BEANS
A white bean with a dense, starchy texture and mild flavor that is widely used in soups and stews.

SCARLET RUNNER BEANS
The whole fresh pods are sliced and eaten: typically boiled, steamed, or fried like a vegetable. Abundant in "green" flavor compounds, like hexanal, they pair well with garlic and lemon.

SOAKED IN SALT WATER
Salt replaces minerals in the bean's cell walls, which soften and let water enter more easily, speeding up cooking.

SOAKED IN BAKING SODA
Baking soda in water destabilizes plant glues to speed up cooking, although it can affect flavor.

COOKED IN TOMATO SAUCE
Beans cooked in acidic sauces (for example, tomato) take longer to soften.

SOYBEANS

Poisonous when raw and unappetizingly bland when cooked, the soybean is an unlikely hero of the culinary world. It forms the basis of dozens of uniquely delicious ingredients, including soy sauce, miso, tofu, and tempeh.

Immature green soybeans (called edamame), when boiled in salted water until tender, have a pleasantly grassy (from hexenal), slightly buttery, pealike flavor. By contrast, fully grown white soybeans are waxy and firm when cooked, owing to high protein levels (double those of other legumes). They can be bitter and astringent and, when damaged, soybeans' rich complement of oils reacts with an enzyme to fragment into strong beany aroma compounds, reminiscent of cardboard, paint, and rancid fat.

TEMPEH
A MEATIER ALTERNATIVE TO TOFU, TEMPEH IS MADE FROM COOKED, FERMENTED WHOLE SOYBEANS, BOUND TOGETHER BY A LIVING FUNGUS.

TOFU
A SOYBEAN CURD MADE FROM PRESSED, CURDLED, SOY MILK, TOFU IS LARGELY DEVOID OF AROMA COMPOUNDS AND HAS LITTLE FLAVOR.

Making soy sauce

Today's soy sauce is a twice-fermented broth of cooked, mashed soybeans and often contains toasted wheat.

Making miso

Miso is made from mashed soybeans fermented for long periods into a thick, intensely flavored paste with sweet, roasted notes.

WHEAT
Roasted and crushed

SOYBEANS
Soaked and cooked

RICE
Koji is grown on salted rice

Roasted wheat and soybeans are combined with koji mold.

COMBINED

The koji mold is blended with the soaked, cooked, and mashed soybeans.

FLAVOR DIRECTORY 117

Common pairings
Add extra depth of flavor to edamame beans with a sprinkle of sea salt and garlic. Chili flakes also work well to add warmth to young beans.

Garlic Edamame Sea salt

Seaweed Miso Ginger

Common pairings
Traditionally miso is eaten with tofu, seaweed, and used in marinades and dressings with garlic and ginger.

SOY SAUCE

Soy sauce is made through fermentation using a starter culture of mold called koji. Over several months, the salty slurry develops acidity and an ever-more complex array of 100+ flavor compounds—caramel-like sweetness, buttery notes, and winelike aromas and increasing umami depth. A powerful aroma compound called 3-methylbutanal is responsible for soy sauce's trademark chocolaty, malty flavor.

TOFU AND TEMPEH

Tofu has a soft, cheeselike consistency but doesn't absorb other flavors—marinades penetrate a few millimeters. It can be fried for a colorful crust. Fermented tofus have a flavorful coat that ranges from sweet and aromatic to pungently cheesy, based on various molds used, extra ingredients, and maturing times. Tempeh is a meatier alternative to tofu that has a subtle nutty, earthy flavor.

Soy sauce and miso varieties

JAPANESE VS. CHINESE SOY
Despite originating in China, many soy sauces sold in the West are Japanese in style, containing equal amounts of wheat and soy. This gives a sweeter taste and milder soybean flavor than the saltier Chinese type.

LIGHT VS. DARK SOY
The shorter-fermented "light" is for general use and as a flavor enhancer. "Dark" is thick, sweet, and best reserved for marinades, braises, and stews.

TAMARI
A wheat-free, thicker Japanese soy sauce, tamari is used to add more body and flavor to stews and stir-fries.

SHIRO MISO (WHITE MISO)
Made with fermented soybeans and koji, often for a shorter period, resulting in the lightest color and mildest flavor. Perfect for delicate dishes like soups and dressings.

AKA MISO (RED MISO)
Uses more soybeans and a longer fermentation period, resulting in a dark red color, strong salty flavor, and robust umami character. Ideal for heartier dishes like stews and marinades.

AWAZE MISO (MIXED MISO)
Combines white and red miso for a balanced flavor profile, sweet and nutty from the white miso and rich and salty from the red miso. Versatile for various dishes.

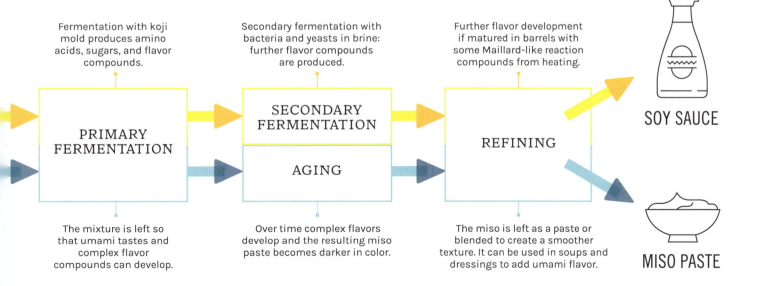

STIR-FRY SCIENCE

Stir-frying is an ancient Chinese technique traditionally done in a high-sided wok over a fiercely hot outdoor stove. It is hugely popular across Asia, thanks to it being a very efficient way to cook with limited fuel.

"Stir-frying" is an imperfect translation of *chǎo*. Inside Chinese restaurant kitchens, little stirring happens; instead chefs energetically toss rice and vegetable pieces out of blisteringly hot woks, which sporadically erupt in flames. This extreme-temperature type of frying is called *bào*, and it imparts a fleeting seared smokiness called *wok hei* ("breath of the wok")—something that is difficult to achieve at home.

Wok hei reactions happen only in oiled pans consistently hotter than 500°F (260°C). At these temperatures, oils smoke and easily ignite. The oil's disintegrated fragments melded with rapid Maillard reactions (pp.74–77) create this elusive flavor.

KEEP ON DANCING

A high smoke point oil (p.40) is an essential if chasing *wok hei*—start cooking only when a thin coating of oil in the pan is smoking. Then add more oil and ingredients immediately after. Presliced, bite-sized ingredients must be kept constantly dancing around the pan so they brown evenly all over and don't char. Experiments show that rapid stirring and tossing cooks faster because airborne pieces cook while they pass through a hot column of steam rising from the pan.

SALTINESS
Light soy sauce adds saltiness, umami, acidity, a subtle soy flavor, and color. Rice wine brings umami, sweetness, and fragrance.

CHEWINESS
Noodles add a satisfying chewy texture to the dish and soak up the flavor of the soy sauce.

CRUNCH
Bell peppers and snow peas bring color, sweetness, and crispness.

TEXTURE
Chicken breast offers a contrasting soft texture and mild, savory flavor.

THE PERFECT STIR-FRY

UMAMI
Shiitake mushrooms introduce a mouth-filling umami depth.

HEAT
Thinly sliced green onions, red chile, and ginger give fiery warmth and top notes of fruitiness.

AROMA
Garlic is a source of aromatic meatiness from sulfur compounds and glutamate (pp.26–29).

MAILLARD REACTION
Peanut (groundnut) oil has a high smoke point, is neutral-flavored, and facilitates high-temperature cooking, for quick browning of the chicken and mushrooms.

COOLING OFF
Each time a moisture-laden morsel strikes the hot metal, the pan's temperature plunges. Add too much too quickly, and food will stew in its own juices rather than searing and browning. To maintain high heat, add fresh ingredients gradually or briefly lift the pan off the stove. For *wok hei* at home, cook ingredients in small batches, set aside, and combine at the end.

CHÃO WITHOUT THE BÀO
Stir-frying over medium heat is less demanding and allows for thicker cuts of meat or vegetables and longer cooking times. Still-firm vegetables and larger meat pieces can be finished by covering with a lid and letting them cook in the steam of added liquids (rice wine, soy sauce, or water).

The perfect stir-fry

French and other Western cuisines typically concentrate key flavors into sauces and gravies, whereas Asian tradition strives for balance and harmony of ingredients, with no single element dominating the rest.

ZEST
FINELY GRATED CITRUS ZEST, PACKED WITH OILS, PROVIDES A HIT OF FLAVOR THAT IS PRIZED BY BAKERS.

BEND THE WHOLE PEEL (PITH AND ZEST) TO BURST THE OIL GLANDS AND SEE THEM ERUPT IN A FINE SPRAY.

PITH
OR ALBEDO HAS HIGH LEVELS OF REPELLENT BITTER SUBSTANCES (PHENOLICS), MAKING IT UNPLEASANT TO EAT.

CITRUS

Once a lavish winter indulgence, citrus fruits are now so commonplace we forget that they are the most important of culinary fruits. This vast, convoluted family offers sweetness, acidity, umami, bitterness, and gel-making pectin.

Each segment of a ripe citrus fruit is packed with small, sausage-shaped bags of juice, called vesicles or sacs, each plumped up with water containing sugars (mostly sucrose), droplets of flavor-rich oil, and a surprising amount of savory-tasting glutamate, especially in oranges and grapefruits. This hidden umami kick explains why orange pairs so well with poultry, and grapefruit powerfully intensifies a marinade's flavor. The citrus rind, or peel, is often discarded, yet it harbors most of the fruit's flavor. Outermost is a fine, colored layer known as the zest (or "flavedo"), inside which are millions of orbs of fragrant oil, termed glands.

SEGMENTS
EACH FRUIT IS DIVIDED INTO SEGMENTS SURROUNDED BY A MEMBRANE.

JUICE
ADD CITRUS JUICE TO BEVERAGES, SAUCES, DRESSINGS, AND DESSERTS FOR A FRESH, TANGY TASTE.

FLAVOR DIRECTORY 121

Citric flavors

Citrus fruits can be grouped into those we eat (mandarin, orange, grapefruit) and those we cook with (lemon and lime), based on the balance of sugar and acid in their flesh. Sweeter varieties, like eating oranges, have 10 times more sugar than acid, whereas those with roughly equal amounts of sugar and citric acid—namely limes—are eye-wateringly sour and best reserved for flavoring other dishes.

Flavor pairings

Musky, sulfur-carrying compounds of citrus zest bring harmony in savory dishes, while sweet-and-sour citrus juice and flesh bring fruity brightness to salads and desserts.

KEY

Sugar   Acid

Orange
This most popular citrus fruit, descended from the smaller mandarin, has a richer flavor, thanks to the 200+ compounds that accompany limonene and citral. The juice is fruitier than the zest, which is best used in baking.

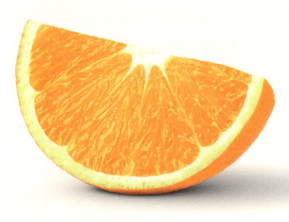

Duck   **Orange**   Almond

 10:1
SWEET/
NAVEL ORANGE

 9:1
MANDARIN

 7:1
BLOOD ORANGE

Grapefruit
This Caribbean fruit is unusual for having bitterness as a feature of its flavor profile. This is due to a substance called naringin, which lessens as fruit ripens and whose bitterness can be tempered with salt or sugar.

Rosemary   **Grapefruit**   Ginger

 6:1
GRAPEFRUIT

Lemon and lime
As well as sour citric acid, terpene flavor compounds dominate: bright, fresh, intensely citrus limonene alongside the lemon's candylike citral. Both compounds degrade quickly after squeezing and are replaced by woodier aromas.

Carrot   **Lemon**   Chanterelle mushroom

Cilantro   **Lime**   Nutmeg

2:1
LEMON

1:1
LIME

APPLES AND PEARS

Apples and pears are pome fruits—fleshy fruits with a fibrous central core containing seeds and a thicker outer layer. They share a juicy crispness and distinctive flavor: taut, water-filled plant cells explode in the mouth, releasing a spray of tart, aroma-packed sweet juice.

Their flavors stem from a fragrant, ester class of aroma compounds (pp.66–67), in contrast with the zingy terpenes of citruses and watermelon's ethereal floral aldehydes. Tightly packed cells are glued together with pectin, giving them a delectable crunch. Ripe fruits soften as pectin is digested by enzymes; tasteless starches and sour acids are broken into sweet sugars. Apples' flavor comes from "apple ester" (ethyl 2-methylbutyrate) with its fruity, applelike scent; butyl acetate, with its banana-like, pear-drop aroma; and hexyl acetate, the pearlike "red" scent of Gala apples.

Apple varieties

EATING/DESSERT

GALA (New Zealand)
Sugar-acid ratio: 40:1
Flavor: Sweet with a mild flavor and a hint of vanilla.

HONEYCRISP (US)
Sugar-acid ratio: 27:1
Flavor: Crisp and juicy with a pleasant tartness but little complexity.

FUJI (Japan)
Sugar-acid ratio: The highest of mass-produced varieties. Up to 60:1
Flavor: Very crisp and refreshing, little aroma.

COOKING

GRANNY SMITH (Australia)
Sugar-acid ratio: 12:1
Flavor: Tart and tangy with green notes.

BRAMLEY (UK)
Sugar-acid ratio: 7:1
Flavor: Very tart, sweetens and softens into a purée with cooking.

DUAL-PURPOSE

BRAEBURN (New Zealand)
Sugar-acid ratio: 16:1
Flavor: Crisp, aromatic, with hints of cinnamon and spice

JONAGOLD (US)
Sugar-acid ratio: 14:1
Flavor: Sweet with a hint of honey and tartness, juicy.

APPLES ARE CRISPER AND DENSER THAN PEARS WITH MORE TIGHTLY PACKED CELLS.

Common pairings
Apples are versatile fruits that can be used with a number of other fruits, including grapes and pears. You can also try with Champagne and apple cider.

Grape · **Apple** · Champagne

Rabbit · **Apple** · Gorgonzola

Uncommon pairings
The sweetness of pears complements the taste of rabbit and other meats like duck and lamb. It also can be used with creamy cheeses like Gorgonzola.

FLAVOR DIRECTORY 123

PEARS
DEVELOP A SOFT TEXTURE WHEN RIPE, WITH VANILLA, HONEY, AND FLORAL NOTES.

TARTNESS

The sprightly tang of apples and pears comes from acid, mostly malic acid, balancing the sweetness of fructose. Although growers are breeding ever sweeter produce, a balanced eater has a sugar-acid ratio of about 16:1. The 2,000-plus different apple varieties can be broadly grouped into dessert or eating apples, cooking apples, dual-purpose apples, and cider apples. Apple varieties that contain medium levels of sugar that are high in acid and rich in puckering tannins are used to make cider.

Pears are also grouped according to their use: dessert/eating pears (Williams/Bartlett, Anjou, Conference, Comice); cooking pears (less sweet, firmer flesh, such as Bosc); canning pears, which survive canning heat and pressure (Williams/Bartlett); and high-tannin pears for fermenting into pear cider (Butt, Hendre Huffcap, and Thorn).

Over time, tiny air gaps between cells enlarge as shrinking cells lose their moisture, eventually becoming cavernous and resulting in a soft and powdery texture.

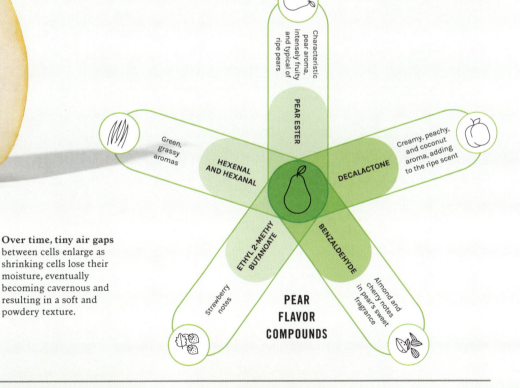

PEAR FLAVOR COMPOUNDS

- **PEAR ESTER** — Characteristic pear aroma, intensely fruity and typical of ripe pears
- **HEXENAL AND HEXANAL** — Green, grassy aromas
- **DECALACTONE** — Creamy, peachy, and coconut aroma, adding to the ripe scent
- **ETHYL 2-METHY BUTANOATE** — Strawberry notes
- **BENZALDEHYDE** — Almond and cherry notes in pear's sweet fragrance

Common pairings
Pears go well with many other fruits, including bananas and strawberries. You can also put them with nuts like almonds and cheeses, including goat cheese.

Apricot · Pear · Strawberry

Soy · Pear · Cauliflower

Uncommon pairings
Pairs partner well with flavors of soy. Try sweet miso and cauliflower or avocado, which contrast beautifully with pears' sweetness.

STONE FRUITS

Common pairings	
Camembert	**Apricot**	Ginger
Coconut	**Plum**	Duck
Roasted peanut	**Prune**	Soft blue cheese
Pork	**Sweet cherry**	Mushroom
Chocolate	**Sour cherry**	Cinnamon
Yogurt	**Mango**	Lemongrass
Raspberry	**Peach**	Almond

From the tropical thrill of the mango to the comforting sweetness of a juicy plum, these much-loved, varied fruits all evolved a single hard seed, or pit, surrounded by succulent flesh that's bursting with fruity flavor.

MANGOES

Mangoes, hailed as the "king of fruits," are the most popular stone fruit globally. Their unparalleled sweetness; sumptuous flavor; and rich, velvety texture makes "mango season," beginning in March, an annual time of celebration in the fruit's native Indian subcontinent. The most flavorful mango varieties, such as the famous Alphonso, boast 270+ different flavor compounds and have syrupy sweet, creamy flesh that combines an intense tropical taste with nuances of black currant–flavored candy, peach, lime, and caramel. Alongside 45g (11 teaspoons) of sugar per fruit—the most of any culinary fruit—and the tang of citric and malic acid, mango's rich and complex flavor comes from piney and citrusy terpenes; fruity esters; strawberry furanones; and creamy, tropical lactones.

Bacon | **Mango** | Parmesan cheese

Bergamot juice | **Peach** | Darjeeling tea

Common pairings
Shared flavor compounds make these ingredients compatible with stone fruits.

Uncommon pairings
A few ideas for less obvious pairings for peaches and mangoes. Herbs like basil and mint also work well with both.

MANGO

THERE ARE OVER 300 MANGO VARIETIES, WITH FLAVORS RANGING FROM CANDY TO CARAMEL.

MANGO

PEACHES, NECTARINES, AND APRICOTS

Peaches, nectarines, and apricots are all rooted in temperate China; peaches and nectarines are essentially the same fruit—a genetic quirk from over 2,000 years ago causing the peach's fuzzy skin to become smooth, giving the sensation of a firmer bite. Apricots are peaches' smaller, sweeter, and tarter sibling but with a more delicate and complex flavor. The creamy, peachy flavor underpinning these related fruits is from lactones, making them subtly reminiscent of tropical fruits. Canned peaches and nectarines are sweeter, softer, and simpler tasting than fresh, lacking acids and many "green" aroma compounds, making them better suited for bakes and sauces. Apricots also carry benzaldehyde—the flavor of almonds (pp.172–173)—and have strong floral qualities from lavender-like linalool and rosy geraniol, both terpenes.

PLUMS AND CHERRIES

Plums and cherries are distant siblings to peaches and apricots and are descended from the same ancient stone fruit parent, but they each have a distinct, fruitier flavor profile. Plums come in large, juicy Japanese varieties as well as smaller, softer European types. Cherries also come in two types: larger sweet varieties, and smaller sour cherries. Both plums and cherries lack the velvety lactone sweetness of peaches and apricots; plums have a floral, piney profile (from terpenes) underpinned by a strong fruity flavor (esters); the very sweet, soft-skinned European plums are picked fully ripe then dried as "prunes," which concentrates sugars and develops their caramel flavors and a potent roselike aroma compound known as a "rose ketone." Cherries have a prominent almond quality like apricots and come in sweet, eating types and high-acid sour ("tart") varieties.

CHERRY
THE BITTER FLAVOR OF SOUR CHERRIES CAN BE MELLOWED WHEN COOKED.

CHERRY

PLUM

NECTARINES
FLAVOR COMPOUNDS IN NECTARINES INCLUDE BENZALDEHYDE, LINALOOL, AND GERANIOL.

APRICOT

NECTARINE

BERRIES

From succulent strawberries bursting with summery sweetness to tangy cranberries perfect for festive sauces, not all these small fruits are true berries—but all are delicious.

BLUEBERRIES

Terpenes and aldehydes (pp.66–67) convey most of this tangy fruit's aroma profile—linalool, with its pleasant floral nose, pinene and limonene bringing pine and lemony hints, and an earthy spiciness from myrcene. Like grapes, the gush of fruitiness that fills the palate when bitten comes from a profusion of rich fruity esters within the pulp.

GRAPES

From over 200 grape flavor compounds come the crisp, green freshness of the green "Thompson," the rich and jammy, musky pleasure of the plum-colored "Concord," and the confectionery-flavored "Cotton Candy" novelty variety. Grapes have a subtle scent but then explode in the mouth with flavor. This is because their skins are concentrated with gently aromatic terpenes, which have citrusy, floral, and herbal qualities, while the flesh contains richer fruity esters, conveying hints of apple, pear, banana, and pineapple.

STRAWBERRIES

Strawberries boast upward of 380 flavor compounds. Their fruitiness springs from esters, as with many fruits, while a summery freshness is delivered by the green apple aroma of hexenal. Yet it is strawberry furanone (furaneol), with its sweet, caramel nuances, that sets them apart. Intensely buttery diacetyl (pp.166–167) further endows this berry with decadence (and its link to cream).

RASPBERRIES

Raspberries belong to the rose family and are not true berries. Instead, they are "aggregate fruits," formed of clusters of tiny, beadlike drupelets, each essentially a miniature berry. A single molecule, raspberry ketone, gives raspberries their distinctive ripe scent, setting them apart from the more complex aroma of strawberries.

Raspberries have a tangier taste due to their higher acid content, including citric and malic acids, which contrasts with strawberries' milder, sweet-acid balance.

CRANBERRIES

This sour, slightly bitter berry is surprisingly complex: predominantly fruity and tart from esters and acids, with background notes reminiscent of cinnamon, almonds, and vanilla—cranberries are perfect for sauces and baked goods.

Grape varieties

THOMPSON SEEDLESS ("SULTANA")
Slightly tart and crisp with fresh, "green"-tasting fruity pulp with hints of blossom. Variety most often used for raisins and sultanas.

RED GLOBE
Large, firm fleshed and very sweet, with a fairly neutral green flavor that carries hints of flowers and citrus.

CONCORD
A rich, jammy, and intensely flavored fruit used for grape juices and in dessert wines. It uniquely carries hits of strawberry and is high in methyl anthranilate—a strongly scented "foxy" compound that has musky qualities and is often used as a grape flavoring commonly added to drinks and confectionery.

BLACK GRAPES HAVE A RICH, SWEET TASTE WITH DEEP, TANGY NOTES, PAIRING WELL WITH GOAT CHEESE.

FLAVOR DIRECTORY 127

Common pairings
Oats, vanilla, peach, banana, currants, and mango.

Banana **Blueberry** Vanilla

Uncommon pairings
Sharp Cheddar cheese, lemongrass, butternut squash, and beef steak.

Cheddar **Blueberry** Lemongrass

Common pairings
Basil, vanilla, cream, and grape.

Cream **Strawberry** Grape

Uncommon pairings
Olive, peanut, chile, and mushroom.

Olives **Strawberry** Mushroom

Common pairings
Chocolate, peach, vanilla, and mint.

Chocolate **Raspberry** Peach

Uncommon pairings
Avocado, tomato, and horseradish.

Avocado **Raspberry** Tomato

BLACKBERRIES HAVE A DEEP, EARTHY FLAVOR, WITH FLORAL NOTES WHEN RIPE.

RED CURRANTS HAVE A TANGY FLAVOR WITH FLORAL AND FRUITY TONES, AND CITRUSY NOTES.

TROPICAL FRUITS

Any fruit that naturally grows near the equator is a tropical fruit. These are some of the most popular of the thousands of species that thrive in warm, wet, sunny climes.

BANANAS AND PLANTAINS

The sweet Cavendish variety has been the world's favorite banana since the 1960s. Unripe green bananas are hard and astringent because their flesh is packed with the indigestible resistant starch found in raw potatoes (pp.104–105). Bananas become creamy and sweet as ripening enzymes shred long starch molecules into small, sweet sugars, mostly sucrose. With ripeness, flavor compounds multiply: bananas' distinctive aroma comes from the ester isoamyl acetate, while a cocktail of other fruity esters and buttery acetoin (pp.66–67) gives the fruit its rounded flavor.

Plantains are larger, less sugary bananas that are a savory staple in many parts of the world. Resistant starch makes them inedible when raw but when boiled or steamed, they develop a honey-sweet flavor with hits of caramel, and toasty pyrazines emerge when roasted or fried. Black-skinned plantains are fully ripe and sweet.

YELLOW PLANTAIN IS OFTEN FRIED OR BAKED, BECOMING GOLDEN AND CRISPY.

CANTALOUPE MELON HAS A SWEET AROMA WITH HONEY AND FLORAL FLAVORS.

FLAVOR DIRECTORY 129

WATERMELONS AND MELONS

Watermelon's watery flesh is colored pink with lycopene, the same carotenoid pigment in tomatoes. Its distinctive flavor erupts when its huge, water-filled cells rupture: defensive enzymes turn traces of fat into an assortment of fragrant aldehydes—the chemical family that gives us grassy hexenal.

PINEAPPLES

Pineapples come from South America and are perhaps the most intensely flavored of tropical fruits. Nearly 300 aroma compounds give pineapples their complex aroma: fruity esters, sulfur-based spiciness, alongside essences of vanilla, caramel, and clove with sherry overtones. Their intense sweetness is heightened with tart citric acid, while a powerful, protein-digesting enzyme called bromelain tingles on the tongue.

COCONUTS

The huge fruits of the coconut palm have supported Pacific Island and Southern Indian communities for millennia and are the lifeblood of their cuisines. Coconuts share some flavor compounds with both cherries and plums (pp.124–125). They are laced with lactones, aroma compounds conveying rich peachy, creamy, and buttery qualities. "Coconut lactone" (gamma-nonalactone), a potent compound, gives its signature creamy coconut flavor with fatty, milky, buttery notes, and is beloved of perfumers.

Common pairings

Chocolate	**Banana**	Honey
Garlic	**Plantain**	Lentils
Dry cured ham	**Watermelon**	Apple
Apple	**Pineapple**	Ham
Dark chocolate	**Coconut**	Peach

Uncommon pairings

Stilton	**Banana**	Bacon
Balsamic vinegar	**Plantain**	Goat cheese
Salmon	**Watermelon**	Coconut
Basil	**Pineapple**	Crab
Turmeric	**Coconut**	Avocado

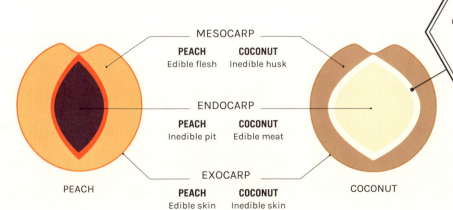

YOUNGER COCONUT FRUITS HAVE A SWEETER TASTE THAN OLDER ONES.

PEACH
- MESOCARP — **PEACH** Edible flesh / **COCONUT** Inedible husk
- ENDOCARP — **PEACH** Inedible pit / **COCONUT** Edible meat
- EXOCARP — **PEACH** Edible skin / **COCONUT** Inedible skin

COCONUT

Fleshy fruits

Coconuts are an oddity, a fleshy fruit in the same family as the cherry and plum but with a thick husk instead of a juicy flesh and an unusual seed with an edible two-layered interior: a creamy-tasting "meat" surrounding sweet, salty, and sour "water."

RICE

Rice, an ancient grain first grown in South East Asia around 9,000 years ago, feeds nearly half of the planet with its 100,000 varieties and grows in almost every climate. Rice's ability to absorb flavors makes it a culinary chameleon, adapting and harmonizing with countless recipes.

> **WILD RICE**
> THIS IS NOT A RICE VARIETY, BUT THE SEED OF A DIFFERENT GRASS PLANT WITH A NUTTY, EARTHY, ROASTED FLAVOR.

WHITE RICE

All rice shares the core flavors of the white, starchy rice kernel. This mostly comes from aldehydes—aroma compounds known for their leafy, oily, and almond scents (see opposite). Grassy, fatty, and citrus peel notes come through hexanal, decanal, and nonanal, as well as an earthiness from mushroom alcohol (pp.142–143). Hints of soybean come through another compound found in cooked beans called 2-pentylfuran.

BROWN RICE

Brown or whole grain rice retains the brown bran coating that is milled away in white rice. This gives it extra layers of flavor, thanks to the additional aldehydes in the seed coat's oils, including almondlike benzaldehyde and 3-methylbutanal (a nutty, malty-scented compound also in beer, meats, and cheeses). This rich complement of compounds aligns with brown rice's broader variety of potential flavor partners.

BLACK RICE

Black rice is whole grain (brown) but with a thicker, chewier, and more flavorful bran layer, which is colored inky black by the same dark pigments found in blueberries (anthocyanins). The darker bran layer has a profusion of nutty, popcorny 2AP and smoky guaiacol, found in barbecued foods and roasted coffee; vanilla sweetness comes from vanillin.

WILD RICE

Although it is called rice, wild rice is a different variety of nutritious aquatic grass that can be used in the same way. The husk is removed in stages of "curing" (fermenting in moist piles) then "parching" (gently roasting). It has flavors, including pyrazines from the Maillard process (pp.74–77), almond-flavored benzaldehyde, caramel furfural, and sweet vanillin, with the essence of vanilla.

Common pairings
Leafy greens, soy, mushroom, and nuts.

Leafy greens · **White rice** · Mushroom

Uncommon pairings
Miso, blue cheese sauce, vanilla ice cream, mango, anchovy, and lemon zest.

Miso · **White rice** · Mango

Common pairings
Nuts, beef, soy, coconut, raisins, and almonds.

Beef · **Brown rice** · Coconut

Uncommon pairings
Feta, butternut squash, tahini, dried cherry, and peanut butter.

Feta · **Brown rice** · Peanut butter

FLAVOR DIRECTORY 131

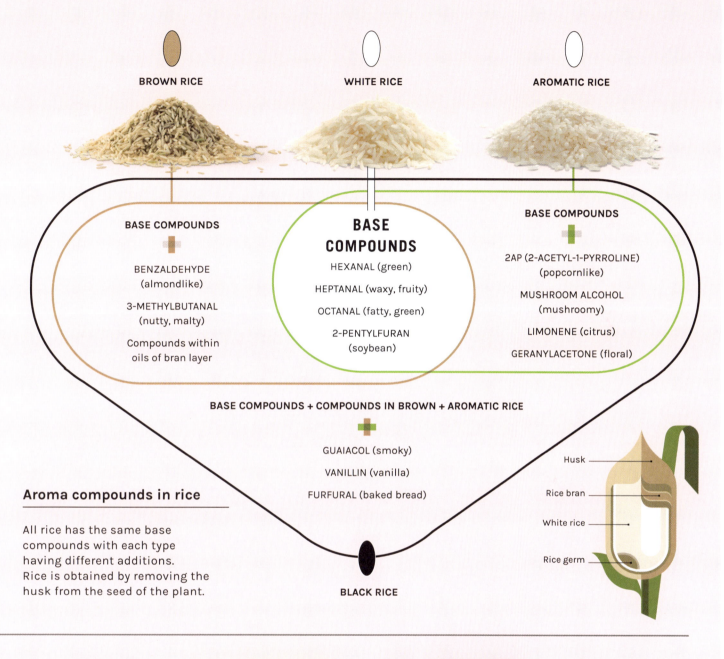

BROWN RICE

BASE COMPOUNDS

BENZALDEHYDE (almondlike)

3-METHYLBUTANAL (nutty, malty)

Compounds within oils of bran layer

WHITE RICE

BASE COMPOUNDS

HEXANAL (green)

HEPTANAL (waxy, fruity)

OCTANAL (fatty, green)

2-PENTYLFURAN (soybean)

AROMATIC RICE

BASE COMPOUNDS

2AP (2-ACETYL-1-PYRROLINE) (popcornlike)

MUSHROOM ALCOHOL (mushroomy)

LIMONENE (citrus)

GERANYLACETONE (floral)

BASE COMPOUNDS + COMPOUNDS IN BROWN + AROMATIC RICE

GUAIACOL (smoky)

VANILLIN (vanilla)

FURFURAL (baked bread)

BLACK RICE

Husk
Rice bran
White rice
Rice germ

Aroma compounds in rice

All rice has the same base compounds with each type having different additions. Rice is obtained by removing the husk from the seed of the plant.

Common pairings
Coconut, eggplant, mushroom, egg, hazelnut, cherry, cranberry, and raisin.

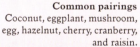

Coconut · **Black rice** · Egg

Uncommon pairings
Lime, chorizo, pistachio, orange, dark chocolate, pork, and peanut.

Lime · **Black rice** · Orange

Common pairings
Black-eyed peas, parsnip, black olive, beef, and parsley.

Parsnip · **Wild rice** · Black olive

Uncommon pairings
Crab, apple, banana, and Cheddar cheese.

Crab · **Wild rice** · Apple

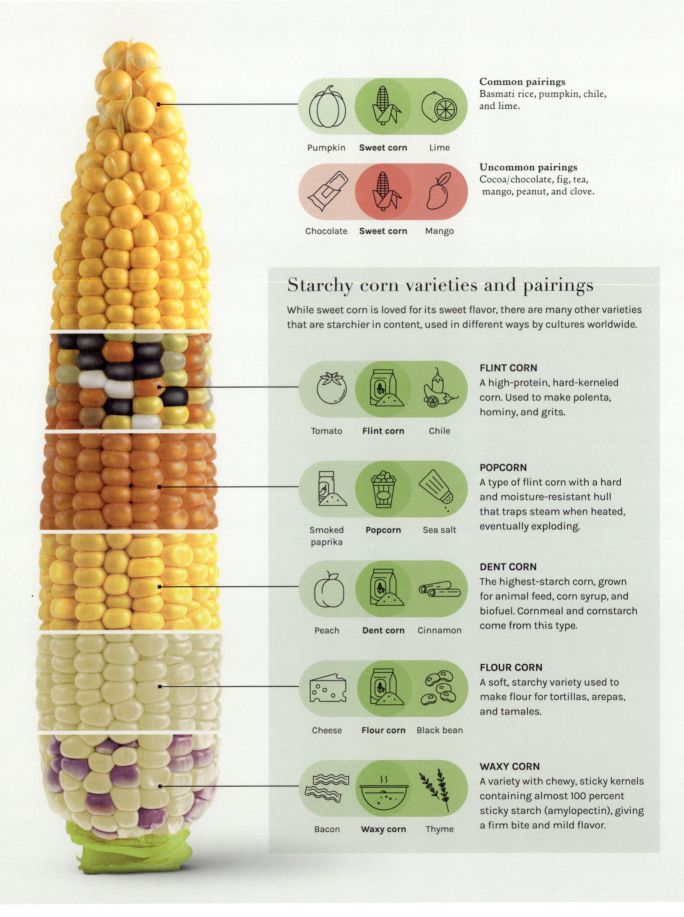

Common pairings
Basmati rice, pumpkin, chile, and lime.

Pumpkin — Sweet corn — Lime

Uncommon pairings
Cocoa/chocolate, fig, tea, mango, peanut, and clove.

Chocolate — Sweet corn — Mango

Starchy corn varieties and pairings

While sweet corn is loved for its sweet flavor, there are many other varieties that are starchier in content, used in different ways by cultures worldwide.

FLINT CORN
A high-protein, hard-kerneled corn. Used to make polenta, hominy, and grits.

Tomato — Flint corn — Chile

POPCORN
A type of flint corn with a hard and moisture-resistant hull that traps steam when heated, eventually exploding.

Smoked paprika — Popcorn — Sea salt

DENT CORN
The highest-starch corn, grown for animal feed, corn syrup, and biofuel. Cornmeal and cornstarch come from this type.

Peach — Dent corn — Cinnamon

FLOUR CORN
A soft, starchy variety used to make flour for tortillas, arepas, and tamales.

Cheese — Flour corn — Black bean

WAXY CORN
A variety with chewy, sticky kernels containing almost 100 percent sticky starch (amylopectin), giving a firm bite and mild flavor.

Bacon — Waxy corn — Thyme

CORN

Also known as maize, corn is the third-largest food source globally after rice and wheat and has been developed for more than 9,000 years from a hard, seeded, thready Mexican grass into the crop we enjoy today. Few crops have undergone as dramatic a transformation from its wild ancestor. This is particularly true for sweet corn, which, thanks to a genetic fluke, cannot turn its sugar into starch and has the sweetness of a fruit, making it the most popular type of corn—and the only type that can be eaten raw.

Corn has a complex flavor that is fresh and "green," while also having a nuttiness and mushroomlike earthiness. All corns also contain glutamate (pp.26–29), which gives them and their flours an addictive umami quality. They also feature a hint of popcorn, from the aroma compound, 2AP (2-acetyl-1-pyrroline), found at high levels in popcorn itself. The flour used for making tortillas, masa harina, is enriched with a depth of flavor not found in other cornstarches through "nixtamalization," an ancient technique for softening kernels' hard hulls.

> SWEET AND WAXY CORN ARE BEST EATEN SOON AFTER PICKING, BEFORE THEIR FLAVORS DIMINISH.

How to cook sweet corn

Fresh corn's fragrance appears only when it is heated; and how you cook it can change its very essence—each method both adding and taking away aroma compounds.

STEAMING
Preserves a fresh, sweet flavor, if done for less than five minutes.

Aroma compounds
Nonanal (musty), mushroom alcohol, limonene (citrus), dimethyl trisulfide (cooked corn).

Flavor descriptions
Fresh, sweet, slight hint of green onion.

BOILING
Boil for a short time to avoid washing out flavor complexity, sweetness, and umami.

Aroma compounds
Acetylthiazoline (nutty), reduced hexanal, dimethyl sulfide (cabbage).

Flavor descriptions
Hints of sweet cabbage and popcorn.

ROASTING
Enhances and adds depth, richness, and fruitiness, accentuating citrus notes.

Aroma compounds
Limonene, myrcene (spicy), prenol (floral), pyrazines.

Flavor descriptions
Rich, fruity, slightly floral, roasted.

GRILLING / BARBECUING
Adds layers of roasted, toasted nuttiness, burnt sugar, and caramel-sweetness.

Aroma compounds
Pyrazines, furans, thiophenes (meaty), guaiacol (smoky), aldehydes, ketones.

Flavor descriptions
Roasted, nutty, earthy, sweet, caramel, smoky.

BREAD

Wheat is a staple food for a third of the world. When water is added to wheat flour, two separate proteins—meatball-shaped gliadin and spaghetti-like glutenin—intertwine to form a uniquely stretchy protein called gluten. Kneading and mixing build and strengthen gluten, transforming a sticky batter into a pliable dough, as fibers align and elongate. Gluten firms as it cooks, giving bread its crumb, pastries their satisfying crunch, and pasta its al dente chew.

Raw wheat seeds (wheat berries) can be eaten whole and have a pleasant earthy, slightly sweet, grassy and subtly nutty taste—much of which comes from their oil-rich bran layer. When wheat cooks, however, magic happens. From 131–158°F (55°–70°C), flour's chalky starch granules inflate with water, swelling the dough or batter, making it plump and springy. Meanwhile, the gluten fibers stretch and harden, ensnaring any enlarging gas bubbles before setting solid at 167°F (75°C). Breads, cakes, and soufflés now stop rising—but wheat's flavor journey has only just started. Uncooked flour's gentle earthy, grassy, slightly waxy flavor fades with each increasing degree as small, fresh-scented aldehyde compounds disintegrate, eclipsed by ever more intense and varied nutty, caramelized, and balsamic aromas. Beyond 266°F (130°C), the surface browns (pp.74–77), giving a crunchy crust and flooding the air with bready, toasted smells.

WHOLE GRAIN
BREAD IS NUTTY AND EARTHY FROM THE BRAN AND GERM, WITH A TOASTED GRAIN AROMA.

CRUST
THE DEEP BROWN COLOR OF THE CRUST DEVELOPS DURING BAKING, THANKS TO THE MAILLARD PROCESS.

GLIADIN + GLUTENIN = GLUTEN

Gliadin and glutenin together form gluten, which is needed to form the strength, elasticity, and structure of bread and other baked goods. When flour is mixed with water, the two proteins bond and help trap gases produced by yeast.

FLAVOR DIRECTORY 135

FLOUR TYPES

During milling, wheat's flavorful bran coating and nutritious germ are removed, leaving long-lasting, finely textured, refined white flour ideal for cakes and pastries. The separated bran can be added back to make brown flour. If brown flour contains wheat's original proportion of bran (around 15 percent), it is termed "whole wheat" or "whole grain." The bran's oils gradually turn rancid and make flour dense and moist, so it has a shorter shelf life.

Traditionally "stone-ground" whole grain flours, which are slowly milled between stones rather than fast-moving metal rollers, do not separate all the bran from kernel and have more aroma compounds and a richer flavor. "Strong" bread flours come from "hard" wheat varieties bred to have more glutenin and gliadin (above 12 percent) and are ideal for kneading into a springy, gas-capturing dough that bakes into a firm-textured, well-risen loaf. Other flour types, such as plain, have differing mixes of hard and "soft" wheat varieties to give lesser amounts of gluten for lighter bakes.

SALT IN BREAD

An essential ingredient in most breads, salt not only elevates bread's flavor but also its height by helping gluten proteins bind more tightly, thus ensnaring more carbon dioxide bubbles. It also puts the brakes on uncontrolled yeast growth, stopping dough from overrising, weakening gluten further. Too much salt kills yeast and makes dough dense.

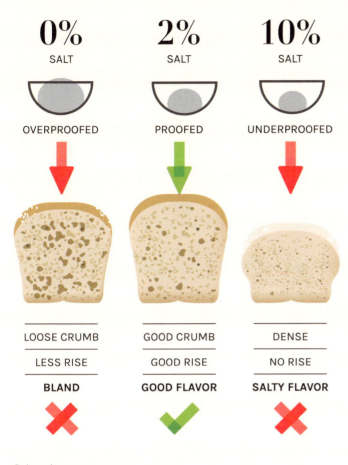

Salt and texture
The amount of salt in the dough affects how it rises and the density of the crumb. For best results, dough should contain 2 percent salt.

Wheat alternatives

SPELT
An ancient cousin of common wheat known for its sweeter, distinctive nuttier flavor and higher protein levels, spelt is a favorite for bread makers wanting a loaf with a more complex taste with a stronger "bread" aroma, and a softer, more tender texture.

DURUM
A wheat species with a deep yellow color and high protein content, durum produces a stronger but less elastic gluten, ideal for pasta. Milled into fine flour or coarse semolina, it's perfect for pasta and breads, like pane di Altamura. Durum bread crusts boast more toasty pyrazines, sweet caramel furans, and nutty pyrroles from the Maillard reaction than standard bread flour.

RYE
Rye is a completely different grass species unrelated to wheat, with its own robust, very complex flavor that is rich, earthy, and a little bitter, carrying notes of mushroom and cooked potato. Rye breads have a dense crumb and chewy texture because wetted rye flour does not form gluten but a dense mass made from sticky proteins called secalins.

SOURDOUGH

Raising (or leavening) agents—whether living or chemical—turn flatbread into puffy rolls and brownies into sponge cakes by releasing gas when wetted and warmed, inflating doughs and batters. Most breads use purified yeast, while cakes, muffins, and soda bread use baking powder or baking soda. Sourdough, however, rises thanks to a unique blend of yeasts and microbes naturally found on wheat grains, in the air, and on bakers' hands.

The wild mix of yeast and microbes is left to grow (or ferment) as a "starter," which is fed regularly with fresh flour and water.

TANGY
FRUITY FLAVORS OF SOURDOUGH COME FROM FERMENTING YEAST AND MICROBES.

KEY
- Microbe
- Primary by-products
- Flavor contributions

Sourdough microbes
The wild yeasts and bacteria in the starter work together to give sourdough bread its flavor.

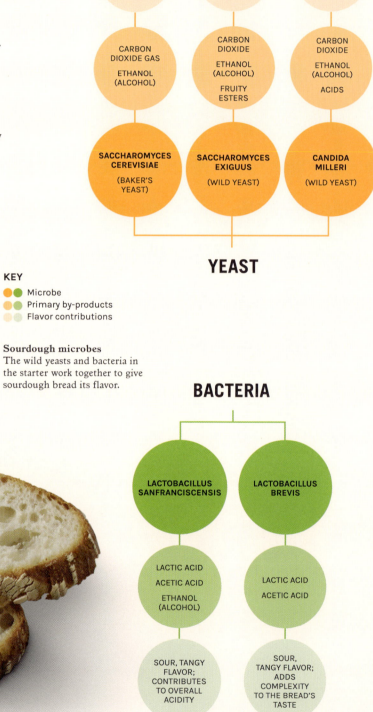

FLAVOR DIRECTORY 137

ENRICHED DOUGH

Dough made with flour, water, yeast, and salt can be enhanced with ingredients like milk, butter, oil, eggs, or sugar, unlocking a world of delicious baked creations.

ADDING FAT

Mixing fat into doughs transforms baked goods: softening stiff gluten for melt-in-the-mouth richness and indulgent buttery or oily flavors. Olive oil makes focaccia tender and adds a fruity, grassy note, while egg yolks in brioche and panettone give softness, color, and a richness.

ADDING SUGAR

Sugar similarly weakens gluten creations by soaking up water and sticking to gluten proteins, giving breads and baked goods a moist texture. Brown sugar and molasses make cookies gooey because of their greater water-holding powers. As the main food for yeast, however, sugar can make breads overrise while proofing. These effects can be lessened by holding off adding sugar and fat until after rising and kneading, when gluten has formed, or by working them in gradually.

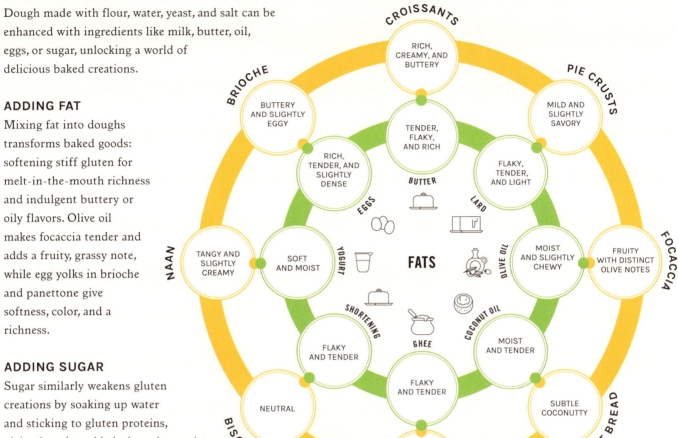

BAKED GOODS KEY
● Fat's effect on texture
● Fat's effect on flavor

BUTTER IN LAMINATED (LAYERED) PASTRIES LIKE CROISSANTS CREATES LAYERS OF FLAKINESS AND IMPARTS A LUXURIOUS, BUTTERY TASTE.

SANDWICH SCIENCE

From the South American arepa to the more modern French croque monsieur, all sandwiches were once peasant foods that now celebrate each region's ingredients, flavors, and culture.

The bread sets the character of the sandwich, but the filling should be the star of the show.

The thickness of the bread should be equal to, or less than, the thickness of the filling. Balance crusty breads with soft fillings, and soft breads with crunch, such as lettuce. Strong-tasting breads like rye are best offset with robustly flavored fillings.

LAYERING UP

Traditionally, the main ingredient is laid at the bottom and topped with condiments and salad. The teeth first sink into the crunch of salad, followed by the intense aromas of what comes next. You can layer condiments or salads above and below the main filling, to prevent moisture from seeping into the bread. With a particularly wet main ingredient, put salad underneath to prevent seepage. Avoid putting slippery ingredients on top of one another, or fillings may squirt out.

FILLING IN

A great sandwich relies on a balance of sweetness, saltiness, sourness, and umami. Worldwide, main fillings are usually high-protein: meat, fish, or egg, although

SWEET AND FLUFFY
White bread brings a mild, slightly sweet flavor with a soft and fluffy texture.

CREAMY
Butter gives richness and creaminess with a distinct, savory flavor and a pleasant aroma.

CRUNCH
Slices of apple have a crisp, juicy crunch and are naturally sweet with a slight tartness.

TENDER
Turkey breast has a mild and slightly savory taste, with a tender texture.

plant-based foods are popular, too. Focus on one strongly flavored "hero" ingredient. Research points to an upper limit of four fillings, after which deliciousness plummets.

SPREADING AND BINDING

Butter and mayonnaise are common in European and North American sandwiches. A high-fat spread forms an oily, water-repellent barrier that shields the bread from moisture, while enhancing flavor (pp.166–167). Smashed avocado, cream cheese, and hummus are alternative spreads. The depth and complexity of cheese flavors serve as "flavor bridges," marrying ingredients that might otherwise jar (pp.70–71). Cheese also adds flavor-boosting fat, salt, umami, and a hint of sourness—enhanced when melted into a creamy glue that binds ingredients together. Other "bridges" include caramelized onions, pickles, and ketchups.

PUNGENT
A tangy and slightly spicy mustard has pungent heat.

NUTTY
Slices of creamy Swiss cheese act as a food bridge, with a buttery, nutty flavor.

PEPPERY
Dark green arugula adds a strong peppery taste.

THE PERFECT SANDWICH

HARMONY
BY CONSIDERING HOW ALL THE COMPONENTS COMBINE, YOU CAN CREATE A BALANCED SANDWICH.

The perfect sandwich

This turkey and Swiss sandwich shows how basic flavors can be balanced: the salty, umami, turkey and cheese are bridged with fruity apple, which also brings a tangy crunch. Arugula adds a bitter note, and the mustard heat. Butter on the bread marries the components nicely.

PASTA AND NOODLES

By boiling or steaming shaped wheat dough, we can create al dente spaghetti and soft ravioli as well as slippery noodles and silky-smooth dumplings. As with bread, gluten is the glue that binds pasta and noodles together, although Chinese noodles have a softer, more supple consistency than Europe's robust creations—partly because of Asia's historical lack of the high-protein "hard" wheats.

HOW DRYING CREATES FLAVOR

Protein-rich semolina (durum) dough is the mainstay of Italian-style pastas; its dense, inelastic gluten (pp.134–135) and coarse particles help it dry into long-lasting pasta shapes and prevent starch from quickly leaching into cooking water. Thoroughly kneaded, shaped, then left to dry, pasta gains layers of flavor through an assortment of chemical reactions. Slowly dried (at 68–104°F/20–40°C over 1–3 days) artisanal pastas gain a caramel sweet, earthy fresh flavor and slightly sticky texture; more modern, high-temperature dried commercial pastas (167°F+/75°C+, in less than 12 hours) have a toasty, nutty, cooked flavor from Maillard reaction compounds (pp.74–77) as well as a deeper yellow color and firmer bite. These differences can guide sauce choices.

Artisan pasta has subtle and balanced flavors; pair with flavors that won't overwhelm them, such as olive oil, fresh herbs, or light seafood. Mass-produced pasta pairs best with strong, hearty, tomato-based, cream, or heavy meat sauces, whose richness complements the pasta's robust flavors.

FRESH PASTA AND NOODLES

Fresh pasta is made from lower-protein, finely milled wheat flour (such as 00 flour) and usually is enriched with whole

SHAPED FOR FLAVOR

SPAGHETTI'S LONG, SMOOTH STRANDS ALLOW FOR COATING WITH LIGHT, OILY SAUCES.

SPAGHETTI   PENNE   LASAGNA   ORZO   FARFALLE

egg or yolks, for succulence and flavor. The dough is kneaded gently to avoid too much dense gluten, then rested for at least 30 minutes to "relax" the entangled, tightly coiled glutenin before rolling and cutting. Fresh pasta is fully hydrated and so cooks quickly in simmering water (2–3 minutes) and, with the exception of spaghetti bolognese, is best partnered with lighter-flavored sauces.

Traditional Asian noodle-making also uses low-gluten flours, resulting in weak gluten doughs. These are sometimes strengthened with kansui (alkaline water) to achieve the firmer, springier texture of Japanese ramen and Chinese lamian ("pulled") noodles. Like fresh pasta, noodles cook quickly but are often preserved by drying. Drying can be done quickly with machines or slowly in the air or direct sun. Slow drying brings out subtler, fresher flavors, while high-temperature drying methods result in a firmer texture and richer flavor. Instant noodles are dried noodles that have been partially cooked and often deep-fried for added flavor.

PASTA COMPOUNDS KEY
- Flavors in artisanal pasta
- Flavors in industrially made pasta

SOBA | RAMEN | UDON | SOBA

SOBA NOODLES

SOBA ARE MADE OF BUCKWHEAT FLOUR AND HAVE A NUTTY FLAVOR.

MUSHROOMS AND TRUFFLES

Neither plant nor animal, fungi inhabit an umami-rich kingdom of their own. Mushrooms and truffles are the fleshy fruiting bodies of the subterranean fungi. Most commercially grown mushrooms are more than 90 percent water, which helps explain why they change in flavor and texture so dramatically when cooked. As they cook, water evaporates, making the texture firmer and the flavor more concentrated. When cooked with fat, the Maillard reaction (pp.74–77) enhances their natural umami and nutty notes, creating crisp, brown edges and layers of savory complexity. It's important not to overcrowd the pan so that they brown rather than steam, causing a rubbery texture.

VITAMIN D
MUSHROOMS ARE ONE OF THE FEW FOODS THAT ARE A SOURCE OF VITAMIN D – SOME PRODUCE IT IN SUNLIGHT.

Mushrooms' celebrated "meaty" flavor comes from their naturally high levels of glutamate and umami boosters like GMP and IMP (pp.28–29). Drying amplifies umami as proteins self-digest into umami-rich fragments and amino acids. Traditionally sun-dried, drying is easy indoors using a low oven or dehydrator. Rehydrate before cooking (for example, in warm water for 20–30 minutes) to soften and release trapped umami. Unlike meat or vegetables, mushrooms cannot be overcooked: their chitin "skeleton"—the same material as insect and lobster shells—won't toughen or collapse with lengthy cooking. All varieties' fresh, "mushroomy" aroma comes from

Mushroom varieties

Mushrooms all offer rich, savory, umami flavors and textures that bring a special quality to dishes.

OYSTER
Mild, nutty flavor and slippery texture, rich in mushroomy octenol.

SHIITAKE
Rich, earthy, smoky flavor and firm, chewy texture.

MATSUTAKE
Strong, slightly spicy flavor and meaty texture.

ENOKI
Mild, slightly fruity flavor and crisp texture.

NAMEKO
Mild, nutty flavor and gelatinous texture.

WOOD EAR
Woody, umami flavor and chewy, jellylike texture.

FLAVOR DIRECTORY 143

Common pairings
Butter, garlic, egg, flat-leaf parsley, thyme, cream, Gruyère cheese, Parmesan cheese, chestnut, potato, and ham.

Butter · Mushroom · Egg

Apricot · Mushroom · Lemongrass

Uncommon pairings
Sherry vinegar, tarragon, dried cranberry, avocado, smoked paprika, spelt, vanilla, lemongrass, and apricot.

"mushroom alcohol" (octenol, highest in gills) and appears only when cut or cooked. Avoid washing mushrooms unless briefly, as rubbing breaks their delicate skin (cuticle), flooding spongy air spaces with water, turning them soggy.

Although mushrooms and truffles are both fungi, they are very different. Truffles fruit underground and are difficult to cultivate commercially; they will grow only in certain seasons in certain types of woodland with the right climate. The most highly prized are the black winter truffle and white truffle, which is mainly found in southern France and northern Italy.

The magic of truffles

BECAUSE THEY EXCHANGE NUTRIENTS WITH HOST PLANTS, TRUFFLES GAIN RICH, COMPLEX FLAVORS.
Truffles' aroma is pungent but elusive: complex, musky, earthy, and umami, it lingers in the mouth and can perfume whatever it is stored next to. They require delicate handling when cooking. Light cooking with fat-rich sauces brings out their flavor best, as the fat helps dissolve and disperse the flavor compounds. Too much heat will diminish truffles' volatile aromas.

GLUTAMATE
THE AMINO ACID IN MUSHROOMS IS A NATURAL FLAVOR ENHANCER, SO MUSHROOM DISHES NEED LESS SALT.

ERYNGII/KING TRUMPET
Meaty flavor and texture.

BUTTON
Mild, slightly earthy flavor and lightly chewy texture.

CHESTNUT
Mild woody, nutty flavor and lightly chewy texture.

PORTOBELLO
Umami, woody flavor and succulent texture.

CHANTERELLE
Delicate nutty, fruity flavor and firm texture.

CEP
Rich umami flavor and meaty texture.

MOREL
Robust earthy, woody flavor and firm meaty texture.

SEAWEED

Seaweeds are primitive marine algae, not plants. With more than 20,000 varieties, they range from tiny plankton to towering giant kelp. Cherished for their rich, savory flavor, they are a popular food around the world.

FLAVOR, TEXTURE, AND AROMA

All seaweeds share a briny, slightly metallic, umami taste and an aroma of the seas. Edible seaweeds fall into three types: green seaweeds (such as sea lettuce and aonori), which grow in the shallows with plantlike flavors; deeper-water brown types (kombu and wakame) with strong savory notes; and red types (nori, dulse), the deepest-growing type with earthy, nutty, and sometimes smoky flavors.

Seaweed's taste comes from the salt and minerals that it harvests from the sea and glutamate, an umami-tasting amino acid it accumulates to store nitrogen, a vital nutrient. Lacking the sweet-tasting sugars found in fruit, seaweed instead produces mannitol, a "sugar alcohol," which has a mild sweetness. This is also synthesized and used as a low-calorie sweetener.

Many seaweeds, especially red and brown, have a soft, slimy texture and firm bite because their cells have thick walls filled with jellylike substances, such as agar and alginate. This allows them to flex in violent ocean currents. Green seaweeds have a crisper, crunchier texture from more brittle, cellulose-based cell walls.

Flavor and aroma come not from the terpenes (pp.66–67) of many fruits and vegetables, but from a different constellation of aroma compounds. Hydrocarbon aroma compounds, rarely found in other foods, have waxy, fatty qualities; "halogenated" compounds, which contain bromine and iodine, carry scents of the sea; these, combined with powerful dimethyl sulfide—also found in cooked corn, cabbage, and shellfish—culminate in a strong marine, slightly medicinal flavor.

DULSE
HAS A STRONG UMAMI FLAVOR, LENDING RICH SAVORINESS TO SOUPS.

DULSE

KOMBU

SEA LETTUCE

SEA LETTUCE
TASTES LIKE A SALTY SPINACH OR KALE. IT CAN BE USED IN SOUP, SALADS, AND SUSHI.

FLAVOR DIRECTORY 145

Seaweed flavors and uses

There are many different kinds of seaweed, and each one has its own flavor compounds and uses.

SEA LETTUCE
Subtle sweet, fruity notes from ethyl acetate, a fruity ester. Mushroom alcohol gives an earthy background flavor.

Blend into pesto for a fresh, oceanic twist. Use with citrus in salads for a fresh balance.

AONORI
Dried into flakes or powder, can be added to dishes to bring a mild, salty, umami flavor. Carries nutty notes.

Cook with nuts or nut oils. Use in soups, salads, and sushi.

IRISH MOSS
Purple and occasionally green with a gentle oceanic flavor with earthy hints.

Made into a gel, it can be used in smoothies, to thicken sauces or soups, and bind desserts.

SEA GRAPES (GREEN CAVIAR)
Tiny grapelike beads have a salty, clamlike flavor. Refreshing green tea aroma from a flavor profile similar to sea lettuce.

Eat raw, in salads.

DULSE
Tastes like bacon when fried or roasted. Its fresh-flavored aldehydes decompose in heat; while Maillard flavors and salty, umami glutamate are concentrated.

Sprinkle flakes on popcorn or salads.

KOMBU
The "king of seaweeds" is prized for its meaty, umami intensity with hexanal, mushroom alcohol, and haylike aromas. Brown when dried.

A staple in Japanese cuisine for making dashi broth.

NORI
Contains aldehydes like grassy hexanal and bready pentanal. Geranylacetone, gives a floral note, and pyrazines bring nuttiness.

Use dried nori sheets to wrap sushi rolls and rice.

SEA SPAGHETTI
Umami flavors with roasted, nutty-flavored pyrazines (dimethylpyrazine, tetramethylpyrazine).

Can be cooked in a similar way to spaghetti.

WAKAME
Mild, sweet, and briny with a refreshing, oceanic saltiness.

Use whole in salads. Its gelatinous consistency adds body to broths and soups.

KEY
- Brown seaweed
- Green seaweed
- Red seaweed

Common pairings
Red and brown seaweeds are used in miso soup and as a seasoning for rice dishes. Kombu is a staple in Japanese cuisine for making dashi.

Rice — Seaweed — Miso

Popcorn — Seaweed — Chocolate

Uncommon pairings
Dulse flakes can be sprinkled on popcorn or used in salads, providing a unique smoky-savory note. Red seaweeds can also pair well with chocolate.

BEEF

This meat comes mainly from steers (neutered male cattle) that mature in two years. Different cuts offer distinct flavors and textures, with tougher parts like shoulder and leg needing slow cooking to tenderize sinew and fat.

FLAVOR NOTES
Raw beef tastes bloody and metallic, which is caused by the iron-rich molecule myoglobin. Cooking releases more than 650 flavor compounds, the most important of which come from the fat. Methods like grilling and frying further enrich these flavors.

The distinctive flavor of cooked beef comes from the Maillard reaction (pp.74–77). It is, therefore, essential to brown the meat using methods like searing or grilling before adding any liquids. Missing this step will leave the meat with a spongy texture and lacking a rich, flavor-packed crust.

SELECTING CUTS
Tough cuts of beef like chuck, brisket, and shank are woven with inedible sinews (connective tissue) made of tasteless collagen that needs time to break down into soft, velvety gelatin. At temperatures between 158–180°F (70–82°C), this transformation slowly turns meat from leathery to succulent. The gelatin also contributes to a rich gravy.

Marbling appears as white flecks within the muscle and develops in animals fed a calorie-rich diet with low exercise. These fine threads of "intramuscular" fat melt at just 130°F (54°C), releasing rich flavor compounds and giving each bite a rich juiciness and distinct, buttery, melt-in-your-mouth sensation. Owing to all the flavor waiting to explode out of beef fat, marbling magnifies the depth and complexity of flavor. Opt for cuts with even marbling (such as rib eye), or breeds known for this characteristic, such as Wagyu.

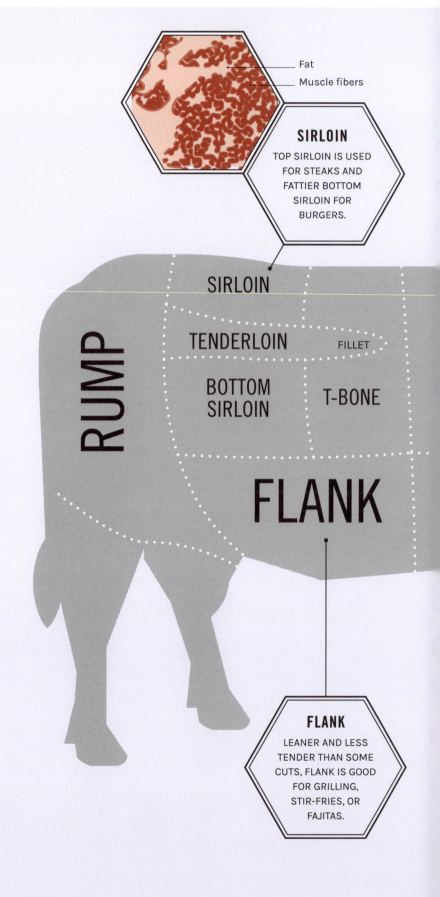

Fat
Muscle fibers

SIRLOIN
TOP SIRLOIN IS USED FOR STEAKS AND FATTIER BOTTOM SIRLOIN FOR BURGERS.

SIRLOIN
RUMP
TENDERLOIN — FILLET
BOTTOM SIRLOIN — T-BONE
FLANK

FLANK
LEANER AND LESS TENDER THAN SOME CUTS, FLANK IS GOOD FOR GRILLING, STIR-FRIES, OR FAJITAS.

FLAVOR DIRECTORY 147

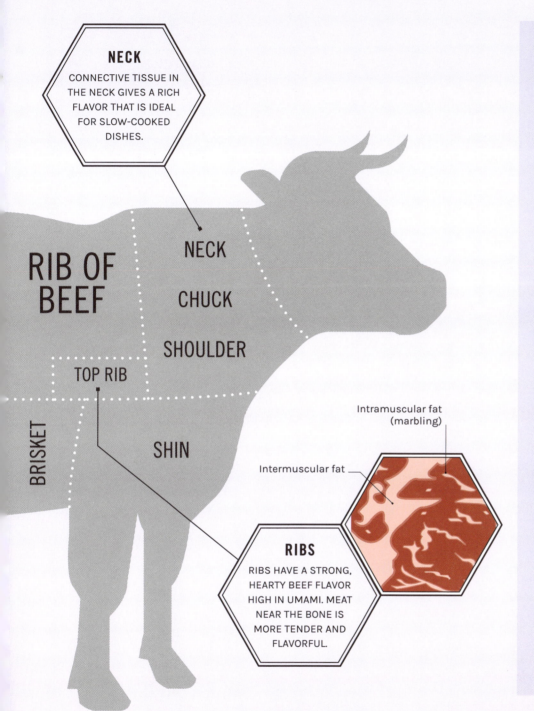

NECK
CONNECTIVE TISSUE IN THE NECK GIVES A RICH FLAVOR THAT IS IDEAL FOR SLOW-COOKED DISHES.

RIB OF BEEF

NECK

CHUCK

SHOULDER

TOP RIB

BRISKET

SHIN

Intramuscular fat (marbling)

Intermuscular fat

RIBS
RIBS HAVE A STRONG, HEARTY BEEF FLAVOR HIGH IN UMAMI. MEAT NEAR THE BONE IS MORE TENDER AND FLAVORFUL.

Beef varieties

GRAIN-FINISHED BEEF
Flavor: Intense meaty flavor with a high fat content. Marbling enhances juiciness and flavor.

Compounds: High-energy grain feed adds extra fat and sulfur-containing compounds for an "American" taste.

How to use: Ideal for grilling and high-heat cooking methods to capitalize on marbling, which melts quickly and gives succulence.

GRASS-FINISHED BEEF
Flavor: Less fat, firmer texture with grassy or herbaceous notes. May taste gamey with hints of clover or wildflowers, varying with diet.

Compounds: A grass-fed diet enriches the meat with terpene aroma compounds and other plant-derived compounds, giving a "green" flavor profile.

How to use: Use cooking methods, such as roasting, to bring out its distinctive flavors.

JAPANESE (WAGYU) BEEF
Flavor: Exceptionally marbled, melt-in-the-mouth tenderness, complex flavor with sweet, fruity aroma and savory umami notes.

Compounds: High fat content (up to 40 percent) and more than 17 flavor compounds give it a signature flavor profile.

How to use Light searing; best served as steak to preserve and highlight its unique fat composition and complex flavors.

Common pairings
Accentuate the classic, roasted flavors of beef by pairing it with nuts, other meats, cocoa, fried or baked potato, or Burgundy wine.

Nuts   Beef   Red wine

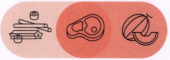

Licorice   Beef   Watermelon

Uncommon pairings
Add licorice root to a slow-cooked beef dish for sweet, smoky depth or watermelon to a cold beef salad for a lighter, fresh taste.

LASAGNA SCIENCE

A global Italian favorite, lasagna originated as a Greek dish layered with dough rather than pasta. Its ingredients, which are more closely paired than most dishes, are rich in fat and umami, possibly explaining why lasagna is perhaps the ultimate in comfort food.

RAGÙ

The thick, meaty sauce, called ragù, forms the foundation of this iconic dish "lasagna al forno."

- **Vegetables and meat:** Diced celery, carrots, and onions are fried in oil until soft and golden, followed by the ground meat (beef or veal are traditionally used)—or a vegetarian alternative—which is sautéed until brown to add a layer of robust Maillard flavors.
- **Wine:** Next comes the wine and liquid ingredients—red wine dissolves ("deglazes") any brown crust on the pan (called a fond), the alcohol quickly dissolving and dispersing flavor compounds. Evaporating (or reducing) the wine vaporizes much of the alcohol while imparting concentrated fruity, tangy, winey flavors.
- **Tomatoes:** Puréed tomatoes, or passata, are then added to bring intense umami undertones without diluting flavor. Tomato is a crucial flavor bridge (pp.88–89), sharing dozens of flavor compounds with the other vegetables as well as with the ground beef, pasta, and Parmesan cheese. A good ragù is left to slowly simmer for several hours, further concentrating flavors, allowing them to meld together, as well as giving time for new flavor compounds to develop.

PASTA

The firm bite of the relatively flavor-neutral pasta sheets offers much-needed textural contrast.

BÉCHAMEL SAUCE

More decadent than the ricotta cheese layers typical of American Italian recipes, a butter-flour-milk béchamel brings an intense creaminess and moistness that balances the meatiness of the ragù. It's often seasoned with nutmeg (p.178), a warming spice that also bridges the pasta with the tomatoes and other vegetables.

The perfect lasagna

This lasagna shows how the flavors of the dish are layered and balanced, working together to make the most tempting mouthfuls of comforting food. The combination of the rich tomato sauce, soft pasta, and creamy sauce is irresistible. You can supplement the meat with vegetables like spinach or zucchini.

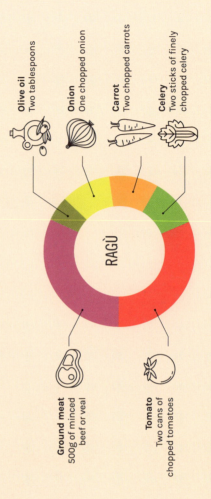

Ragù
The rich, comforting sauce used in lasagna contains ground meat and tomatoes as its main ingredients, with vegetables, olive oil, and wine added for extra depth of flavor.

Ground meat
500g of minced beef or veal

Tomato
Two cans of chopped tomatoes

Olive oil
Two tablespoons

Onion
One chopped onion

Carrot
Two chopped carrots

Celery
Two sticks of finely chopped celery

+ Seasoning
Salt and freshly ground black pepper

+ Wine
Mild, Italian red or white wine can be used

Cooking with alcohol

ALCOHOL EVAPORATES EASILY—AT JUST 172°F (78°C)—MEANING IT QUICKLY VAPORIZES IN A BOILING DISH: after 15 minutes, 60 percent is gone and by an hour, 75 percent. It never vanishes: even after 2.5 hours, 5 percent of the original alcohol remains.

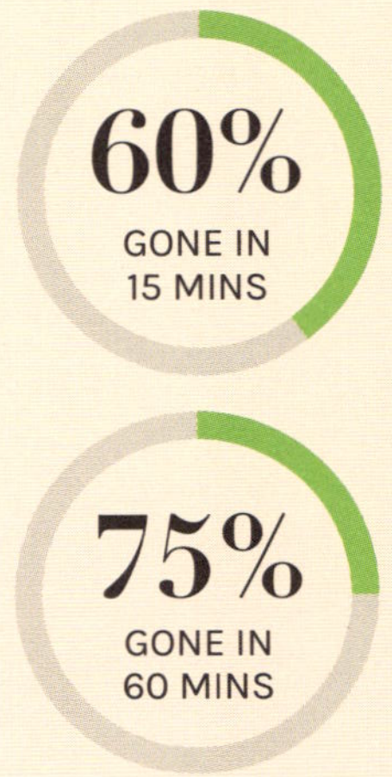

60% GONE IN 15 MINS

75% GONE IN 60 MINS

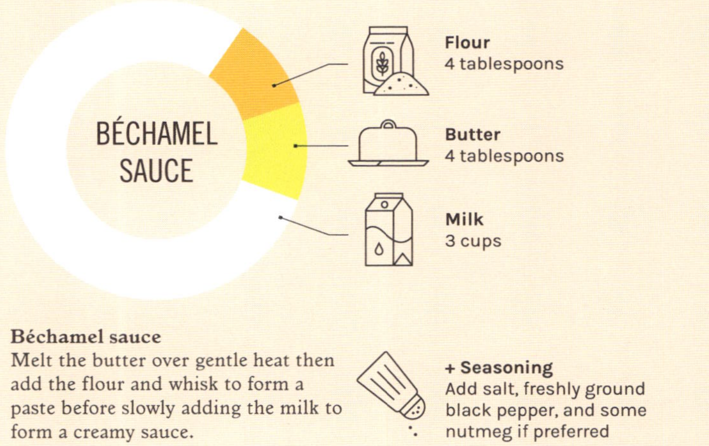

Flour 4 tablespoons

Butter 4 tablespoons

Milk 3 cups

+ Seasoning Add salt, freshly ground black pepper, and some nutmeg if preferred

BÉCHAMEL SAUCE

Béchamel sauce
Melt the butter over gentle heat then add the flour and whisk to form a paste before slowly adding the milk to form a creamy sauce.

Grated Parmesan cheese
Sprinkled over a final layer of béchamel and oven baked until brown

Pasta
Sheets of pasta are used to absorb the flavors of the meat and sauce

Ragù
A rich sauce that adds depth and flavor to the dish

Béchamel sauce
A rich, creamy layer that adds mild flavor

POULTRY

Poultry—including chicken, duck, goose, and turkey—is affordable, flavorful meat, ranging from mild and versatile to rich and gamey. It is generally mild tasting, with its depth of flavor being highly dependent on fat content.

More than 250 chemical compounds have been associated with the flavors of poultry meat, and 500 have been associated with its aroma when cooked. It is the Maillard reaction (pp.74–75), the thermal breakdown of fat, and the interaction of these two processes that creates the flavors and aromas of poultry.

Species that fly only in short bursts (chickens and turkeys) have a type of muscle fiber in their breasts that produces a white meat.

This is lean and mild tasting. The breast muscle of species that fly long distances (ducks and geese) have more oxygen-supplying myoglobin, which produces a dark meat. Ducks and geese also have a thick layer of fat under the skin, so their meat cooks well at high temperatures, either roasted or grilled, because it is essentially self-basting.

MAXIMIZING FLAVOR

There are challenges when roasting a whole bird as different parts of the bird cook at different rates. Roasting, grilling, or frying poultry produces rich, fatty aromas and flavor compounds, although these methods can dry out breast meat. White breast meat stays juicy if boiled or poached but then doesn't have the same rich

CITRUS IS OFTEN USED IN POULTRY COOKING TO CUT THE SLIPPERY MOUTHFEEL OF FATTY MEAT.

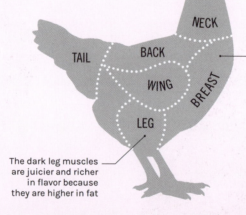

Chicken flavors
Chicken and turkey have subtle flavors and serve as a canvas for other ingredients.

The white breast meat is mild and low in fat

The dark leg muscles are juicier and richer in flavor because they are higher in fat

FAT CONTENT	CHICKEN	TURKEY
BREAST MEAT (SKINLESS)	3%	2%
LEG MEAT (SKINLESS)	7%	7%

Common pairings
Garlic, ginger, lemongrass, oregano, rosemary, sage, tarragon, and thyme.

Garlic — Chicken — Sage

Uncommon pairings
Cardamom, celery seeds, and fennel.

Cardamom — Chicken — Fennel

Common pairings
Cranberry, oregano, rosemary, sage, and thyme.

Cranberry — Turkey — Rosemary

Uncommon pairings
Cumin, paprika, parsley, and pecan nuts.

Cumin — Turkey — Paprika

FLAVOR DIRECTORY 151

GOOSE FAT
HAS A HIGH BURNING (SMOKE) POINT AND SUBTLE FLAVOR—PERFECT FOR COOKING ROAST POTATOES.

flavor compounds. Techniques such as brining, basting, and resting help ensure moisture is retained.

Hanging or aging ducks and geese helps to increase the flavor and tenderize the meat. These birds are traditionally "hung" to allow air to flow around all sides, which helps with moisture evaporation and subsequently the natural breakdown of proteins by enzymes still found in the muscle tissue.

STOCK

Poultry carcasses can be used to make stock, which can then be used to form a rich basis for soups and sauces and countless other dishes in the kitchen. Boiling a chicken carcass with herbs and vegetables for 10 hours at 158°F (70°C) makes for a clear, pure chicken stock. Using a pressure cooker can reduce that cooking time dramatically.

Brining and marinades

BRINING CAN BE USED TO KEEP POULTRY MOIST DURING COOKING.

Brining poultry meat can increase water content by 10 percent or more, preserving moistness and succulence. Dissolved salt enters the meat, followed by water, and causes muscle proteins to unravel and expand into a soft gel. Acids, such as lemon or vinegar, break down proteins, tenderizing the meat, "cooking" it slightly.

DUCK	GOOSE
5%	7%
12%	17%

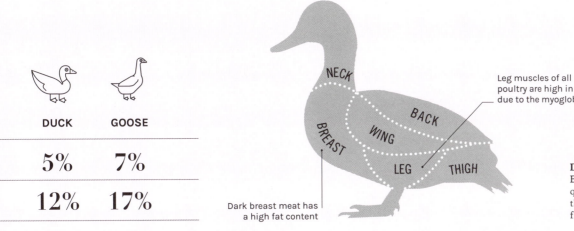

Leg muscles of all poultry are high in iron due to the myoglobin

Dark breast meat has a high fat content

Duck flavors
Both duck and goose are quite bold tasting and therefore demand robust flavors to accompany them.

Common pairings
Chinese five-spice, ginger, orange, rosemary, Sichuan pepper, and star anise.

Ginger — Duck — Star anise

Uncommon pairings
Balsamic vinegar, cherry, pineapple, and tamarind.

Cherry — Duck — Pineapple

Common pairings
Anise, Chinese five-spice, cinnamon, citrus, garlic, rosemary, and thyme.

Cinnamon — Goose — Citrus

Uncommon pairings
Blackberry, cherry, and sage.

Blackberry — Goose — Sage

PORK

Pork is the most popular meat globally and offers flavors with sweet, fruity, and floral tones. It has a slight natural sweetness, and its flavor can vary from mild and savory to rich and meaty, depending on the cut. Pork tenderloin, for example, has subtle flavors while pork belly is rich. When cooked, the Maillard reaction (pp.74–77) browns the meat while creating caramelized tones.

Pork fat has a fairly clean, neutral taste that varies depending on the pig's diet and breed (see right). Fat enhances flavors during cooking as it melts, absorbing and amplifying aroma compounds. Fat distribution across the pig's body affects the flavor and texture of different cuts. For instance, the belly contains alternating layers of fat and muscle, and as the fat melts ("renders"), it "bastes" the meat, frying the surface to add a rich, flavorful crust. In the shoulder, marbled fat combines with collagen to melt during slow cooking, creating a juicy, succulent texture and deep flavor.

CURING

Pork can be cured through salting, smoking, or fermentation to create foods like bacon, ham, and salami. Salt inhibits harmful bacteria and removes moisture from the meat, preserving it. Enzymes in the meat break down proteins into umami-rich meaty compounds, while fat degradation creates "piggy" flavors. Depending on the method, the meat may be further dried, smoked, or aged in controlled conditions, intensifying its texture and taste.

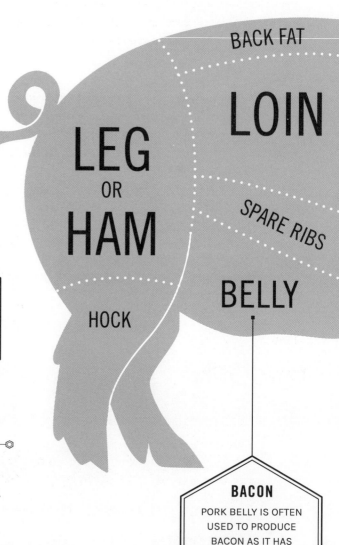

BOAR ODOR
THE PHEROMONE ANDROSTERONE IN MALE PIGS CAN CAUSE A DISTASTEFUL ODOR AND FLAVOR IN THE MEAT.

BACON
PORK BELLY IS OFTEN USED TO PRODUCE BACON AS IT HAS LAYERS OF FAT, WHICH ADD RICH FLAVOR.

Sausages

MOST CULTURES MAKE A FORM OF SAUSAGE, USED TO PRESERVE MEAT. PORK IS OFTEN A KEY INGREDIENT DUE TO ITS HIGH FAT CONTENT, ensuring sausages aren't too dry even if dry cured. Spanish chorizo is flavored with smoked paprika and then smoked, while Italian salami is fermented and covered in mold. Chinese sausages (lap cheong) are often heavily spiced and dry cured, while German Bratwurst and English bangers are fresh sausages that are cooked before eating.

FLAVOR DIRECTORY **153**

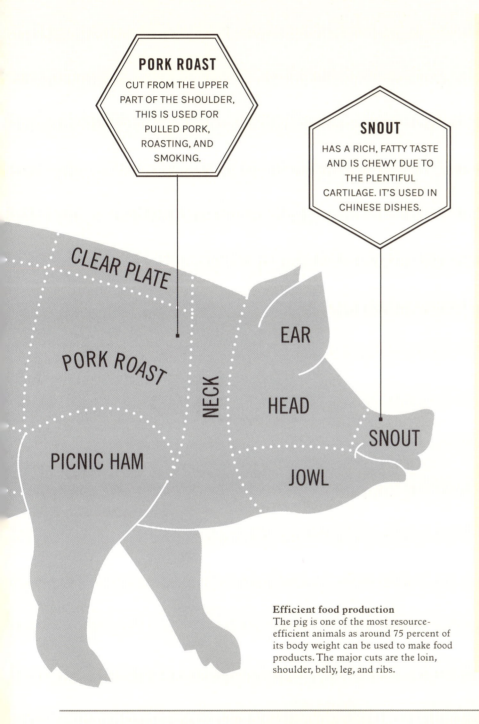

PORK ROAST
CUT FROM THE UPPER PART OF THE SHOULDER, THIS IS USED FOR PULLED PORK, ROASTING, AND SMOKING.

SNOUT
HAS A RICH, FATTY TASTE AND IS CHEWY DUE TO THE PLENTIFUL CARTILAGE. IT'S USED IN CHINESE DISHES.

Efficient food production
The pig is one of the most resource-efficient animals as around 75 percent of its body weight can be used to make food products. The major cuts are the loin, shoulder, belly, leg, and ribs.

Heritage breeds

The breed of pig and where and how they are traditionally reared makes a big difference to the flavor of their meat.

NORTH AMERICA

RED WATTLE PIG
Rearing: Adaptable to most climates.
Known for: Lean and flavorful meat.

DUROC
Rearing: Hardy animals that suit most conditions and temperatures.
Known for: Lean meat with a sweet flavor.

UK

GLOUCESTER OLD SPOT
Rearing: In orchards, feeding on apples.
Known for: Tender and flavorful meat.

SPAIN/PORTUGAL

IBERIAN BLACK PIG
Rearing: Free ranging, foraging on acorns and herbs.
Known for: Rich, nutty flavor.

HUNGARY

MANGALITSA PIG
Rearing: Cold climates, eating anything.
Known for: Flavorful, highly marbled fatty meat with wild boar gaminess.

CHINA

MEISHAN PIG
Rearing: Indoor or outdoor habitats.
Known for: Marbled, flavorful meat.

Common pairings
Apple, Chinese five-spice, sage, thyme, marjoram, and pineapple.

Apple — Pork — Sage

Uncommon pairings
Caraway, dill, fennel, tarragon, peach, and maple syrup.

Peach — Pork — Fennel

LAMB, MUTTON, AND GOAT

Sheep and goats are closely related. Their flavor and cooking uses vary according to the age of the animal: lamb (sheep, under 1 year) is mild and tender; hogget (sheep, 1–2 years) firmer and more gamey; mutton (sheep, 2+ years) like goat, is rich and bold.

LAMB

This red meat has a slightly earthier, gamier flavor than beef, which comes from the type of fatty acids found in the fat. Lamb raised on a combination of grain and grass tends to be milder in flavor than those that are reared on grass alone. The age of the animal (about one year) ensures that the meat has developed a depth of flavor and sufficient fat but remains tender. Some cuts of lamb, such as cutlets, are cooked hot and fast, which creates a caramelized crust while the center remains pink and tender. Other cuts, like the shoulder or leg, are best cooked low and slow so the meat falls away from the bone. You can enhance the flavor of lamb by marinating before cooking using ingredients such as garlic, rosemary, olive oil, and herbs like thyme. Lamb leg is sometimes prepared by piercing the leg all over and filling the piercing with a sprig of rosemary and slice of garlic wrapped in an anchovy. The anchovy disintegrates during roasting and bastes the meat in salts and oils as it melts away.

MUTTON

Meat from older sheep is richer, firmer, and more flavorful, with a higher fat content and a dark red color. Its strong, gamey flavor can be an acquired taste, and it's not widely popular in North America. It is prominent in Middle Eastern and Mediterranean cuisine, with Mongolia being the world's number-one consumer.

GOAT

As goats are generally older than sheep when eaten, goat tends to have a tougher texture, and (due to its leanness) can dry out quickly. Although low in fat, it is high in connective tissue, so slow cooking is best to create tender morsels of meat. Its strong, gamey flavor pairs well with other bold flavors. Goat is a key ingredient in slow cooked African and Caribbean stews and curries.

RICH FAT
THE MARBLING OF THE FAT IN THIS CUT MAKES IT SUCCULENT AND MELT-IN-THE-MOUTH.

SLOW COOK
THE HIND SHANK IS RICH IN FLAVOR WITH A TOUGH TEXTURE, IDEAL FOR BRAISING OR SLOW COOKING.

Common pairings
Anchovy, garlic, lemon, mint, potato, rosemary, and salt.

Uncommon pairings
Chocolate, coffee, grapefruit, mackerel, pumpkin seed, and whiskey.

FLAVOR DIRECTORY 155

RACK OF LAMB
THIS PRIME CUT COMES FROM THE RIB.

MARINATE
GOAT MEAT IS TRADITIONALLY MARINATED FOR EIGHT HOURS BEFORE BEING ADDED TO A STEW OR CURRY.

GAMEY
FATTY ACIDS GIVE GOAT AND LAMB THEIR DISTINCT GAMEY FLAVOR—IN THE MEAT AS WELL AS THE MILK.

HEAD
CHEEK
NECK
TONGUE
RIB
SHOULDER
BREAST
FORE SHANK

Heritage sheep breeds

Some traditional, often rare, breeds from around the world are valued for their unique characteristics and flavor. Many are ancient and have been bred over centuries, often for wool or for meat. These breeds are favored for their meat:

NORTH AMERICA

GULF COAST NATIVE
Rearing: Hot and humid climates.
Known for: Subtle earthy flavor.
Uses: Roasted rack of lamb.

HOG ISLAND
Rearing: Free-roaming or pasture fed, hardy.
Known for: Tender, clean, and slightly sweet tasting meat.
Uses: Slow-roasted marinated cuts.

UK

SOUTHDOWN
Rearing: Adapted to temperate climates, hardy and resilient.
Known for: Extremely tender meat.
Uses: Grilled chops or steaks.

ICELAND

ICELANDIC
Rearing: Hardy, adapted to cold climates.
Flavor: Mild and sweet with earthy notes.
Uses: Smoked dishes.

AFRICA/MIDDLE EAST

DAMARA
Flavor: Rich flavor, less gamey than some breeds.
Uses: Stews, braises, roasts, and grills.

AUSTRALIA

WILTIPOLL
Rearing: Hardy, adaptable, and self shedding.
Flavor: Lean meat with mild flavor.
Uses: Slow-cooked dishes or roasts.

Common pairings
Chile pepper, cilantro, curry, paprika, thyme, and turmeric.

Chile — Goat — Paprika

Pomegranate — Goat — Soy sauce

Uncommon pairings
Pomegranate, rosemary, sesame, and soy sauce.

GAME MEAT

Game comes from wild animals that are hunted rather than farmed. The most popular game meats are venison (deer), wild boar, pheasant, and rabbit. Game animals are generally leaner than their domestic counterparts and eat a more varied diet that fluctuates across different seasons, with no artificial additives, hormones, or antibiotics. This influences the flavor, texture, and color of the meat.

Game meat is generally more intensely flavored than farmed meat and potentially tougher in texture, depending on the age of the animal. Its earthier, musky flavors often make it an acquired taste. Rabbit is the mildest with a subtle sweet flavor that can be very tender when cooked well—cooking slow and low or in stews keeps meat moist and tender. Pheasant is one of the mildest of the game birds, but richer in flavor than chicken, with a slightly nutty undertone. It can be roasted whole, or the legs can be braised while the breast is best pan-seared or cooked sous vide (sealed in water). Wild boar is more intense and less fatty than domestic pork and has rich, mushroom-like flavors. Different cuts are cooked much like domestic pork, but wild boar lends itself particularly well to smoking. Venison is perhaps the gamiest flavored of these meats and has a distinct ironlike taste, though if aged and cooked properly, it can have a velvety texture. Cuts are cooked much like beef, but resting is crucial to keeping it moist and tender.

MYOGLOBIN
HIGH LEVELS OF THIS IRON- AND OXYGEN-BINDING PROTEIN GIVE GAME MEAT ITS DARK COLOR.

Common pairings
Apple, bay, juniper berries, sage, and thyme.

Apple · **Pheasant** · Sage

Uncommon pairings
Chestnut, elderberry, fig, persimmon, and quince.

Fig · **Pheasant** · Quince

Common pairings
Bay, garlic, mushroom, prune, rosemary, and thyme.

Garlic · **Rabbit** · Mushroom

Uncommon pairings
Fennel, hazelnut, lavender, and preserved lemon.

Fennel · **Rabbit** · Hazelnut

Common pairings
Bay, blackberry, cherry, juniper berry, and wild mushroom.

Blackberry · **Venison** · Cherry

Uncommon pairings
Blood orange, chestnut, chicory root, cocoa, and rose hip.

Blood orange · **Venison** · Chestnut

Common pairings
Apple, garlic, prune, rosemary, and sage.

Prune · **Wild boar** · Rosemary

Uncommon pairings
Crab apple, green walnut, mulberry, and pine nut.

Mulberry · **Wild boar** · Green walnut

OFFAL

Offal refers to the internal organs of animals that can be eaten and is less popular in some cultures and decreasing in popularity elsewhere as people are able to afford more desirable cuts of meat. While offal does have distinctive flavors, it is likely the textures that can be most challenging to the modern palate. Yet offal is cheap and nutritious and makes use of the whole animal. Some still-common dishes that incorporate offal include haggis (stomach, heart, and lungs), steak and kidney pie, sausages (intestine), and liver and onions. Liver and kidneys are perhaps the most palatable and therefore the most popular.

LIVER

Liver has a smooth, buttery texture, regardless of its source. Its distinctive flavor is strongest in lamb and pig, mildest in calf and chicken. Liver is often made into pâté, though can also be fried or smoked. It's important to not overcook liver as it can become rubbery.

KIDNEYS

Calf, lamb, and pig kidneys are the most readily available, with calf the most tender, pig the firmest, and lamb in between. Kidneys are rich in umami, with a metallic, gamey taste. They can have a urine smell, so thorough cleaning is essential: remove the white fat layer, membrane, internal fat, and tubes. Soaking in cold water or milk for up to three hours reduces blood and strong flavors. Salting to cut bitterness, then briefly cooking over high heat, ensures a tender, flavorful result.

MILK BATH
SOAKING LIVER IN MILK FOR SEVERAL HOURS BEFORE COOKING HELPS REDUCE STRONG FLAVORS.

Offal varieties

SWEETBREADS (THYMUS/PANCREAS)
Mild flavored, crispy on the outside when fried and creamy on the interior.

TONGUE
Mild, meaty flavor with a slightly gelatinous texture.

TRIPE (STOMACH)
Subtle flavor with a chewy or spongy texture.

GIZZARDS (POULTRY ONLY)
Gamey flavor, naturally tough but tender when slow-cooked.

HEART
Very meaty flavor with a firm, dense texture.

MARROW
Rich and buttery flavor that melts in the mouth.

OXTAIL
Intense umami flavor with gelatinous texture.

BRAIN
Delicate flavor with a silky, custardlike texture.

Common pairings
Black pepper, garlic, mustard seeds, shallot, sage, and thyme.

Black pepper · Kidney · Shallot

Uncommon pairings
Allspice, caper, cilantro, ginger root, green peppercorns, and sorrel.

Ginger · Kidney · Allspice

Common pairings
Brandy, onion, mustard seeds, parsley, sage, and thyme.

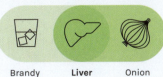

Brandy · Liver · Onion

Uncommon pairings
Blood orange, chestnut, green apple, Sichuan peppercorns, and tarragon.

Blood orange · Liver · Green apple

FISH

Fish, on average, accounts for just under 16 percent of the animal protein we eat, although this rises to more than 20 percent in Asian and African countries. Aquaculture, commercial fishing methods, and advances in processing have made fish more accessible to more people in the last century.

Fish, perhaps more than other animals, are prone to taking on flavor based on their diet and environment. They are usually categorized into two groups: white fish and oily fish. White fish, including cod, haddock, plaice, and halibut, has a delicate flavor and takes well to gentle herbs and seasoning that don't mask the fish's natural flavor. Oily fish, including tuna, salmon, mackerel, and anchovy, has richer, more robust flavors due to the oil content throughout the flesh. It can handle being paired with more intense flavors. All types of fish benefit from acidic flavors such as lemon.

MACKEREL

HAS SAVORY UMAMI QUALITIES AND A RICH, BUTTERY FLAVOR FROM ITS HIGH LEVELS OF OIL.

SEA BASS

HAS A MILD, SWEET FLAVOR THAT CAN TURN MORE NUTTY WHEN GRILLED OR ROASTED.

Common pairings
White fish, including cod, haddock, and halibut, all pair well with capers, dill, garlic, lemon, parsley, and thyme.

Lemon — White fish — Parsley

Fennel — White fish — Green tea

Uncommon pairings
Fennel, green tea, juniper berry, and makrut lime leaves.

FLAVOR DIRECTORY 159

OILY FISH

OIL DISTRIBUTED THROUGHOUT THE BODY (5 PERCENT OR MORE)

MEAT NOT AS FLAKY

EAT SUSHI, GRILLED, PAN-SEARED, SMOKED

WHITE FISH

OIL CONCENTRATED IN THE LIVER (LESS THAN 2 PERCENT)

MEAT WHITE, FLAKY

EAT POACHED, FRIED, GRILLED

PRESERVING

Evolved for the chilly depths, fish—especially oily species—spoil quickly without preservation or processing. Numerous preservation techniques have been developed around the world, many of which help strong flavors grow.

Oily fish, such as salmon, trout, and herring, are often cured using a combination of salting, drying, heating, and smoking. Smoking adds unique flavors, such as a peaty character from a peat fire. Salting and drying is often used, particularly with cod. This method also concentrates flavor compounds and increases the firmness of the flesh even after it has been desalted and rehydrated.

Raw fish dishes

Fish can be eaten raw by dressing or super-freezing (freezing immediately after it is caught to −40°F/C or below). This gives a fresh, clean taste with a tender texture.

SASHIMI
Thinly sliced fish, such as salmon or tuna, often super-frozen at sea then thawed for safety.

CEVICHE AND CRUDO
Fish or shellfish is thinly sliced and cured in citrus juice for immediate consumption.

POKE
Often tuna or octopus that is fresh or super-frozen, cubed, and marinated in soy sauce and sesame oil.

Common pairings
Pair oily fish such as tuna, mackerel, and salmon with black pepper, chile pepper, dill, ginger, lemon, or wasabi.

Chile   **Oily fish**   Lemon

Green almond   **Oily fish**   Soy sauce

Uncommon pairings
Green almonds, maple syrup, pink peppercorns, soy sauce, or sumac.

CRUSTACEANS

Crustaceans, a group that includes shrimp, crabs, and lobsters, are often considered a luxury item, despite the effort required to extract relatively small amounts of meat from their shells. Their meat is sweet and succulent, with tasting notes that include butter, cheese, musty, vinegar, pungent, and sweaty. The white meat found in the claws, legs, and muscular body sections (in the tail of shrimp and lobster) is firm and flaky with a mild, sweet flavor. This is usually preferred for main dishes. Dark meat is found in the body cavity (crab) or head (lobster and shrimp), in and around organs, and is soft with a pastelike consistency and a very rich and intense flavor. Dark meat is perfect for enriching sauces, making pâtés and spreads, or as a base for soups.

UMAMI
INOSINATE (IMP) AND GUANYLATE (GMP) ADD UMAMI TONES TO SEAFOOD FLAVORS (PP.26-29).

COLOR
CRUSTACEANS TURN PINK WHEN COOKED AS CAROTENOID PIGMENT ASTAXANTHIN IS FREED FROM PROTEINS.

FLAVOR DIRECTORY 161

COOKING

The most traditional method of cooking is boiling or steaming in salted water. The sweet flesh pulled from the shell is delicious simply dressed in melted butter with a touch of garlic and parsley. Crustaceans can also be grilled, pan-seared, poached, or prepared raw as part of ceviche or crudo.

Crab and lobster are often paired with rich sauces that are hollandaise-, butter-, or cream-based and can contain alcohol, such as brandy or Champagne. The firm meat and delicate taste of shrimp, on the other hand, makes it a versatile partner to stronger flavors such as chile and lime.

STOCKS AND BISQUES

The discarded shells from seafood are best used as a basis for stock and bisque, a rich, creamy shellfish soup made from stock blended with the rest of the ingredients and then strained multiple times and finished with cream. To enhance the flavor of the shells, they are often first roasted until fragrant and then crushed to increase the surface area. They are then added to a pot with onions, carrots, celery, garlic, leek, bay leaf, and other herbs, along with water and wine, and boiled into a stock. Bisque is strongly flavored, with a balance of savory, slightly sweet, and rich, buttery notes.

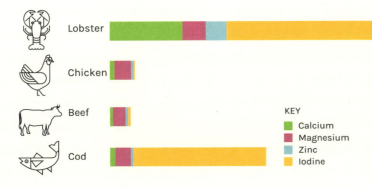

Relative mineral levels
Shell formation requires minerals and as a result, crustaceans are highly efficient at absorbing dissolved minerals in their aquatic environment. Compared with other sources of protein, crustaceans have significantly higher levels of minerals such as calcium, magnesium, zinc, and iodine. This makes crustaceans a great source of essential minerals.

MOLLUSKS

Mollusks typically have shells, such as oysters, mussels, scallops, snail, and cockles, though cephalopods, such as octopus and squid, do not. Many are "suspension feeders," taking plankton and other nutrients out of the water. Their flavor is, therefore, strongly influenced by their environment and what they eat, and they can accumulate toxins from the environment, such as mercury. Careful processing and preparation methods can address most of these concerns.

Mollusks generally have sweet, salty flavors with a creamy or plump mouthfeel texture. They are often steamed and pair well with lemon, garlic, and a creamy white wine. Scallops are delicious briefly grilled, fried, or broiled and paired with the stronger flavors of bacon or Spanish chorizo—the crunchy Maillard crust (pp.74–77) perfectly complements the silken interior.

SQUID AND OCTOPUS

Octopus and squid offer more meat than other shellfish. They are carnivores with tough muscles and plentiful cartilage, giving them a meatier texture than shelled mollusks, although they can become rubbery if not fresh or prepared properly. Octopus, in particular, is best tenderized before cooking by pounding, soaking, and/or freezing and thawing.

Squid and octopus have an umami taste and mild marine flavor from sulfur compounds. Animals that feed more on crustaceans, such as crabs and shrimp, have a stronger umami flavor than those with a mollusk and fish diet.

Due to their dense structure, squid and octopus lend themselves well to being grilled, braised, stewed, fried, or sautéed. Much like scallops, these cooking methods create a flavorful browned surface with a contrasting soft interior. Calamari is the classic fried squid dish and is usually served with a slice of lemon and dipping sauces. The key to avoiding a rubbery texture is hot and fast (when grilling) or low and slow (if stewed).

OYSTER   CLAM   SCALLOP

FLAVOR DIRECTORY 163

Common pairings
Lemon, Champagne, hot sauce (for example, Tabasco), horseradish, and garlic.

Lemon — **Oyster** — Champagne

Green apple — **Oyster** — Cucumber

Uncommon pairings
Grapefruit, Granny Smith apple, sake, cucumber, and jalapeño chile.

Common pairings
White wine, fries, shallots, garlic, tomato, parsley, butter, and cream.

White wine — **Mussel** — Fries

Smoked paprika — **Mussel** — Cider

Uncommon pairings
Curry powder, smoked paprika, cider, green curry paste, and Spanish chorizo.

Common pairings
Bacon, butter, lemon, peas, asparagus, and white wine.

Bacon — **Scallop** — Asparagus   Miso — **Scallop** — Pineapple

Uncommon pairings
Maple syrup, pineapple, miso, cherry, and balsamic reduction.

Common pairings
Lemon, olive oil, garlic, tomato, oregano, and red wine.

Red wine — **Octopus** — Olive oil   Fennel — **Octopus** — Orange

Uncommon pairings
Fennel, orange, ouzo, smoked paprika, and harissa.

Common pairings
Garlic, parsley, tomato, lemon, olive oil, and white wine.

Garlic — **Squid** — Tomato   Ginger — **Squid** — Coconut milk

Uncommon pairings
Coconut milk, ginger, sherry, vinegar, Spanish chorizo, and mango.

FRESH
SEAFOOD HAS A PLEASANT BRINY SCENT. FISHINESS COMES FROM TRIMETHYLAMINE (TMA), MADE BY BACTERIA.

Oysters

OYSTERS ARE CONSIDERED A DELICACY AND, UNLIKE MOST SEAFOOD, ARE OFTEN EATEN RAW IN THEIR HALF SHELL.

They have a mild flavor and pair well with salt and a hot sauce. The true appeal lies in their texture—when served fresh and cold, oysters are firm, plump, and juicy, delivering a burst of briny sweetness with each bite. However, if they are old or of low quality, they can become rubbery, fibrous, or even gritty.

MUSSEL

MILK AND CREAM

Milk has been part of our diet since Neolithic times and remains fundamental to cooking today. A blend of fat globules and proteins dispersed in liquid, milk is one of the most nutritious substances we cook with. Its main components are water, fat, protein, carbohydrate (lactose), and minerals.

Most commercially sold milk is pasteurized (heated to destroy any pathogenic bacteria) and homogenized (which makes the fat globules smaller so the fat doesn't separate out). Cow's milk from many farms is blended together, which means there is not a great deal of flavor variation. Lactose in milk gives a mild sweetness, while the fat content brings creamy, buttery flavors. Earthy and grassy

ENZYMES IN CREAM AND MILK ARE DESTROYED BY PASTEURIZATION, EXTENDING THEIR SHELF LIFE.

MILK FAT CONVEYS MILK'S FLAVOR AND AROMA. THIS IS WHY SKIM MILK TASTES BLAND.

LIGHT CREAM

CLOTTED CREAM

CRÈME FRAÎCHE

SKIM MILK

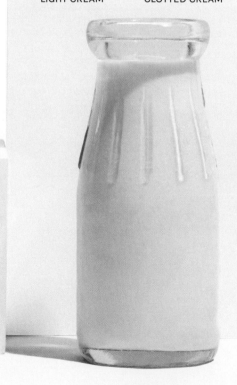

HEAVY CREAM

WHOLE MILK

notes in milk depend on the diet of the animal. Cooking with milk can deliver caramelized, more savory flavors.

When cultured or fermented through the addition of bacteria (usually *Streptococcus* and *Lactobacillus*), milk is used to create products like yogurt, sour cream, and kefir (pp.168–169). This process thickens the milk and adds nutty, tangy flavors.

COOKING WITH MILK

Milk is important in cooking, notably as the foundation of béchamel sauce (pp.148–149), to which it gives a mild flavor and smooth texture. It is also used in authentic ragù alla bolognese to cut through the acidity of the wine and tomatoes. In custard, the natural minerals in milk help egg yolk proteins mesh together, while the sugar and water content slows this process down, resulting in a smooth custard.

Milk takes on flavors from ingredients that are stored nearby. This also means it lends itself well to being infused with flavor, such as with garlic and Parmesan cheese in Alfredo sauce, with blueberries in yogurt, or with nutmeg for a custard.

CREAM

Cream has a similar flavor profile to milk but with a richer texture and mouthfeel due to the higher fat content. Heavy cream and clotted cream have the richest flavors. Like milk, cream can develop more complex, sour flavors when fermented to make sour cream or crème fraîche, for example.

GOAT'S MILK CONTAINS SHORT-CHAIN FAT MOLECULES, GIVING IT A "GOATY" FLAVOR.

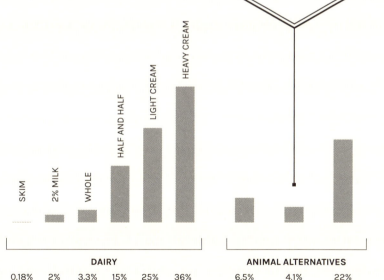

Fat in milks
Different milks vary in textures, flavor profiles, and mouthfeel. All these factors depend on the fat and protein content; the higher the fat content, the thicker the product and the richer the flavor.

BUTTER

The age-old process of churning shatters and coalesces the ivory-white fat globes in milk, turning the liquid into rich-tasting gold, which, when drained of excess water, transforms into the solid that we know as butter. Butter is a unique blend of water, fat, proteins, and sugar, and as any chef will tell you, it has the power to transform the flavor of a dish.

- **Salted vs. unsalted:** Typically added after churning, salt enhances butter's flavor (pp.14–17). Salted butter is generally used for spreading rather than cooking, so the cook can control how much salt enters a dish.
- **Cultured (lactic) vs. "sweet cream":** Butter in Europe is normally partially fermented (cultured)

Butter and ghee production

Different processes are used to create butter products, from butter that is around 80 percent fat to ghee, which is 100 percent fat with richer flavors from cooking.

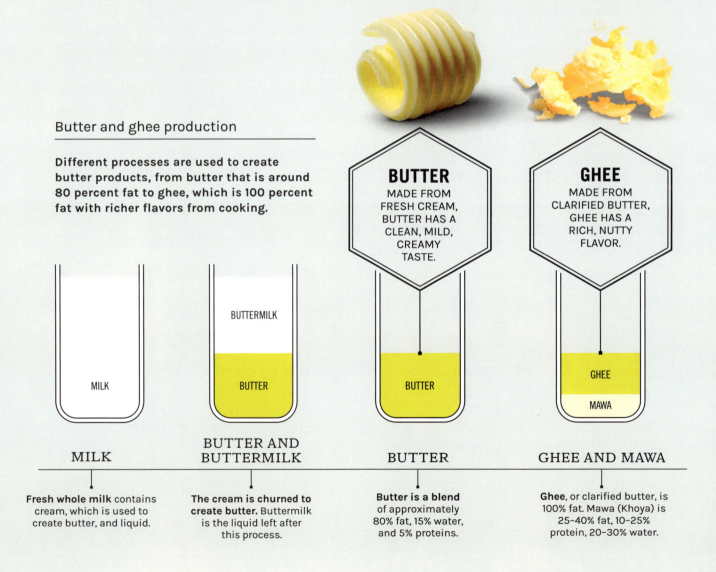

BUTTER — MADE FROM FRESH CREAM, BUTTER HAS A CLEAN, MILD, CREAMY TASTE.

GHEE — MADE FROM CLARIFIED BUTTER, GHEE HAS A RICH, NUTTY FLAVOR.

MILK
Fresh whole milk contains cream, which is used to create butter, and liquid.

BUTTER AND BUTTERMILK
The cream is churned to create butter. Buttermilk is the liquid left after this process.

BUTTER
Butter is a blend of approximately 80% fat, 15% water, and 5% proteins.

GHEE AND MAWA
Ghee, or clarified butter, is 100% fat. Mawa (Khoya) is 25–40% fat, 10–25% protein, 20–30% water.

with bacteria that produce lactic acid, imparting some sourness and a fuller, more buttery flavor. Butter that lacks this process is called "sweet cream," which is paler colored and the norm in North America.

- **Whey butter:** Made from the liquid left over from cheesemaking (whey), this tangy butter has a slightly cheesy flavor. It is popular in Sweden, where it is known as "messmör."
- **Clarified butter:** pure (99+ percent) butter fat extracted from either sweet or cultured butter, clarified butter has an intense buttery flavor, a high smoke point (p.40), and is very long lasting—making it popular in warmer regions. It is traditionally made by simmering and skimming/straining the separated milk solids. Termed "ghee" in India, it is the main cooking fat on this subcontinent, and in this form, it can be slightly browned with toasty, caramel Maillard flavors (pp.74–75). Another dairy product, called mawa and used in South Asia, is made by simmering milk until the water evaporates, leaving a solid, creamy mass.

FLAVOR COMPOUNDS AND PAIRING

There are few ingredients that do not benefit from the fat, flavor, and creamy, rich texture of butter. The two related flavor compounds diacetyl and acetoin have the distinct sweet, buttery, creamy, and milky flavor, while 230+ other aroma compounds make it a match for countless partners, among which fruits, cheeses, cured hams, nuts, and bread are high scorers.

Regional varieties

NORTH AMERICA

AMISH
(84–85 percent fat):
Traditionally made by the Amish community, this is a versatile, high-fat, creamy, textured butter.

UK

DEVON/double cream butter
(80 percent fat):
Made from double/thick cream, this butter has a luxurious creaminess.

IRELAND

IRISH BUTTER, notably Kerrygold
(82 percent fat):
Recognized worldwide for its creamy texture, sweet taste, and rich yellow hue, which is attributed to the grass-fed diet of Irish cows.

FRANCE

BEURRE CHARENTES-POITOU
(82 percent fat):
Cultured at low temperatures and coming from Western France, this very smooth and creamy butter is mildly nutty.

BEURRE D'ISIGNY
(82 percent fat):
A longer fermentation gives this butter from Normandy a sweet, creamy taste and notes of hazelnut, along with a vivid yellow color from carotenoids in the grass.

LUXEMBOURG

BEURRE ROSE
(82 percent fat):
The rich, flavored national butter of Luxembourg.

SPAIN

MANTEQUILLA DE L'ALT URGELL Y LA CERDANYA
(82 percent fat):
A soft, spreadable, and acidic butter with complex flavors.

MANTEQUILLA DE SORIA
(83 percent fat):
This traditional Spanish product is a pale-colored butter with sweet fruit and nut aromas.

TURKEY, MIDDLE EAST, AND NORTH AFRICA

(fat content varies)
Often made locally and in small batches owing to the need for refrigeration, butter products from these regions are often cultured and then clarified. There are many variations: "sade tereyağı" in Türkiye, "smen" in North Africa, "samneh" in Lebanon, and "nit'ir qibe" in Ethiopia.

Common pairings
Butter works with bread, garlic, herbs, lemon, and Parmesan cheese as well as vanilla, cinnamon, and honey in sweet baked goods.

Cheese — **Butter** — Bread

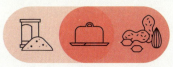

Curry powder — **Butter** — Nuts

Uncommon pairings
Try adding curry powder to butter for a spicy spread. Add matcha powder or chopped nuts and eat with toast.

YOGURT, KEFIR, AND CHEESE

Milk can be fermented to make yogurt, kefir, cheese, and many other foods that are enjoyed around the world. As milk is highly nutritious but spoils quickly, preservation was the first reason to ferment it, and over millennia, dozens of variants have evolved to delight us with their flavors and texture.

One of the key processes in dairy fermentation is the breakdown of lactose (the sugar found in milk) into lactic acid (pp.84–85). This makes it more digestible, kills harmful bacteria, and gives a tangy taste. Different microbes produce different foods, each with their own flavor.

YOGURT

Yogurt is formed by fermenting milk with *Lactobacillus bulgaricus*, *Streptococcus thermophilus*, and other bacteria. Known as "thermophilic" microbes, they prefer a warm environment at around 104–113°F (40–45°C). Yogurt is popular in Middle Eastern and Indian cooking, and it pairs well with herbs and spices often used in these regions. It is frequently used to thicken curries or to make dips with honey, for example.

KEFIR

Kefir is one of a small number of dairy ferments made with both bacteria and yeast, known as a SCOBY (symbiotic culture of bacteria and yeast). Unlike other ferments, kefir uses small, grainlike clusters containing microbes. The flavor profile and texture reflect a complex relationship between these microbes, producing tangy, creamy flavors with hints of yeast. Kefir pairs with desserts for sharpness or serves as a tangy base for savory soups.

CHEESE

Although cheese falls into different categories, many share similar flavor compounds in varying amounts. Soft cheeses are characterized by being young and creamy and often have a surface mold. Within that, they can range from gentle to very strong flavors depending on the microbes introduced. Gentle sweet, nutty notes come from aldehydes; sulfides offer stronger funky, cabbagy tones; and lactones' sweet, buttery notes.

Hard cheeses are generally more aged and have a lower water content, giving them a longer shelf life than soft cheeses. This can vary from a few months

YOGURT
HAS A CREAMY, BUTTERY FLAVOR FROM DIACETYL COMPOUNDS AND FRESH, APPLE NOTES FROM ACETALDEHYDE.

KEFIR
HAS A SMOOTH VISCOSITY FROM KEFIRAN, SHARPNESS FROM ACETIC ACID, AND BANANA NOTES FROM ISOAMYL ALCOHOL.

FLAVOR DIRECTORY **169**

	FETA	BRIE	STILTON	MATURE CHEDDAR	PARMESAN
ORIGIN	GREECE	FRANCE	UK	UK	ITALY
FLAVOR	CREAMY, RICH	SOFT, MILD, BUTTERY	RICH, CREAMY, CRUMBLY	TANGY, NUTTY, COMPLEX	NUTTY, SALTY, UMAMI

A rich global food type
Every part of the world has its own cheeses with flavors shaped by local climate and the type of cow, goat, or buffalo used to produce it.

in the case of a mild Cheddar to many years for Parmesan cheese, which has intense umami from glutamate; crunchy umami bursts from crystals of solidified amino acids; and sharp, tangy notes from small fat molecules.

Blue cheeses can be either soft or hard. Their defining feature is that they have the spores of mold (*Penicillium roqueforti* and *Penicillium glaucum*) added to the curds or injected directly into the shaped cheese. They have earthy, musty flavors from methyl ketones; sharp, rancid flavors from butyric acid; and mushroom notes from alcohols such as "mushroom alcohol" (1-octen-3-ol).

BLUE CHEESE HAS MANY OF THE SAME SAVORY, UMAMI FLAVOR COMPOUNDS FOUND IN MISO PASTE.

Common pairings
Honey, almonds, berries, cinnamon, apple, garlic, and cucumber.

Honey · **Yogurt** · Berries

Uncommon pairings
Bacon, pickles, avocado, kimchi, and chocolate.

Kimchi · **Yogurt** · Bacon

Common pairings
Kefir pairs well with honey, berries including blueberry, strawberry, and raspberry.

Blueberry · **Kefir** · Honey

Uncommon pairings
Use with harissa in dips or with sweet potato in a soup.

Harissa · **Kefir** · Sweet potato

Common pairings
Apple, goat cheese, pear, grapes, ham, salami, and honey.

Apple · **Cheese** · Pear

Uncommon pairings
Pineapple, apricot, cumin, and beets.

Pineapple · **Cheese** · Apricot

EGGS

Eggs are important in baking and cooking, both in a supporting role and as a star ingredient. They are incredibly versatile in that they can just as easily be found in a dessert such as meringue, or a main dish like an omelet.

There are over 140 aroma compounds associated with eggs. The pungent "eggy" smell and taste of eggs is the result of high levels of sulfuric compounds, particularly hydrogen sulfide. The yolk and white offer very different taste experiences. Egg white has a subtle metallic flavor, and it can be delicate and tender, such as when perfectly poached, or firm and bouncy when boiled. The yolk is rich in fats and has a more complex, buttery taste with subtle umami notes. The yolk provides the luxurious silky mouthfeel of mayonnaise, where it serves as an emulsifier between the oil and vinegar.

YOLK COLORS

The pigment molecules known as carotenoids contribute to the pale yellow to orange color of egg yolk, orange indicating higher levels of these plant pigments. There are cultural differences in terms of yolk color preference—in Asia deep orange is preferred, while in the US a lighter yolk is sought after, with European countries generally somewhere in the middle. Supplements such as marigold flower petals, corn, dark green leafy vegetables, squash, pumpkin, and red peppers (paprika) are added to the diet of laying hens to give the yolks a richer yellow color.

Egg substitutes

SOME FOODS THAT ARE HIGH IN SULFUR COMPOUNDS CAN EMULATE THE FLAVOR and aroma of eggs. Black herbal salt (Kala namak) and the Indian spice asafoetida (Devil's Dung) are two such ingredients that can impart "eggy" flavors. Other options to replace egg flavors are nutritional yeast, miso paste, and silken tofu. The best choice depends on the recipe being used.

YOLKS OF CHICKEN EGGS CONTAIN AROUND 5G FAT, CONTRIBUTING TO THEIR RICH FLAVOR.

EGG WHITES ARE FAT-FREE, PROTEIN-RICH, AND MILD IN FLAVOR WITH SULFURIC, METALLIC NOTES.

FLAVOR DIRECTORY **171**

Egg varieties

QUAIL EGG
Delicate, slightly rich flavor with buttery notes and slightly more gamey than chicken eggs.

CHICKEN EGG
The most commonly eaten eggs have a mild flavor and can absorb flavors of other ingredients.

GOOSE EGG
Rich, robust, creamy flavor. Can have grassy notes, depending on the diet of the goose.

DUCK EGG
Rich, creamy texture with a firmer mouthfeel than chicken's eggs. Higher fat content.

GUINEA FOWL EGG
Rich, gamey flavor influenced by the bird's diet; can have vegetation and seed flavors.

PHEASANT EGG
Buttery, gamey, nutty flavors. Yolks are creamy with firm whites.

COOKING

Eggs can be cooked as a single ingredient, usually on a gradient of soft to hard yolks, such as in soft- or hard-boiled eggs. They can also be fried, poached, or scrambled, all of which bring their own flavor and texture profiles, from the crispy brown edges of the classic fried to the creamy, fluffy scrambled egg. Eggs are also culinary shape-shifters. Whisking egg whites causes the proteins to unfold and trap air bubbles, creating the scaffolding for savory (soufflé) and sweet dishes (meringue) alike.

PRESERVING

Eggs can be preserved with acid, salt, or alkali, extending shelf life while developing bold new flavors. Pickled eggs, boiled and stored in malt vinegar, are a tangy British pub classic. In China, salted eggs are brined whole, with salt slowly permeating the shell—firming the rich yolk while the watery white remains liquid. Century eggs (pídàn) are alkaline cured, with duck eggs aged in a clay, ash, salt, and rice bran paste. Over months, the white transforms into dark, savory jelly, while the yolk turns creamy, rich, and pungently umami.

GLAZE
THE MAILLARD REACTION GIVES EGG-WASHED BAKED GOODS THEIR ATTRACTIVE BROWN COLOR.

Common pairings
Salt, chives, Cheddar cheese, mushroom, hot sauce (sriracha), avocado, bacon, and basil.

Cheese — Egg — Avocado

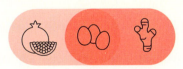

Pomegranate — Egg — Turmeric

Uncommon pairings
Sumac, harissa, turmeric, matcha, tahini, pomegranate molasses, ginger, dukkah, miso, and horseradish.

NUTS

Nuts are mostly edible seeds surrounded by a hard shell. Many of those we eat, such as almonds, walnuts, and hazelnuts, grow on trees, while peanuts grow underground and are technically legumes (pp.114–115). There is evidence that nuts have been part of our diet for as long as humans have existed. They are used in cuisine all over the world, from pistachio baklava in Greek and Persian food to peanut satay in Indonesia and salted peanuts in cola in the South of the US.

The ease with which nuts can be grown, their relative abundance, high nutritional value, versatility, and unique flavors make them a fantastic ingredient to complement other flavors or to lead a dish. Many nuts have a sweetness and creaminess that pairs with countless other ingredients. They also contain oil, which serves as their reservoir of flavor.

WALNUTS

Walnuts are rich in heart-friendly omega-3 fats, but it is these healthy oils that make them quickly turn rancid. As such, walnuts are often preserved in some way, such as pickling or storing in alcohol or syrup. Cooked walnuts have a nutty, toasty flavor from pyrazines.

HAZELNUTS

Hazelnuts are a valuable foraged food as well as a commercial crop. Their most distinctive flavor comes from the ketone flavor compound filbertone, which increases in intensity after cooking. Hazelnuts are sweet and fruity from filbertone, which is rarely found in other foods and gives them a unique quality. They also have sweet, fruity, caramel flavors from furaneol and when uncooked have a fresh grassiness from hexanal.

JUGLONE IS A COMPOUND FOUND ONLY IN WALNUTS, GIVING THEM A DISTINCT EARTHY, ASTRINGENT FLAVOR.

46% OF CASHEWS' WEIGHT IS MADE UP OF FAT, WHICH GIVES THEM A CREAMY TEXTURE.

Popular nuts
Some of the most eaten nuts include pine nuts, almonds, cashews, pecans, Brazil nuts, and walnuts. Each has its own distinct flavor.

Common pairings
Cheese, honey, banana, pear, and cinnamon.

Cheese — Walnuts — Honey

Uncommon pairings
Miso, tea, maple syrup, bacon, mustard, peas, and grapes.

Miso — Walnuts — Bacon

Common pairings
Chocolate, caramel, apple, pear, coffee, and vanilla.

Coffee — Hazelnuts — Vanilla

Uncommon pairings
Pink peppercorn, chile, lavender, balsamic vinegar, and basil.

Pink peppercorn — Hazelnuts — Chile

Common pairings
Peach, apricot, cinnamon, cardamom, chocolate, honey, and spinach.

Cinnamon — Almonds — Cardamom

Uncommon pairings
Turmeric, blue cheese, beets, rosemary, miso, and saffron.

Turmeric — Almonds — Blue cheese

Common pairings
Chocolate, honey, coconut, coffee, wine, and tea.

Chocolate — Brazil nuts — Coconut

Uncommon pairings
Miso, ginger, truffle oil, and mushrooms.

Ginger — Brazil nuts — Miso

ALMONDS

Almonds are the seeds of a stone fruit in the family of trees that includes plums and apricots. They're most notable for their use in marzipan and desserts. The signature marzipan flavor comes from benzaldehyde. A citrusy sweetness comes from linalool and a subtle vanilla flavor comes from vanillin.

BRAZIL NUTS

Coming from the tropical forests of South America, Brazil nuts have a rich, creamy, indulgent flavor with earthy and nutty tones. The inside of the nut is quite sweet, and so works well in truffles and cakes. Very high fat levels (69 percent) give these a smooth mouthfeel and creaminess. Aldehydes like hexanal add earthy notes and esters including ethyl acetate have floral undertones. Pyrazines bring a nutty, roasted aroma.

THERE IS EVIDENCE OF ALMOND MILK GOING BACK TO THE MIDDLE AGES WITH A RECIPE IN "THE FORME OF CURY" RECIPE BOOK, AROUND 1390.

CHESTNUT FLOUR HAS BEEN USED AS A KEY STARCH SOURCE FOR CENTURIES. IT IS VERSATILE ENOUGH TO BE USED TO MAKE PASTA, CAKES, AND BREAD.

PEANUT — PISTACHIO — HAZELNUT — MACADAMIA — PECAN

AROUND
9–11LB
(4–5KG) OF OLIVES ARE USED TO MAKE A 34 FL OZ (1 LITER) BOTTLE OF OLIVE OIL.

VIRGIN OLIVE OIL
HAS HIGH LEVELS OF ANTIOXIDANTS, ALLOWING IT TO BE STORED FOR LONG PERIODS.

LIGHT OLIVE OIL

VIRGIN OLIVE OIL

EXTRA-VIRGIN OLIVE OIL

Olive oil production

THE PRODUCTION OF OLIVE OIL BEGINS WITH THE HARVESTING AND CRUSHING OF THE OLIVES, FOLLOWED BY A PROCESS CALLED MALAXATION, which has a direct effect on the flavor and quality of the oil. During this phase, the olives are churned to a paste under temperature-controlled conditions and small droplets of extracted oil coalesce to form larger droplets. The oil is then separated from any water via decanting or centrifugation, to create the natural virgin olive oil. If the oil is of low grade and containing flavor defects, then it can be subject to further refinement but will no longer be classed as "virgin."

PHENOLIC COMPOUNDS, SUCH AS **OLEUROPEIN** AND **HYDROXYTYROSOL,** CONTRIBUTE TO THE PUNGENCY AND BITTERNESS OF OLIVE OIL, WHILE OLEOCANTHAL INVOKES PEPPERY NOTES.

OLIVE OIL CONTAINS OLEIC ACID, WHICH HELPS LOWER **"BAD" LDL CHOLESTEROL** AND IS ONE OF THE MAJOR CONTRIBUTORS TO THE HEALTH BENEFITS OF OLIVE OIL.

AROMA COMPOUNDS SUCH AS HEXANAL IMPART A GREEN, FRUITY AROMA.

OLIVE OIL

A staple of the Mediterranean diet, olive oil is drenched in culinary versatility and boasts supreme nutritional benefits. Classified in grades, it offers a unique freshness and pungency, peppery undertones, with a rich, well-rounded flavor.

Olive oil is made by the pressing of olives, which grow on trees native to the Mediterranean Basin. In this region, different varieties, climates, and growing conditions produce olive oils each with its own individual flavor. As olives mature on the tree, their color changes from green to yellow to purple to black, becoming sweeter, richer, and less bitter.

Picking olives at the right stage of the ripening process is vital for making the highest-quality olive oil. The sweet spot for this is found to be when they still possess a tinge of green, as this is when the olives contain the greatest concentration of aromatic compounds. Notably, polyphenols (a class of taste compounds) are central to the pungency and bitterness of olive oil, and which also function as antioxidants and help prolong shelf life.

Olive oils are graded depending on their purity, the best being virgin olive oils, which are from crushed olives by mechanical means with no chemical or thermal treatment. This gentle method maximizes the delicate flavors and nutritional content, setting them apart from other vegetable oils. Due to its delicate flavor, virgin olive oil is best saved for the finishing touches to a dish, drizzling over salads or simply soaked up with bread. The highest-quality oils are termed "extra-virgin."

STORAGE
TO PROTECT OLIVE OIL FROM LIGHT AND OXYGEN, IT IS STORED IN DARK BOTTLES OR METAL CANS.

Olive colors

GREEN/YELLOW (LESS RIPE)
The best olives for making extra-virgin olive oil. Contain the highest level of polyphenol compounds, producing an intense, pungent oil with strong bitterness and peppery aftertaste. Pairs well with punchy, well-flavored dishes and red meat or with sweet balsamic vinegar or fresh tomato to contrast its pepperiness.

YELLOW/PURPLE (PARTLY RIPE)
Produces a medium-strength olive oil with a green, fruity taste; grassy notes; and mild bitterness. A great all-arounder for frying, drizzling over roasted vegetables, or adding to pasta dishes.

BLACK (FULLY RIPE)
Not to be confused with "Californian" black olives, which are unripe olives turned black chemically, fully ripe olives are fruity and flavorful and produce oil that has a smooth, buttery, fruity taste with little bitterness.

Common pairings
Bread, salad, pasta, cheese, meat, spices, and herbs, including basil and rosemary.

Bread — Olive oil — Pasta

Dark chocolate — Olive oil — Popcorn

Uncommon pairings
Popcorn, sushi, egg, yogurt, dark chocolate, and sea salt.

BLACK PEPPER, GINGER, AND MUSTARD

Spices like black pepper, ginger, and mustard breathe life into food, turning monochrome meals into tantalizing technicolor. Black pepper brings hot, spicy, citrusy notes while ginger has woody and citrus flavors, and mustard adds pungent, sharp compounds.

BLACK PEPPER

Often added unthinkingly to Western cuisine with the ever-present pepper mill, the pungent compound piperine gives this surprisingly fiery spice its bite. Black pepper is versatile: it can be used to bring warmth to dishes as well as a gentle pine aroma from pinene, hints of citrus (limonene), alongside a subtle turpentine-like background (myrcene). Preground pepper loses these top notes, while white pepper lacks its aromatic dark coat, is harsher, and carries dunglike nuances. White pepper is usually chosen for its pale color and is used in many Chinese and Asian dishes.

GINGER

One of the first spices to reach Europe, this warming ingredient forms the backbone of many Asian dishes and is a go-to flavoring in Western baking. Ginger flavor comes from zingiberene, a compound found in few other spices. The fresh knobbly underground stems should be peeled just before cooking to preserve the citrusy, sweet, and floral flavors (from citral, linalool, geraniol, and others). Heat comes from gingerols, which break down to sweet zingerone when cooked or transform into the very fiery shogaol when dried (pp.44–45).

MUSTARD

From the stovetops of India to the hot dogs of American stadiums, mustard is an international flavoring. Mustard's powerful seeds, which come from a spindly brassica plant, are bland when whole and dry. As with its sulfuric kin (pp.109), flavor and heat develop following damage. Flavor builds quickly in the minutes

Pepper flavor

TO ENJOY PEPPER'S FULL COMPLEXITY, IT IS VITAL TO PRESERVE SUBTLE TERPENE COMPOUNDS, WHICH EVAPORATE WHEN EXPOSED TO AIR.

GRIND WHOLE PEPPERCORNS IMMEDIATELY BEFORE USING TO MINIMIZE FLAVOR LOSS.

PREGROUND SPICE IS GOOD ONLY FOR ADDING HEAT.

Common pairings
Salt, garlic, olive oil, Parmesan cheese, and lemon all work well with black pepper.

Salt · **Black pepper** · Garlic   Strawberry · **Black pepper** · Pineapple

Uncommon pairings
Black pepper works with some unexpected sweet foods, including strawberry, pineapple, watermelon, apple, mango, and chocolate.

Common pairings
Ginger is often used with garlic in Asian cuisine and shares many compounds with lemon and honey.

Honey · **Ginger** · Lemon   Dark chocolate · **Ginger** · Beet

Uncommon pairings
Ginger pairs well with many different ingredients, including cheeses, dark chocolate, and beet.

FLAVOR DIRECTORY 177

after moistening ground mustard seeds before ebbing away, unless drenched in acid (such as vinegar), which stalls the flavor-generating myrosinase (p.44) while preserving existing flavor compounds. Yellow seeds, used in American mustard and pickling, are mild; brown seeds are fierier, and are used in Indian cooking and Dijon mustard; black mustard seeds are the most potent and aromatic. Mustard is high in mucilage—an emulsifier that binds oil and water—and so can be used to prevent vinaigrettes and sauces from splitting.

GINGEROL
COMPOUND GIVES FRESH GINGER ITS PUNGENT HEAT AND SPICY FLAVOR.

Mustard varieties

There are many types of mustards, with their own unique flavors and properties. The color depends on the seeds used: black, brown, or yellow.

DIJON MUSTARD
SMOOTH AND TANGY WITH SPICY FLAVORS.

YELLOW MUSTARD
MILD TASTE THAT IS LESS PUNGENT THAN OTHER VARIETIES.

ENGLISH MUSTARD
VERY STRONG, SPICY FLAVOR WITH HEAT AND SHARPNESS.

BROWN MUSTARD
SPICY AND COARSE IN TEXTURE.

WHOLE GRAIN
MADE WITH WHOLE MUSTARD SEEDS, THE FLAVOR IS MILD TO SHARP.

AMERICAN MUSTARD
YELLOW MUSTARD WITH VINEGAR AND TURMERIC; SWEET AND MILD.

NUTMEG AND MACE

The comforting warmth of nutmeg and mace hides their fiery history. Both come from the stone fruit of the Indonesian *Myristica fragrans* tree and were at the center of brutal spice wars in the early 16th century.

Nutmeg and mace are brimming with oils containing bitter, defensive flavor compounds and intensely aromatic terpenes. These substances create bittersweet, warm, and woody qualities, mace having a subtler but more complex flavor than nutmeg. The most important compounds are musky and balsamic myristicin, which are accompanied by pinelike pinene and peppery sabinene. A background of medicinal eucalyptus from potent eugenol makes both spices natural partners to clove.

Both spices carry an unusual group of chemicals called neolignans, which clamp onto cold temperature-sensing nerves in the mouth, like menthol in mint (pp.198–199), but with an eerie cooling effect that is 30 times more potent than menthol and lasts three times as long.

AROMATIC
NUTMEG CARRIES HINTS OF LEMONGRASS AND TOBACCO. IT'S SWEET WITH PEPPERY UNDERTONES.

How nutmeg grows

Nutmeg is the dried seed found inside the fruit of a tropical evergreen *Myristica fragrans* tree. The mace is wrapped around the seed.

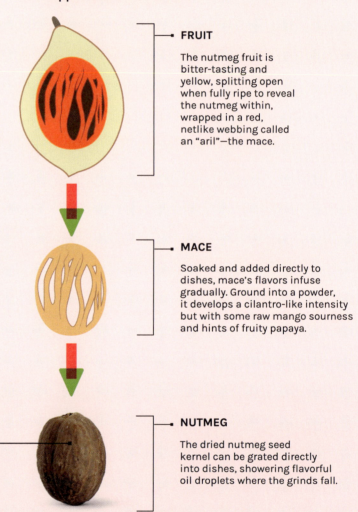

FRUIT
The nutmeg fruit is bitter-tasting and yellow, splitting open when fully ripe to reveal the nutmeg within, wrapped in a red, netlike webbing called an "aril"—the mace.

MACE
Soaked and added directly to dishes, mace's flavors infuse gradually. Ground into a powder, it develops a cilantro-like intensity but with some raw mango sourness and hints of fruity papaya.

NUTMEG
The dried nutmeg seed kernel can be grated directly into dishes, showering flavorful oil droplets where the grinds fall.

Common pairings
Cabbage, cinnamon, and cocoa are good partners with nutmeg. Dairy foods, including milk, cream, and cheese are also classic pairings in sauces.

Cabbage Nutmeg Cocoa

Avocado Nutmeg Papaya

Uncommon pairings
Some more unusual flavors such as avocado, papaya, tomato, cauliflower, and roasted Brussels sprouts pair well with nutmeg.

CLOVES

Powerful and penetrating, cloves are one of the most ancient spices and have a place in cuisines worldwide. Cloves are unusual for being dried flower buds, rather than seeds, which are harvested before they bloom then dried to maximize flavor. Like nutmeg, for millennia the coveted clove tree was found only in the spice islands.

Cloves can easily overpower other foods and ingredients. Their flavor comes from eugenol—a potent aroma compound that has a piercing eucalyptus aroma and a slightly warm and numbing effect in the mouth. Cloves are the richest natural source of this chemical, which is also used in medicine: it makes up 90 percent of cloves' oil. Slightly peppery and woody qualities come from the terpene caryophyllene and sweet vanilla notes from vanillin. Whole cloves will slowly release oils into a dish as it cooks, but their tooth-shattering hardness means they are best removed before serving. Ground cloves deliver a faster, more intense flavor release at the expense of the whole spice's subtler nuances. A classic partner to nutmeg, with which it shares over 120 flavor compounds, and in sweet dishes, clove plays a key role in countless spice blends and has myriad delicious pairings.

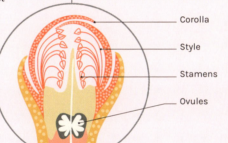

Flower buds
Cloves are the buds from an evergreen tree native to the North Moluccas Islands in Indonesia. The unopened flower petals form the ball at the top. They are harvested and dried before being used in cooking.

LESS IS MORE
USE GROUND CLOVES SPARINGLY AS THEIR INTENSE FLAVOR CAN OVERPOWER OTHER INGREDIENTS.

MIX IT UP
CLOVES ARE ESSENTIAL FOR SPICE MIXES LIKE CHINESE FIVE-SPICE, RAS EL HANOUT, AND GARAM MASALA.

Common pairings
Pork and peach can be used effectively with cloves. Other pairings include ginger and rosemary.

Pork — Cloves — Peach

Blue cheese — Cloves — Peas

Uncommon pairings
Peas and strong blue cheeses like Gorgonzola, Roquefort, and Stilton pair well with cloves.

CHILES

Chiles are famed for the burning sensation they produce, leading to the release of endorphins, feel-good dopamine, and an identical biological response to being burned. This comes from the chemical capsaicin, named after the chile plant's official name, *Capsicum annuum*.

Chiles come from Central and South America and Mexico remains a major producer. The plant evolved fiery capsaicin to repel predators, although birds are immune so can eat and disperse seeds. Heat is measured in Scoville Heat Units (see below). While a fresh jalapeño has a Scoville rating of 2,500–8,000, its heat can vary with ripeness. Capsaicin is stable, so cooking, smoking, or drying does not reduce heat significantly. Chiles lose aroma compounds during drying but retain their heat, making dried chiles ideal for adding heat.

PAPRIKA

The popular spice paprika is actually made from dried chiles specially selected for having low levels of the mouth-burning compound capsaicin. With a Scoville rating generally below 1,000 (with sweet paprika rating lower and hot paprika rating higher), the spice is prized for its sweet, smoky, and earthy qualities.

ACID AND FAT
USE ACIDS (VINEGAR, CITRUS) TO INTENSIFY CHILE HEAT AND FATS (YOGURT, MILK) TO TONE IT DOWN.

PAPRIKA
CONTAINS CAPSAICIN, ALTHOUGH IT IS AT LEVELS 40 TIMES LESS THAN CAYENNE.

Scoville heat scale

This measures how spicy or hot a chile pepper is. Values are calculated based on how much sugar water it takes to dilute until heat is no longer detectable by a panel of tasters. Top of the scale is capsaicin, with 16 million Scoville Heat Units (SHUs).

PAPRIKA	JALAPEÑO	CAYENNE	SCOTCH BONNET	GHOST PEPPER
SCOVILLE SCORE: BELOW 1,000	SCOVILLE SCORE: 2,500–8,000	SCOVILLE SCORE: 30,000–50,000	SCOVILLE SCORE: 100,000–350,000	SCOVILLE SCORE: 1,000,000+

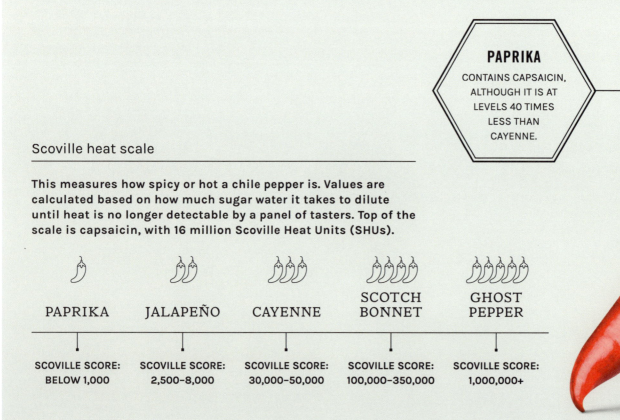

PAPRIKA

FLAVOR DIRECTORY **181**

Common pairings
Cilantro, lime, Cheddar, chicken, and tomato.

Cilantro **Jalapeño** Lime

Uncommon pairings
Greek yogurt, strawberry, dark chocolate, pear, and cucumber.

Yogurt **Jalapeño** Strawberry

Common pairings
Cumin, caraway, scallops shrimp, lamb, lentil, and potato.

Cumin **Paprika** Caraway

Uncommon pairings
Maple syrup, pear, apple, caramel, cucumber, pumpkin, and cashew.

Pumpkin **Paprika** Pear

Common pairings
Allspice, mango, pork, ginger, garlic, and pineapple.

Allspice **Scotch bonnet** Pineapple

Uncommon pairings
Sage, rum, and passion fruit.

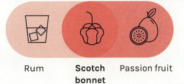
Rum **Scotch bonnet** Passion fruit

Chile varieties

PAPRIKA
Origin: Hungary
SHU: Below 1,000
Flavor: Gentle sweetness from beta-ionone. Mild when fresh, they are often smoked before drying and grinding. Stunning red color from tasteless carotenoid pigments, capsanthin and capsorubin.
Used in: Goulash.

JALAPEÑO
Origin: Mexico
SHU: 2,500–8,000
Flavor: Grassy, fresh, fruity from hexanal, hexanol, and bright "bell pepper pyrazine" (2-methoxy-3-isobutylpyrazine).
Used in: Salsa.

CHIPOTLE
Origin: Mexico
SHU: 2,500–8,000
Flavor: Chipotle peppers are smoked jalapeños, offering a sweet, smoky flavor with a little bitterness from phenolic compounds.
Used in: Adobo sauce, beef chili.

FACING HEAVEN
Origin: China
SHU: 10,000–50,000
Flavor: Used dry it has earthy flavors. Floral, citrus notes from nonanal and decanal.
Used in: Mapo tofu, stir-fried beef, and other Sichuan dishes.

BIRD'S EYE
Origin: Southeast Asia
SHU: 50,000–100,000
Flavor: Dominated by capsaicin. Beta-caryophyllene gives a slight woodiness, and clove.
Used in: Thai green curry, hot sauce, spicy stir-fried noodles.

SCOTCH BONNET
Origin: Caribbean
SHU: 100,000–350,000
Flavor: Tropical fruity notes from fruity esters, such as banana-scented Isoamyl acetate (p.128), alongside sweetly fragranced beta-ionone.
Used in: Jamaican jerk chicken.

GHOST PEPPER (BHUT JOLOKIA)
Origin: India
SHU: 1,000,000+
Flavor: Intensely hot, with fruity esters, floral linalool, and lemony limonene.
Used in: Chutneys and curries.

VERSATILE
THE JALAPEÑO IS VERY POPULAR GLOBALLY AND ESSENTIAL TO MEXICAN AND TEX-MEX CUISINE.

JALAPEÑO

SCOTCH BONNET

CURRY SCIENCE

Eaten in India for millennia but exported and adapted by European colonizers, curries are heavily spiced dishes of vegetables, pulses, meat, or fish adored internationally.

PEANUT
OIL IS NEUTRAL IN FLAVOR AND FACILITATES HIGH-TEMPERATURE COOKING.

CRUNCH
Roasted peanuts bring a satisfying crunch and a toasted nutty aroma.

FLORAL FRESHNESS
Aromatic fresh Thai basil leaves are added before serving for a burst of fresh herbaceous flavor.

RICHNESS
Coconut milk brings sweet, creamy richness with a high fat content.

FIRMNESS
Waxy potatoes are chosen so that they hold their form.

Although the Western term "curry" originates from the Tamil word kari ("sauce"), and many of the classic spices originate in the Indian subcontinent, the word is used for various spiced dishes from Thailand, Vietnam, Jamaica, and South Africa. The foundation of a curry is often a paste made from spices and fresh aromatic ingredients such as shallots, garlic, ginger, chiles, coconut, tomatoes, curry leaves, or lemongrass, which are pounded or puréed and cooked in oil to release their flavor compounds at the start of cooking. The spices are selected to showcase the main ingredients, whether that's rich, intense spice and chile heat in a slow-cooked lamb curry, or fresher, more citrusy spices for a fish or vegetable-based curry.

Spices are usually used in blends of at least four so that the strong flavor compounds of each spice balance each other out and none dominates, adding depth and nuance. Examples include Thai curry paste, Indian garam masala, Middle Eastern baharat, Moroccan ras el hanout, and Japanese Katsu curry powder.

UMAMI
Meltingly soft braised beef, plus caramelized onions and garlic, bring savory umami depth.

SOURNESS
Tamarind paste brings sourness and fish sauce adds acidity, along with umami and saltiness.

TOASTINESS
Onions, garlic, and shallots toasted in their skins add a toasty aroma, caramelized flavor, and deep color.

SPICY
Thai lime leaves and lemongrass pair with Indian spices, including cumin, cardamom, cloves, and chiles to add heat.

THE PERFECT CURRY

THE BUILDING BLOCKS OF CURRY

Curries also benefit from the distinctive sweet base flavor of alliums, such as garlic or shallots, along with ginger, which are layered with the spices and simmered with a rich ingredient like coconut or peanuts to soften the flavor and bring sweetness and richness. Tomatoes add the sweetness, acidity, and umami needed to underscore the flavors. Bite-sized pieces of the main ingredient are added, along with liquid, and gently simmered until tender. The flavors continue to develop after cooking, which is why curries often taste even better the next day.

The perfect curry

This Thai Massaman curry layers traditional Thai aromatics such as lime leaves, lemongrass, fish sauce, coconut, and tamarind paste with classic Indian spices of cumin, chiles, cloves, and cardamom. Coconut milk adds richness and toasted peanuts add pops of flavor and textural contrast. Traditionally cooked with a slow-braised red meat such as lamb or beef, along with potatoes that absorb the flavors beautifully, a Massaman curry is a rich, luxurious, and complex dish.

TURMERIC

Turmeric is a knobbly rootlike growth (a rhizome), closely related to ginger, that hails from the Indian subcontinent. Its earthy, musky aroma is conveyed by a unique compound called turmerone.

This spice comes in a spectrum of shades and flavors, from the sweet and mild sunflower-yellow Madras variety, used in curry powders, to the richer, sunset-orange Alleppey type. This is higher in flavorful oils and contains twice as much curcumin—the yellow, clothes-staining pigment found almost exclusively in turmeric and lauded for its health-giving properties. An ensemble of other compounds, including eucalyptus-like cineole and peppery caryophyllene, completes turmeric's pungent, spicy, herbal, and subtly citrus profile.

Fresh turmeric has some hints of citrus and ginger, and it can be used like ginger by peeling and frying in slivers, slices, or as grated pieces with other aromatic ingredients. Ground turmeric has a stronger, earthier flavor but lacks the bright, zesty flavors of fresh, half the oils having been lost through the sterilizing, lengthy drying, and intensive grinding processes.

Common pairings
Ginger, cinnamon, cumin, clove, lentils, fennel, and root vegetables.

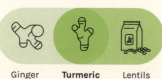

Uncommon pairings
Rosemary, dill, mango, vanilla, and grapefruit.

CUMIN

Coming from a wispy-leaved, desert-loving plant native to the Eastern Mediterranean and West Asia, cumin is woven into the culinary tapestry of India, the Middle East, Latin America, and North Africa. Small, intensely flavored cumin seeds are one of the most ancient spices, once used as a table condiment like pepper by the ancient Egyptians. The seeds are used whole or ground into powder and are a key ingredient in garam masala and curry powders.

Cumin has a spicy, earthy, herbal flavor from a unique aroma compound, cuminaldehyde, also present in myrrh and eucalyptus but few other spices. Cumin seeds are often toasted or fried, which releases heady, nutty, and smoky kitchen-filling aromas from an effusion of meaty, roasted-flavored pyrazines. They are also easy to grind and their oils release notes of pine and licorice from an array of terpene aroma compounds. As with other spices, preground cumin offers slightly more muted flavors than freshly roasted and ground versions. Once ground, it should be used within six months for the best flavor.

PINE AND LICORICE

MUTED FLAVOR ← **PREGROUND** ← **SEEDS** → **FRESHLY GROUND**

→ **HEATED** → **NUTTY AND TOASTED**

Cumin uses

This versatile and strongly flavored seed can be used whole, freshly ground, or preground. When toasted, nutty flavors are released that can be used in curries, breads, soups, and stews.

Common pairings
Cinnamon, coriander seed, garlic, onion, black pepper, root vegetables, and roasted meat.

Cinnamon   **Cumin**   Root vegetable

Orange   **Cumin**   Coconut

Uncommon pairings
Orange, avocado, garden cress, cocoa, and coconut.

CINNAMON AND CASSIA

CEYLON CINNAMON

THIN AND PAPERY, MULTIPLE LAYERS

FLAVOR
COMPLEX | SWEET | WARM | CITRUSY

50–70%
Cinnamaldehyde

>0%
Coumarin

5%
Eugenol

Often confused for their similar sweet and aromatic flavor, cinnamon and cassia are the dried bark of two related tropical trees. Cinnamon comes from South India and Sri Lanka (formerly Ceylon), cassia from China and Southeast Asia.

True ("Ceylon") cinnamon and cassia ("Chinese cinnamon") owe their trademark spicy, warm aroma to cinnamaldehyde, a unique compound that warms the mouth by activating heat pain fibers (pp.42–43). Cassia has a bolder, brasher flavor profile owing to it having more of this pungent substance and a higher complement of sweetly aromatic coumarin, a chemical that smells like mowed hay but which can damage the liver if eaten in excessive amounts. The two are not interchangeable: cassia is cheaper than cinnamon and lacks true cinnamon's aromatic breadth: eucalyptus aroma from eugenol, floral lavender qualities from linalool, as well as a licorice, sweetshop aroma from safrole.

CASSIA

THICK, ROUGH, SINGLE-LAYER QUILLS

FLAVOR
BOLD | SPICY | HOT

70–90%
Cinnamaldehyde

1–5%
Coumarin

>1%
Eugenol

CASSIA HAS A HOTTER, STRONGER FLAVOR THAN CEYLON CINNAMON.

Common pairings
Carrot, apple, allspice, vanilla, almonds, and mango.

Uncommon pairings
Goat cheese, mushroom, pineapple, and coffee.

Carrot — **Cinnamon** — Mango

Goat cheese — **Cinnamon** — Mushroom

Spinach — **Cassia** — Sweet potato

Chocolate — **Cassia** — Beans

Common pairings
Spinach, tea, pork, pine nut, and sweet potato.

Uncommon pairings
Chocolate, beans, lamb, pear, coconut, and pistachio.

FLAVOR DIRECTORY 187

ALLSPICE ("PIMENTO")

Allspice is an aromatic Jamaican berry whose flavor mimics cinnamon, nutmeg, and clove by happy circumstance of sharing their aroma compounds. Widely celebrated in Caribbean and Latin American cuisines, it is a delightfully full-bodied, aromatic spice.

Allspice's evocative aroma permeates all parts of the allspice tree; in the Caribbean, whole leaves are used to infuse flavor and the wood is used as charcoal for smoking meat. Allspice oils' clovelike character stems from an abundance of powerful eugenol along with its sweeter related compound methyl-eugenol, which has a spicy, earthy note and is also in nutmeg and cinnamon. Caryophyllene brings peppery, fresh-cut wood aromas, echoing nutmeg (it is also in hops and basil), while smaller amounts of warming cinnamaldehyde accentuate its connection with cinnamon (see left).

Allspice berries are dried and often ground before being used in a variety of dishes around the world.

Allspice's flavor comes from the oil glands in the husk

THE HUSK

PIMENTO
ALLSPICE WAS MISNAMED "PIMENTO" FROM THE SPANISH WORD FOR PEPPER, "PIMENTA."

SWEET AND SAVORY
ALLSPICE COMPLEMENTS FOODS FROM PORK TO CAKES.

Common pairings
Cinnamon, clove, ginger, citrus, gin, root vegetables, and pork.

Clove — Allspice — Pork

Beet — Allspice — Apple

Uncommon pairings
Cocoa nibs, beet, spearmint, soybean, rum, apple, and rosemary.

CILANTRO/CORIANDER

Now grown and used around the world, every part of the cilantro plant is edible, but its leaves are probably the most widely used herb internationally. They can be used to add flavor to a wide variety of dishes, sweet and savory.

Cilantro leaves and seeds (known as coriander) have been used since antiquity in cooking and medicine and are featured as key ingredients in a variety of cuisines, including Mexican, Indian, across Asia, as well as in the Mediterranean and the Middle East. Although from the same plant, the seeds and leaves have a different flavor profile: the stronger-tasting seeds have a bitter, warm, uniquely floral and citrus aroma owing to a wealth of fragrant linalool in the seed oil, while the leaves have less linalool and offer a gentler citrusy aroma and herby taste.

PAIRING AND BRIDGING

- **Coriander seeds:** The potent floral and citrusy linalool means that coriander pairs closely with citrus fruits, including grapefruit and lime peel, as well as fresh-tasting herbs such as basil, mint, marjoram, and lemon balm. Try making a sweet soy sauce marinade with grapefruit juice and roasted ground coriander seeds to glaze a salmon fillet, chicken, tofu, or vegetables before roasting.

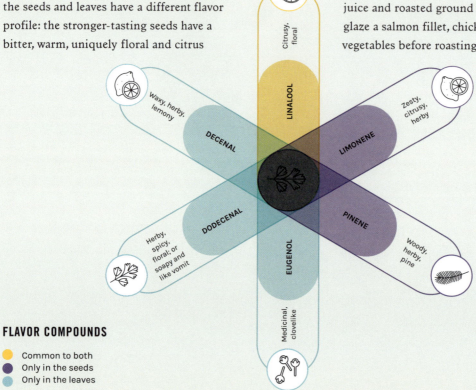

FLAVOR COMPOUNDS
- Common to both
- Only in the seeds
- Only in the leaves

Common pairings
The medicinal undertones of eugenol make cilantro ideal for pairing with clove and cinnamon.

Clove · Cilantro · Cinnamon

Strawberry · Cilantro · Egg

Uncommon pairings
Try adding some chopped cilantro to a bowl of fresh strawberries or add to a plate of scrambled eggs for a delicious savory note.

FLAVOR DIRECTORY **189**

• **Cilantro:** As well as floral linalool and the distinctive waxy/soapy flavors of aldehydes, the medicinal undertones of eugenol makes the herb ideal for pairing with cloves and cinnamon. Use to make clove-infused white rice flavored with finely chopped cilantro and lemon juice.

HOW TO COOK

Whole coriander "seeds" are actually dried fruits, with two seeds inside each. When you grind them (ideally after roasting or toasting them), the fibrous husks are mixed in. These woody pieces are highly absorbent and soak up liquid, making the spice a useful ingredient for thickening sauces.

Select cilantro leaves from healthy plants or buy from reputable growers and try to buy them when in season. When the cilantro plant grows in stressed conditions (such as with too much/little light, water, or heat), then its leaves accumulate a particularly unpleasant aldehyde called E-2-decanal, tainting the herb with a smell reminiscent of damp towels and bed bugs.

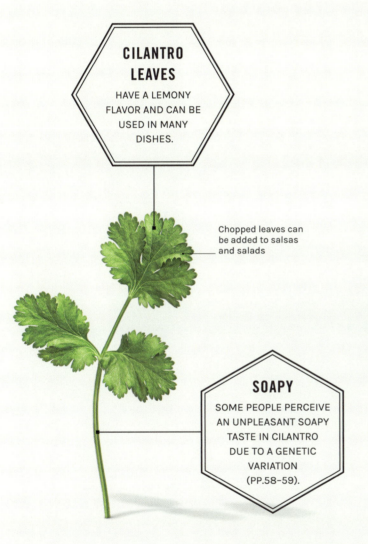

CILANTRO LEAVES HAVE A LEMONY FLAVOR AND CAN BE USED IN MANY DISHES.

Chopped leaves can be added to salsas and salads

SOAPY SOME PEOPLE PERCEIVE AN UNPLEASANT SOAPY TASTE IN CILANTRO DUE TO A GENETIC VARIATION (PP.58–59).

Cilantro varieties

There are two main types of cilantro plant, Indian and European.

EUROPEAN
The European variety has smaller fruits and more of the floral linalool compound.

INDIAN
The larger-fruited Indian type has a spicier flavor and different flavor profile, thanks to extra compounds not found in the European variety.

Common pairings
Herbs such as basil and lemon balm, and citrus fruits pair well with coriander seeds.

Basil   Coriander   Lemon balm

Chocolate   Coriander   Herbal tea

Uncommon pairings
Freshly ground coriander seeds can be added to a dark chocolate dessert or an herbal tea for aromatic warmth.

FENNEL

Fennel is an herb, a vegetable, and a spice. The entire plant is edible and infused with anethole—the sweet, slightly medicinal flavor of anise and licorice. Commonly used in fish recipes, fennel also works in Mediterranean stews and spice mixes.

FLAVOR COMPOUNDS

The dominant flavor compound in fennel, anethole, is 13 times sweeter than sugar with an intense, warm, licorice-like aroma. Other flavor compounds include estragole, which is similar to anethole but with more herby, floral qualities and the main aroma compound in basil. Fenchone is very bitter-tasting with a cool, medicinal, camphor (mothballs) aroma. Limonene brings a fresh, citrusy aroma, while herby, pinelike flavors come from pinene and sweet, floral, and slightly balsamic aromas come from anisaldehyde.

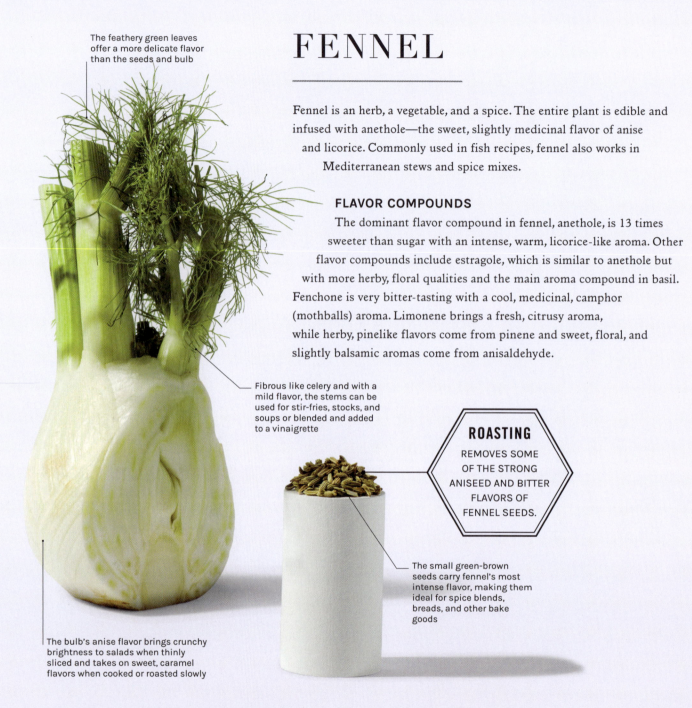

The feathery green leaves offer a more delicate flavor than the seeds and bulb

Fibrous like celery and with a mild flavor, the stems can be used for stir-fries, stocks, and soups or blended and added to a vinaigrette

The bulb's anise flavor brings crunchy brightness to salads when thinly sliced and takes on sweet, caramel flavors when cooked or roasted slowly

ROASTING REMOVES SOME OF THE STRONG ANISEED AND BITTER FLAVORS OF FENNEL SEEDS.

The small green-brown seeds carry fennel's most intense flavor, making them ideal for spice blends, breads, and other bake goods

---

Common pairings
Garlic, basil, olive oil, seafood, lemon, chicken, and shellfish.

Seafood · Fennel · Olive oil

Dark chocolate · Fennel · Strawberry

Uncommon pairings
Dark chocolate, citrus fruit, strawberry, and cinnamon.

PARSLEY

FINELY CHOP PARSLEY BEFORE USE TO RELEASE MORE OF ITS AROMATIC COMPOUNDS.

CURLY LEAF PARSLEY HAS A MILDER FLAVOR THAN FLAT-LEAF AND ADDS FRESHNESS USED AS A GARNISH.

Parsley is an underestimated herb with a surprisingly complex flavor profile for enhancing myriad dishes. It is the foundation of a number of classic herb blends and dishes. Like many herbs, parsley's fresh green, grassy flavor comes from hexanal. Its distinctive character comes from a range of other compounds, with amounts varying between the two main varieties. Menthatriene and apiole are dominant in flat-leaf parsley, menthatriene having a crisp, green, woody parsley flavor, while apiole (also known as parsley camphor) contributes a fresh, herbaceous parsley flavor. Further flavors come from myristicin (dominant in curly leaf parsley), which is warm and spicy (similar to nutmeg), limonene, which adds a citrusy note, and phellandrene, which brings a peppery, citruslike scent.

You can chop and use the stalks as they contain the same flavor compounds as the leaves, although in smaller amounts

Parsley varieties

FLAT-LEAF PARSLEY (Italian parsley)
Looking like cilantro, flat-leaf parsley is the best pick for flavor. Its bold, herby character and subtly citrus flavor shines through in salads, soups, sauces, and herb blends such as "fines herbes" and "bouquet garni."

CURLY LEAF PARSLEY
Curly leaf parsley is mainly bred for its deep forest-green color and showy crinkled leaves, rather than flavor. Having up to a fifth less flavor-rich oil than flat-leaf, curly leaf parsley lacks its more intensely flavored cousin's green freshness and instead has a muted bitter, warm, and slightly spicy flavor.

Common pairings Lemon, garlic, white fish, olive oil, tomato, and mushroom.

Lemon — Parsley — White fish

Peach — Parsley — Ginger

Uncommon pairings Apple, nutmeg, ginger, peach, pomegranate, cocoa, and dark chocolate.

DILL

One of the most ancient medicinal herbs, this unassuming wiry plant is an indispensable forest of flavor for cooks—its leaves and seeds offering deliciously fresh citrusy, aniselike flavors. As with all plants, aroma compounds exist for plant survival. The brighter, more diverse flavor profile of the leaf contrasts with the simpler, more robust spicy earthiness of the seed because the leaves must deter many herbivores, attract pollinators, and fight infection, while the seeds' focus to resist underground infection needs fewer, but more concentrated, protective compounds.

The leaves contain dill ether (floral/herby dill), hellandrene (woody, herby terpene), myristicin (spicy, nutmeglike), limonene (citrus), eugenol (spicy clove), damascenone (honeylike fruity), cymene (hints of citrus, earth, and wood). The seed aromas include carvone (caraway), limonene (citrus), eugenol (spicy clove), and vanillin (vanilla).

UNLEASHING THE FLAVOR

As with most herbs, the moment dill is chopped, its aroma compounds start evaporating and being broken down by defensive enzymes. Always use it immediately after cutting or blanch briefly in near-boiling water for 30 seconds to destroy the enzymes to keep its zingy taste for longer.

> IN THE MIDDLE AGES IN EUROPE, DILL WAS USED IN WITCHCRAFT, AS A LOVE POTION, AND A MEDICINE.

Dill herb varieties

COMMON DILL
The most common variety, with bright, feathery leaves. Used to garnish fish, and in salads.

FERNLEAF
A smaller plant, provides a green herb with a taste of fennel, anise, and celery.

BOUQUET
A taller plant with bigger leaves. Sweet and aromatic with anise and caraway flavors.

Common pairings
The fresh leaves pair well with lemon, fish, potato, and celery.

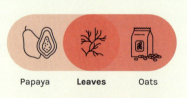

Lemon — **Leaves** — Fish

Papaya — **Leaves** — Oats

Uncommon pairings
Beef, mango, papaya, strawberry, oats, and cranberry.

Common pairings
Use the seeds in recipes with cinnamon, nutmeg, parsnip, celeriac, and bread.

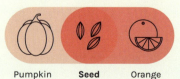

Parsnip — **Seed** — Bread

Pumpkin — **Seed** — Orange

Uncommon pairings
Pumpkin, gin, orange, juniper berry, and chocolate.

BASIL

Originally from India, basil is known for being a Mediterranean herb—its glossy emerald-green leaves deliver an invigorating sweet and savory flavor with hints of mint, anise, and pepper. When threatened, basil produces more aromatic compounds, to ward off pests. Basil plants that are slightly stressed (for example, by underwatering) can have more pronounced flavors, a useful tip for gardeners and cooks.

Basil's very high water content and delicate leaves mean that by the time it has dried, almost all of the flavorful oil (50–80 percent) has evaporated away, leaving dusty, bland flakes. Like other soft-stemmed herbs, stems can be chopped and used alongside leaves and are best added late into cooking or as a garnish to preserve their essence.

Basil varieties

SWEET BASIL
The most common, fragrant and sweet. Used widely in Mediterranean dishes.

LEMON BASIL
High in the flavor compound limonene, a citrus flavor that pairs well with seafood or salad. Popular in Thai food.

INDIAN "HOLY BASIL"
Has strong woody, peppery qualities from caryophyllene (found in black pepper), ideal for heavily spiced dishes.

THAI BASIL
Thai basil has flavors of licorice and anise from plentiful estragole.

CINNAMON BASIL
A distinct cinnamon nuance from methyl cinnamate—one of the key aroma compounds in the spice.

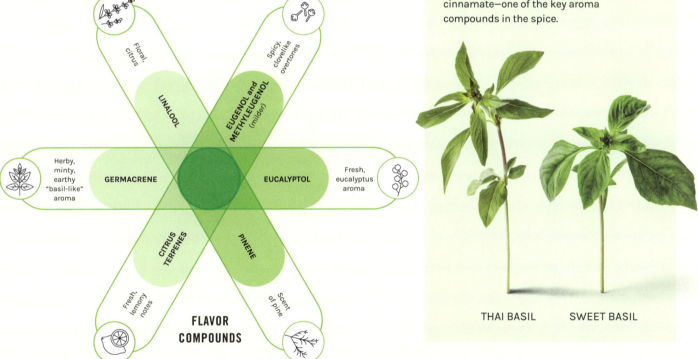

THAI BASIL   SWEET BASIL

Common pairings
Tomato, garlic, olive oil, lemon, oregano, and rosemary are all used with basil in numerous Italian recipes.

Tomato   **Basil**   Olive oil

Coconut   **Basil**   Melon

Uncommon pairings
Melon, dark chocolate, cocoa, and coconut.

OREGANO AND THYME

Oregano, known as the "pizza herb" in North America, is a cornerstone of Italian cuisine and one of the world's most popular herbs. Thyme, another robust Mediterranean herb, has very similar core flavor compounds as oregano but in different proportions.

"Oregano" is a catch-all term for some 40 *Origanum* species, all with small, fuzzy leaves that have a similar peppery, citrusy, savory, woody, and sometimes bitter flavor.

"Common oregano" (*Origanum vulgare*) is the most popular, with its strong savory, slightly pungent flavor, although depending on where you live, "oregano" might be a similar-tasting but completely unrelated herb. Marjoram (*Origanum majorana*) is one type of oregano with a distinctly sweeter, fresher, and more floral flavor. In some Spanish regions, however, "oregano" is referred to as "marjoram," adding to the confusion.

OREGANO — RETAINS ITS FLAVOR WHEN DRIED, OFFERING AN INTENSE SEASONING.

Crush leaves before adding to dishes, to speed oil release

Sprinkle fresh oregano or marjoram leaves over dishes just before serving

Use in meat and vegetable rubs and marinades

OREGANO MARJORAM

Common pairings
Basil, thyme, rosemary, garlic, green vegetables, tomato, and olive oil.

Rosemary · **Oregano Marjoram** · Garlic

Lime · **Oregano Marjoram** · Coconut

Uncommon pairings
Lime, gin, nutmeg, cardamom, black currant, cocoa, and coconut.

FLAVOR DIRECTORY 195

FLAVOR COMPOUNDS

Thyme, with its dark green pointed leaves, is related but looks very different from oregano and has a distinctly woody, lemony flavor. Its gentler taste makes it more versatile, and it is often used in French cuisine. Numerous thyme varieties exist, with flavors like lemon, mint, pineapple, caraway, and nutmeg, offering endless sweet and savory pairing possibilities.

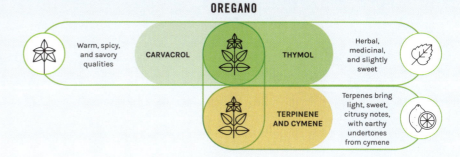

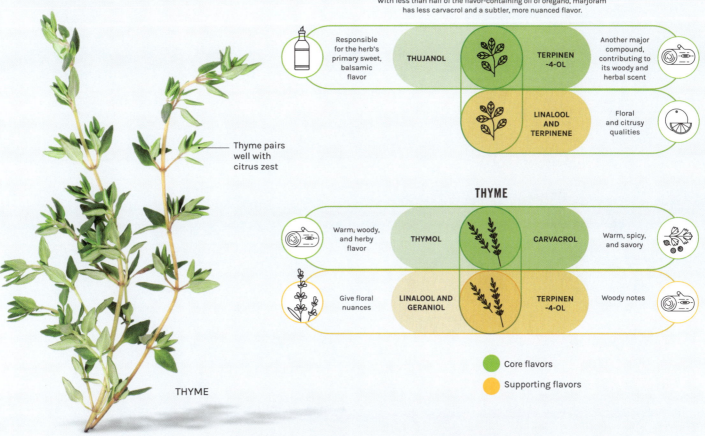

Thyme pairs well with citrus zest

THYME

● Core flavors
● Supporting flavors

Common pairings
Citrus zest, tomato, garlic, oregano, dill, beef, and poultry.

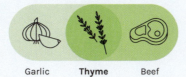

Garlic — Thyme — Beef

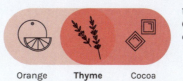

Orange — Thyme — Cocoa

Uncommon pairings
Orange, cinnamon, lime, clove, apple, and cocoa.

SAGE

The soft, velvety, fuzzy leaves of sage are a treasure-trove of flavor, carrying a potent herbal aroma with earthy hints of mint and eucalyptus. Often partnered with meats and a fundamental flavoring in traditional Western cooking, sage is equally delicious in other international cuisines—and even in desserts.

FLAVOR COMPOUNDS

As with most herbs, grassy and herby terpenes make up the mainstay of flavor. The core flavor compounds are:
- **Thujone:** the main flavor of sage is powerfully herbal, warm, and subtly minty.
- **Borneol:** earthy, mossy (lost in dried sage)
- **Hexenal:** green and grassy background (not found in dried sage)
- **Eucalyptol:** eucalyptus and medicinal.

Supporting compounds found in sage include:
- **Pinene:** adds a fresh, resinous note of pine
- **Camphor:** sharp, clean, and penetrating medicinal aroma
- **Linalool:** floral, with a hint of spice, and citrus, also found in lavender.

DRIED VS. FRESH

All the fresh grassy hexenal and most of the floral-scented compounds vaporize when leaves are dried, leaving a less rounded, harsher, medicinal flavor that is useful for adding early or midway through cooking. Dried sage is sold as very intense powder (ground) or as milder-tasting coarse flakes (rubbed); both are excellent in rubs or marinades.

DRIED SAGE HAS A STRONGER FLAVOR THAN FRESH LEAVES, WITH HINTS OF MINT, EUCALYPTUS, AND LEMON.

7 FRESH SAGE LEAVES

1 TEASPOON Powdered dried sage

OR

2 TEASPOONS Rubbed dried sage

Sage varieties

PURPLE SAGE
Striking purple leaves have a milder flavor than common sage.

PINEAPPLE SAGE
Hints of tropical fruit and flowers come from a fruity ester, geranyl acetate, and rose-scented geraniol.

GREEK SAGE
A spicier, punchier flavor, thanks to more medicinal eucalyptol and penetrating camphor than other sage varieties.

BABY (BLACK CURRANT) SAGE
High levels of limonene, smoky guaiacol, and sugars as well as fruity esters give this variety a sweet fruitiness like that of black currant.

COMMON SAGE

Common pairings
Peppercorn, squash, rosemary, mint, oregano, butter, and meat.

Squash Sage Butter

Star anise Sage Fig

Uncommon pairings
Star anise, lemon, black currant, fig, pear, carrot, and cocoa or dark chocolate.

ROSEMARY

Rosemary's woody pine flavor has a strong medicinal undercurrent of camphor and top notes of mint, lemon, sage, and pepper. Known for enhancing the flavor of meats, rosemary's tough needlelike leaves slowly release their flavorful oils, lending itself well to slow-cooked dishes.

Rosemary really shines when added early to a dish to allow oils to escape from its tough leaves—and the earlier it is added, the stronger the flavor infusion. Like sage, rosemary is a powerful herb that needs a light touch if it is not to overpower other ingredients. Finely chopping leaves accelerates flavor release, dialing up flavor further, and is ideal for meat and vegetable rubs. Dried rosemary lacks the fresh green and citrus notes of fresh but delivers a more intense herbal flavor (rosemary-scented verbenone increases with drying) and is also excellent in rubs.

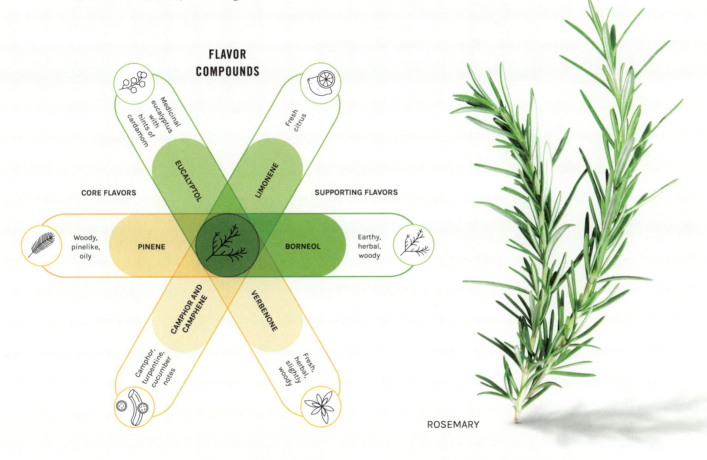

ROSEMARY

Common pairings
Tomato, garlic, olive (and oil), meat, potato, stone fruit, thyme, sage, and oregano.

Potato — Rosemary — Stone fruit

Uncommon pairings
Strawberry, chocolate, ginger, orange, and herring.

Chocolate — Rosemary — Ginger

MINT

For introducing a refreshing, energizing dimension to a dish, few things beat mint. The herb's bizarre mouth-chilling powers make it a favorite not only for flavoring sweets, desserts, chewing gums, and toothpastes but also for bringing vibrancy to savory dishes.

There are two main culinary types of mint: sharp and intensely minty peppermint and sweeter, grassy, more lemony spearmint. Mint's refreshing and cooling sensation comes from menthol, which activates the same nerves in our skin and mouth that sense cold temperatures. This creates the illusion of coldness, much like capsaicin triggers hot-pain nerve fibers to cause a sensation of pungent heat (p.43). Menthol also binds to pain nerves, numbing them.

Dried mint has 30 percent less cooling menthol, 50 percent less menthone, and fewer other minty compounds, while woody, spicy, waxy, and soapy notes become prominent as several minor compounds (caryophyllene, germacrene, and others) increase markedly.

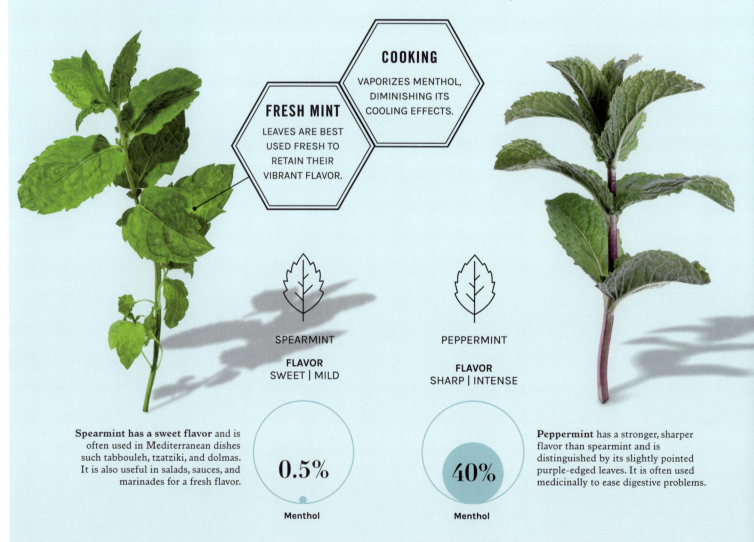

FRESH MINT
LEAVES ARE BEST USED FRESH TO RETAIN THEIR VIBRANT FLAVOR.

COOKING
VAPORIZES MENTHOL, DIMINISHING ITS COOLING EFFECTS.

SPEARMINT
FLAVOR
SWEET | MILD

0.5%
Menthol

Spearmint has a sweet flavor and is often used in Mediterranean dishes such tabbouleh, tzatziki, and dolmas. It is also useful in salads, sauces, and marinades for a fresh flavor.

PEPPERMINT
FLAVOR
SHARP | INTENSE

40%
Menthol

Peppermint has a stronger, sharper flavor than spearmint and is distinguished by its slightly pointed purple-edged leaves. It is often used medicinally to ease digestive problems.

Mint varieties

SPEARMINT
Flavor profile: milder than peppermint, with a sweet, light, refreshing taste dominated by (R)-carvone.
Uses: all-purpose mint flavoring, perfect for meats and in salads, cocktails, and desserts.

PEPPERMINT
Flavor profile: strong, cooling, intense mint flavor. Very rich in menthol.
Uses: herbal tea, desserts.

CHOCOLATE MINT
Flavor profile: minty with a subtle chocolate undertone from compounds such as sweet and smoky benzofuran.
Uses: desserts, ice creams, and garnishes.

LEMON MINT
Flavor profile: lemon and citrus from limonene and citral; flowery and fruity notes from geraniol and neral, rounded off with floral linalool.
Uses: try in cocktails, fruit salads, and use for garnishes.

APPLE MINT
Flavor profile: mintiness fades into fruity, floral, and slightly sweet with a hint of apple from a trio of fruity esters and flowery linalool.
Uses: ideal for fruit salads, jellies, and summer drinks.

LEMON MINT SHARES COMMON AROMA COMPOUNDS WITH CITRUS FRUITS.

CHOCOLATE MINT

LEMON MINT

APPLE MINT

Common pairings
Lamb, peas, yogurt, cucumber, and potato.

Lamb — Mint — Peas

Feta — Mint — Berries

Uncommon pairings
Berries, feta, mango, lentils, fennel, and vanilla.

SAFFRON

Known as the "king of spices" and with a regal price tag to match, saffron's uniquely warming, honeyed, delicate haylike flavor is irreplaceable. Just three fragrant red threads come from each harvested crocus flower—and their precious flavor needs careful coaxing out. Saffron's flavor improves over time—the bitter picrocrocin gradually degrades into fragrant safranal, reaching a peak of flavor around two years after harvesting. Color, however, fades over time as crocin breaks down.

Before adding to cooking, the traces of oil in each thread are best drawn out by soaking ("blooming") in warm water or milk for at least 20 minutes.

Heating saffron threads to 158–194°F (70–90°C) before using also gives their flavor a major boost, converting more bitter picrocrocin into sweet-smelling safranal.

When cooking with saffron, add the soaked threads early to maximize color and late for the best flavor.

GROUND
SAFFRON, WHICH IS EASILY ADULTERATED, SHOULD BE AVOIDED. LOOK FOR ISO CERTIFICATION.

3
THREADS PER FLOWER

FLAVOR COMPOUNDS

A trio of compounds gives saffron its ethereal, musky flavor and golden color.

- **Crocin:** a ruby red pigment that turns sunshine yellow in water.
- **Picrocrocin:** gives a lingering, slightly bitter taste.
- **Safranal:** a mowed-hay, musky-scented terpene aroma compound and saffron's primary flavor, found in only a handful of foods (see uncommon pairings).

COLOR CHANGES

FRESHLY PICKED SAFFRON CONTAINS A RED PIGMENT CALLED **CROCIN**	ADD TO WARM WATER OR MILK TO TURN CROCIN YELLOW
DEEP CRIMSON	GOLDEN AMBER

FLAVOR CHANGES

WHEN PICKED, SAFFRON CONTAINS A BITTER TASTE COMPOUND CALLED **PICROCROCIN** → ADD HEAT AND DRY → WHEN HEATED, PICROCROCIN TURNS TO AN AROMA COMPOUND CALLED **SAFRANAL**

150+ AROMA COMPOUNDS ARE RELEASED WHEN SAFFRON IS HEATED AND DRIED

Common pairings
Rice, potato, carrot, mushroom, pea, ginger, butter, and lemon.

Carrot · **Saffron** · Butter

Fig · **Saffron** · Green tea

Uncommon pairings
Fig, peach, tea, green tea, grapefruit, and vanilla (all contain safranal); lemongrass and beef.

VANILLA

The alluring ivory flowers of the vanilla orchid are a fitting crown for the creamy, honeyed flavor of the plant's dried fruits (pods). From ice cream, chocolate, and marshmallows to cookies, cakes, and savory dishes, vanilla imbues food with velvety sweetness.

Fresh vanilla pods resemble French green beans but have an unpleasant, bitter taste. It can take up to eight months to transform them into the soft, aromatic brown pods we recognize. Painstaking steps include blanching, fermenting ("sweating"), drying, and conditioning. Natural enzymes and microbes convert sugars, acids, and bland compounds into vanillin, vanilla's core flavor, alongside a complex blend of more than 250 sweet, creamy, fruity, floral, smoky, prune, and even cheesy flavor compounds.

FLAVOR COMPOUNDS

- **Vanillin:** the principal top-note flavor compound, delivering the familiar warm, sweet, creamy vanilla flavor, produced synthetically for many foods.
- **Guaiacol:** sweet, spicy, smoky nuances.
- **Methyl cinnamate:** a fruity, balsamic ester with flavors of ripe red cherries and strawberries, also in cinnamon.
- **Furfural:** sweet, caramel, and bready, also in roasted nuts, breads, and coffee.
- **Anisaldehyde:** sweet, floral, anise or licorice-like, marzipan.
- **Hydroxybenzaldehyde:** sweet, floral, and slightly almondlike.

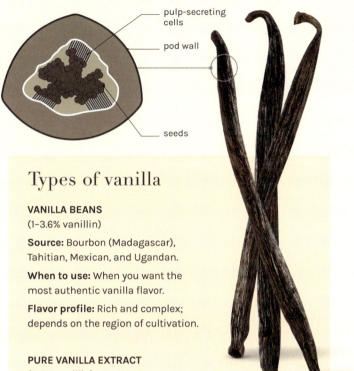

Types of vanilla

VANILLA BEANS
(1–3.6% vanillin)

Source: Bourbon (Madagascar), Tahitian, Mexican, and Ugandan.

When to use: When you want the most authentic vanilla flavor.

Flavor profile: Rich and complex; depends on the region of cultivation.

PURE VANILLA EXTRACT
(1–2% vanillin)

Source: Real vanilla beans, water, and alcohol.

When to use: When you want an authentic flavor.

Flavor profile: Strong, authentic flavor.

SYNTHETIC VANILLA EXTRACT
(1% vanillin)

Source: Synthetic vanillin.

When to use: When a less expensive option is needed.

Flavor profile: One-dimensional flavor.

VANILLA PASTE
(0.1–1.6% vanillin)

Source: A blend of vanilla extract and vanilla bean specks.

When to use: When you want a more intense flavor and the visual appeal of vanilla bean specks.

Flavor profile: Subtle floral and woody undertones.

Common pairings
Chocolate, apple, cream, and coffee.

Chocolate · Vanilla · Apple

Potato · Vanilla · Mushroom

Uncommon pairings
Butternut squash, tea, tomato, mushroom, and potato.

BAY LEAVES

Champions have long been adorned with garlands of bay (laurel) leaves and despite some chefs shunning bay leaves as "tasteless," their complex blend of pine, clove, floral, and eucalyptus can make a meal a real winner.

Bay leaves are tough and slow to give up their scented oils, so should be added early in cooking. They are best used as a background flavor to enhance other dominant ingredients. Leaves need heating, simmering, and time for their fragrant oils to escape and infuse a dish but can easily overwhelm so need fishing out before a bitter eucalyptus taste takes over.

Bay varieties

Varieties such as California Bay laurel, Indian bay leaf, and West Indian bay leaf aren't true bay leaves, which are known as "Mediterranean" or "Turkish," but are similarly flavored leaves from other plants.

CALIFORNIA BAY LAUREL
A heftier, harsher eucalyptus and menthol flavor than true "Mediterranean" (or "Turkish") bay, thanks to high levels of a potent ketone aroma compound called umbellulone, not found in any other ingredient and known to cause headaches. Use sparingly.

INDIAN BAY LEAF
Coming from cassia trees (p.186), the very distinct spicy and woody flavor of this small, slender leaf, also known as tej patta, lends delicate notes of allspice, cinnamon, and dried orange peel. Spicy, woody qualities come from a sabinene aroma compound, also in nutmeg (p.178), and make it a favorite in curries and spicy dishes.

WEST INDIAN BAY LEAF
A highly fragrant warm, sweet-spicy aroma, reminiscent of clove, comes from eugenol, with peppery, and lemony notes coming from myrcene and limonene. Ideal in soups and stews.

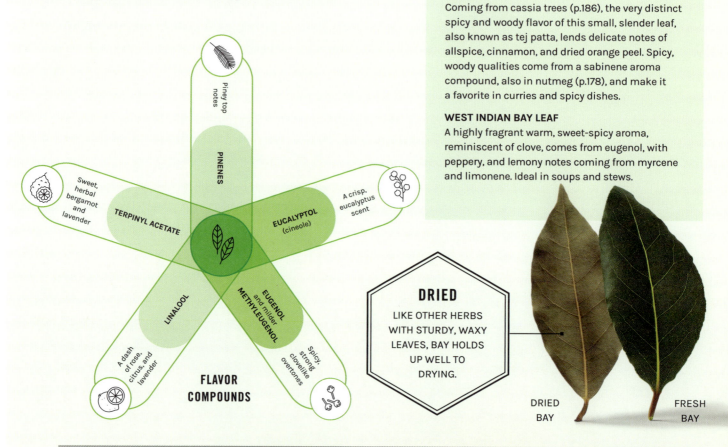

DRIED — LIKE OTHER HERBS WITH STURDY, WAXY LEAVES, BAY HOLDS UP WELL TO DRYING.

DRIED BAY | FRESH BAY

Common pairings
Tomato, mushroom, black pepper, rosemary, lentils, potato, root vegetables, beef, and lamb.

Mushroom | Bay | Tomato

Orange | Bay | Pineapple

Uncommon pairings
Dark chocolate, orange, nutmeg, cardamom, pineapple, and celeriac.

CURRY LEAVES

Despite their name, curry leaves are not related to curry powder. Uniquely musky and lemony scented, these glossy South Indian leaves are popular in Sri Lankan and Indian cooking and are best used fresh and fried with spices to add flavor to dishes.

Curry leaves have a mildly bitter and herby scent, with a citrusy flavor and anise and nutty undertones. They come from the curry tree (*Murraya koenigii*), which is native to India but also grown in Sri Lanka and Southeast Asia, as well as Australia. Unlike bay leaves, which dry well, curry leaves lose flavor as they dry, with up to 90 percent of sulfury 1-phenylethanethiol dissipating as water evaporates.

Curry leaves are most often used in dishes such as dhal, curries, and stews as well as chutneys and dips. They're best added early in the cooking process to allow their rich flavors to develop. Fresh curry leaves are more flavorful than dried versions and can be stored for a couple of weeks in the fridge.

FLAVOR COMPOUNDS

Core flavor compounds in curry leaves include 1-phenylethanethiol, a sulfur compound imparting a musky, sulfury, burnt aroma. Linalool, which contributes a sweet citrusy and floral flavor, is also present, as well as hexenal with its fresh, grassy, applelike scent. Supporting compounds include pinene, which has resinous pine scents, and eucalyptol, bringing the penetrating flavor of eucalyptus.

BLOOMING

FRYING CURRY LEAVES ("BLOOMING") IN OIL WITH SPICES MAKES THEM COME ALIVE.

Common pairings
Red meat, rice, potato, onion, mushroom, lentils, cumin, cinnamon, and cloves.

Red meat · Curry leaves · Potato

Uncommon pairings
Hazelnut, plaice, sardine, mint, orange, ricotta, and cheese.

Plaice · Curry leaves · Hazelnut

TEA

All teas come from the leaves of the same south Chinese shrub, *Camellia sinensis*, but are processed in different ways. Black tea is made from picked leaves that have been left to air-dry and turn brown (oxidize). Natural pigments and traces of fat and protein are broken down into taste and aroma compounds and new reddish brown pigments (thearubigins) are created. Oolong tea is partly oxidized, while green and white tea leaves are only slightly oxidized, or not at all. Pu-erh comes from fermented green tea leaves.

Tea bags often contain lower leaves from which much of the aromatic oils have evaporated, resulting in a flatter-tasting, more bitter infusion. Whole-leaf tea takes time to swell in hot water, after which a fuller palette of aroma and taste compounds grows.

Extracting flavor from tea leaves needs hot water and time. The hotter the water, the faster flavor compounds, tannins, and bitter compounds are released. Nonoxidized teas (green, white, yellow) become flat tasting because the catechins they contain quickly degrade above 176°F (80°C).

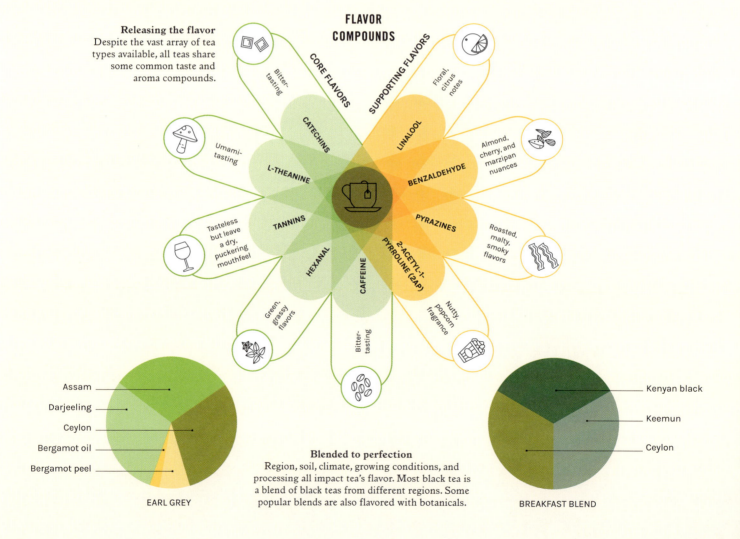

Releasing the flavor
Despite the vast array of tea types available, all teas share some common taste and aroma compounds.

Blended to perfection
Region, soil, climate, growing conditions, and processing all impact tea's flavor. Most black tea is a blend of black teas from different regions. Some popular blends are also flavored with botanicals.

Tea varieties

The umami depth and more than 600 different flavor compounds of tea leaves make them incredibly versatile ingredients for pairing with food.

Common pairings

GREEN TEA
Flavor profile: Lively, sweet, vegetal, grassy, or seaweed notes.
Key compounds: Catechins, hexenal, caffeine.
Examples: Sencha.

Mango   **Green tea**   Peanut

WHITE TEA
Flavor profile: Delicate, slightly sweet floral or fruity notes.
Key compounds: Benzaldehyde, linalool.
Examples: Bai Mudan White Peony, Baihao Yinzhen Silver Needle.

Peach   **White tea**   Feta cheese

OOLONG TEA
Flavor profile: Varies from creamy and buttery to earthy and woody.
Key compounds: Pyrazines, damascone.
Examples: Tie Guan Yin, Da Hong Pao.

Citrus fruit   **Light oolong tea**   Cheese

BLACK TEA
Flavor profile: Full-bodied malty caramel or fruit notes.
Key compounds: Thearubigins, tannins, damascone, 2-acetyl-1-pyrroline (2AP).
Examples: Darjeeling, Assam, Lapsang Souchong.

Dark chocolate   **Black tea**   Strawberry

PU-ERH
Flavor profile: Earthy, woody, nutty, sweet notes.
Key compounds: Geosmin (earthy), linalool, mushroom alcohol/octenol, methoxyphenyls.
Examples: Sheng (raw), Shou (ripe).

Mushroom   **Pu-erh**   Dark chocolate

PU-ERH IS THE MOST COMPLEX OF TEAS IN TERMS OF FLAVOR, CONTAINING OVER **1,000** FLAVOR COMPOUNDS

COFFEE

Originally from Ethiopia, coffee is loved around the world for its caffeine hit and its invigorating aromas and flavors, from spicy fruit to chocolate and charred wood. Coffee can be savored alone or used to enrich and enhance a variety of dishes.

Coffee's profusion of flavor comes from the bitter, grassy-tasting seeds, called "beans," from a cherrylike fruit. These are dried and roasted until brown. The way coffee is roasted controls its flavor and color. Green beans cool as they dry when dropped into the roaster, before slowly turning brown as the Maillard reaction (pp.74–77) takes off at 302°F (150°C). This produces haylike aromas then sweet, bready flavors. Caramelization builds, turning sugars into caramel, toffee, and burnt sugar aroma compounds, while trapped steam accumulates inside the bean. At around 374°F (190°C), the beans split open. Termed the "first crack," pressurized steam ruptures the seed and roasted coffee flavors erupt as glistening oil starts seeping out. Fruity, sometimes spicy flavors develop.

ARABICA COFFEE
CONTRARY TO WHAT WAS ONCE BELIEVED, ARABICA COFFEE IS FROM ETHIOPIA, NOT ARABIA.

Then roasted, nutty flavors develop with some sweetness and progressively stronger bitter flavors of tobacco. Trapped carbon dioxide gas builds up inside the beans and they explode open again at around 428°F (220°C)—the "second crack"—popping loudly like corn with the release of smoky, charred aromas.

FLAVOR COMPOUNDS

- **Methylfurfural:** adds to the sweet, caramel-like flavors in coffee. It's a product of the sugar breakdown (caramelization) and the Maillard reaction and contributes to the pleasant and sweet notes.
- **Furfural:** imparts a sweet, bready, almondlike, or caramel aroma. This compound is made from the breakdown of sugars and the Maillard reaction.
- **Acetic acid:** alongside other acids (citric, malic, formic, etc.). This contributes to a bright, crisp flavor profile. It's produced from the breakdown of carbohydrates and in the Maillard reaction.

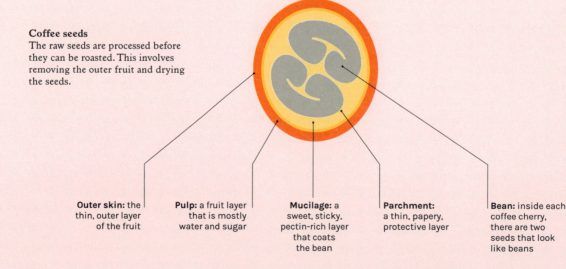

Coffee seeds
The raw seeds are processed before they can be roasted. This involves removing the outer fruit and drying the seeds.

Outer skin: the thin, outer layer of the fruit

Pulp: a fruit layer that is mostly water and sugar

Mucilage: a sweet, sticky, pectin-rich layer that coats the bean

Parchment: a thin, papery, protective layer

Bean: inside each coffee cherry, there are two seeds that look like beans

FLAVOR DIRECTORY 207

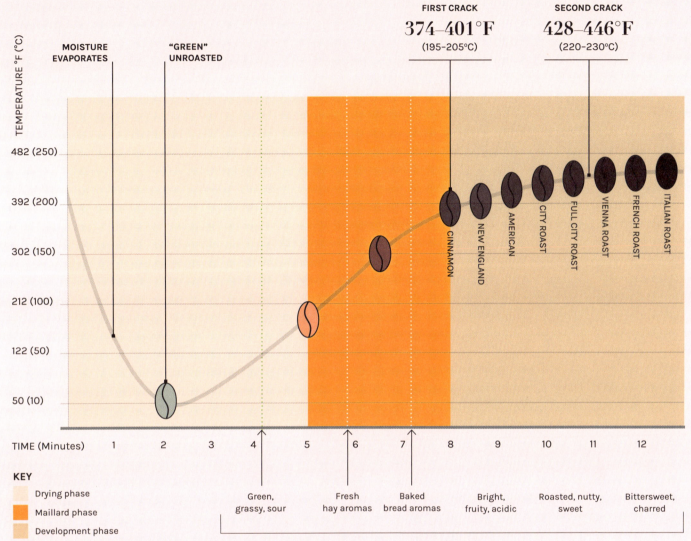

As the coffee beans are roasted, different flavors develop, from a light cinnamon roast through the darkest Italian roast. The names have developed over time from the flavor or place where that style of coffee is popular.

• **Furfuryl alcohol:** Offers a sweet, burnt, or woody aroma and contributes to the body and aromatic complexity of the coffee.
• **Pyridine:** Provides a bitter, pungent aroma, often associated with roasted or burnt characteristics. It contributes to the perceived "strength" or "roastiness" of the coffee.

• **Cyclopentanone:** Known for sweet, caramel-like notes, adding to the complexity of the coffee's aroma profile. Formed from the breakdown and pyrolysis (burning) of sugars during roasting.
• **Phenols:** Contribute woody, smoky, or spicy notes, formed through pyrolysis in the later roasting stages. Higher levels of phenols bring a richer flavor.

CHOCOLATE

One of the most loved foods, chocolate can be eaten as a dessert, drunk as a beverage, and used in savory dishes. It's made from sweetened cocoa that comes from cacao seeds. Dark and milk chocolates have varying levels of cocoa, sugar, and milk solids.

The most significant flavor compounds include:
- **Pyrazines:** Nutty, roasted notes. Formed during roasting, these are key to the chocolate aroma.
- **Alcohols and esters:** Fruity, winey, and floral notes from fermentation of the pulp, particularly in fine cocoa varieties. For example, ethyl acetate (pineappley ester) and linalool (floral, citrus).
- **Aldehydes and ketones:** Crucial for malty, sweet almond, and dairylike chocolate flavors, which form within the bean itself as it ferments. Examples include vanillin (vanilla, creamy, sweet), 2-methylbutanal and 3-methylbutanal (malty, chocolaty).
- **Acids:** Fermentation generates acetic acid and other acids; too much leads to sour, bitter, or vinegary off-flavors. These are typically neutralized with alkalis (Dutch processing) to give cocoa powder a mellower taste and a darker hue.
- **Bitter compounds and tannins:** Stimulants caffeine and theobromine are among the dozens of defensive bitter compounds in raw cacao beans. Other bitter compounds and tannins are partly destroyed during processing.

DIFFERENT TYPES

Chocolate is sweetened cocoa mass (solids and/or fat), often flavored with vanilla and mixed with an emulsifier (usually lecithin) to give a smoother finish. It is usually made by separating the cocoa into solids (cocoa powder) and fats (cocoa butter), then recombining them in differing proportions and sweetening them. Milk solids (milk powder), added to milk and white chocolate, give a softer texture and a creamy flavor.

The glassy shine, telltale crack, and melt-in-the mouth delight of fine chocolate comes from the fat in cacao. Cooled gradually and carefully (tempering), the fat molecules align and interlock into perfect lattices. Cooled quickly, an unstable mishmash of fat molecules results in a dull, soft-textured chocolate that soon develops a white bloom from fats rising to the surface. Mass produced, confectionery chocolate often swaps cocoa butter for cheaper vegetable oils like palm oil, lacks tempered chocolate's snap and shine, and can leave a greasy mouthfeel.

Making chocolate

The flavor of chocolate comes from the pulp-covered seeds of the cacao tree that are fermented, dried, roasted, and ground, each stage adding to the over 600 aroma compounds that make up chocolate's aroma and addictive flavor.

FERMENTATION AND DRYING

The pulp surrounding the cacao seeds ("beans") ferments, producing fruity and floral esters and acids, essential for flavor development. Drying lowers moisture to 7%, concentrating some compounds, and readying for roasting.

ROASTING AND WINNOWING

Roasting develops the flavors, then winnowing removes the shell, releasing bean fragments (the "nibs").

FLAVOR DIRECTORY **209**

Common pairings
Nuts, citrus, wine, roasted red meat, coffee, berries, dried fruit, ginger, cinnamon, and chile.

Uncommon pairings
Passion fruit, fried onions, puréed avocado, whiskey, olive oil, bacon, blue cheese, lavender, and caviar.

Dark chocolate may boost your well-being, as it releases a cascade of feel-good compounds that have been linked to improved mood. However, there is debate as to whether chocolate contains enough of these compounds to have any effect.

Cacao varieties

 Forastero: Basic cocoa flavor, strong and robust, used for 90 percent of the world's cocoa.

 Criollo: Rare, aromatic, with smooth, mild flavors that are nutty, earthy, and floral. Used in premium chocolate.

 Trinitario: A cross of Criollo and Forastero, combining strong basic cocoa notes with some aromatic, fruity, or winelike tones.

 Nacional: Grown in Ecuador, famed for its floral, nutty, and spicy characteristics.

WHITE CHOCOLATE CONTAINS COCOA BUTTER BUT NO COCOA SOLIDS; ITS FLAVOR COMES FROM SUGAR, MILK POWDER, AND VANILLA.

GRINDING

The nibs are heated and ground, releasing cocoa butter and forming a paste known as cocoa mass or liquor, which serves as the basis for chocolate.

REFINING AND CONCHING

The chocolate mixture is smoothed, mixed, and aerated, removing some bitter compounds and deepening creamy, malty flavors.

TEMPERING

Cooling carefully controls the crystallization of cocoa butter, giving the chocolate a silken mouthfeel, glossy finish, and satisfying snap.

MOLDING

Final shaping affects flavor perception; smooth-edged chocolates taste creamier and less bitter than straight-edged ones.

WINE

From the humble grape comes a head-spinning range of flavors, from juicy blackberries and zesty lemons to toast, chalk, oak, spices, even leather—making wines versatile kitchen companions and flavor-pairing superstars.

Alcohol's burning bitterness and wine's puckering dryness and acidity make wine an acquired taste. Wine's many flavors come from either the grapes themselves (primary aromas/flavors), fermentation (secondary aromas/flavors), and aging in bottles or oak barrels (tertiary aromas/flavors). Sweet wines have grape sugars left after fermentation while dry wines lack these sugars, putting acidity and tannins center stage. Young wines that are one to three years old are fruitier while those that are five to 10 years old are more complex.

Different grape varieties and terroirs (the soil and the climate in which the grapevines grow) create distinct flavor profiles. New World wines (outside Europe and the Middle East), where it is warmer, are made with grapes that are sweeter and less acidic, making wines fruitier and more alcoholic (sugar being food for alcohol-producing yeasts).

Glass size and shape

GLASSES WITH LARGE BOWL SIZES AND SMALLER OPENINGS GIVE MAXIMUM AROMA RELEASE and intensity for both red and white wines, so take claims of wine-specific glasses with a sip of skepticism.

Tall flutes are best for fizzy wines as bubbles are larger when they burst, spraying more aroma compounds skywards.

Popular grape varieties

RED

CABERNET SAUVIGNON
Widely used in blends, this is abundant in fresh, green-tasting pyrazines (methoxypyrazines p.66 and methylpyrazines). Flavors range from roasted pepper to brandied cherry.

MERLOT
Fewer tannins and subtler flavors than cabernet, merlot's prized flavors include tomato, plum, and cherry pie.

PINOT NOIR
This grape thrives in cooler climates, where gentle, earthy fruitiness gives well-balanced wines.

SYRAH/SHIRAZ
Termed Syrah in France and Shiraz in Australia, cooler climate Syrah wines boast blackberry, plum, black pepper, olive and herby flavors, while New World versions offer ripe fruitiness with chocolate and vanilla undertones when aged in oak.

GRENACHE/GARNACHA
Often blended with other varieties, these intensely sweet grapes create wines with few tannins, ripe red berry flavors, and a hefty alcoholic kick.

WHITE

SAUVIGNON BLANC
Refreshing, high acidity, dry wines with aromas of lemon, green apple, grass, and wet stone, often with tropical top notes of guava, kiwi, and passion fruit in warm-climate wines.

CHARDONNAY
Powerful flavors of apple, pear, and citrus. Chardonnay is often aged in oak barrels, introducing toasted, nutty, and spicy notes. It is also famous for rounded buttery tastes and balanced acidity due to fermentation—releasing diacetyl, the aroma compound of butter (pp.166–167).

RIESLING
Riesling's bright primary flavors of green apple, pear, and citrus are complemented by strong floral aromas from linalool and "rose ketone" (damascenone). With age, wines develop rich notes of honey, dried fruit, and nuts.

PINOT GRIGIO/GRIS
In Italy, Pinot Grigio is a light, crisp wine with notes of pear, green apple, and citrus. French winemakers, making Pinot Gris, create richer, spicier wines evoking ripe peach, honey, and ginger.

MOSCATO
Moscato has strong floral aromas (orange blossom and rose) and sweet stone-fruit (peach and apricot), refreshing, aromas. It is often slightly sparkling (known as frizzante).

RED WINES ARE BEST ENJOYED AT
64–72°F
(18–22°C) TO ENHANCE AROMA AND REDUCE BITTERNESS.

FLAVOR DIRECTORY **211**

GRAPES
Primary flavors come from molecules in the grape itself such as terpenes (floral, citrus notes), esters (fruitiness), and phenolics (bitterness, astringency).

FERMENTATION
During fermentation, microbes and yeasts eat up the sugars in the grapes, creating more esters, alcohols, and acids, bringing complex flavors of banana, apple, butter, and many more.

AGING
Aging adds tannins, flavors of vanilla, toast, and smoke, imparted from contact with the inside of wooden barrels as the wine is left to mature.

OTHER CATEGORIES

ROSÉ WINE
PINK-COLORED WINE WITH FRESH, FRUITY, AND SOMETIMES FLORAL NOTES.

ORANGE WINE
MADE BY INCLUDING SKINS AND SEEDS OF WHITE WINE GRAPES FOR A WINE THAT HAS TANNINS AND SOME RED WINE FLAVORS.

SPARKLING WINE
WINES THAT UNDERGO A SECOND FERMENTATION (IN-BOTTLE OR IN A TANK), PRODUCING BUBBLES AND A FIZZY TEXTURE, OFTEN WITH NOTES OF FRUIT, TOAST, AND YEAST.

DESSERT WINE
SWEET, WITH RICH, HONEYED, OR FRUITY FLAVORS.

FORTIFIED WINE
A WINE WITH ADDED SPIRITS, INCREASING ALCOHOL CONTENT AND STOPPING FERMENTATION, RESULTING IN A SWEET OR DRY STYLE WITH RICH AND COMPLEX FLAVORS.

Common pairings
Seafood such as oyster, shrimp, and scallop, green salads, chicken, risotto, cheeses such as Brie and Camembert.

Scallop   **White wine**   Chicken

Uncommon pairings
Pickled vegetables, including carrot, cucumber, and kimchi. Charred cauliflower, popcorn, and wasabi peas are other options to try.

Cauliflower   **White wine**   Popcorn

Common pairings
Red meat, game meat like duck and rabbit, Parmesan cheese, pasta in tomato-based sauces, and pizza.

Red meat   **Red wine**   Parmesan

Uncommon pairings
Bacon, pulled pork, roasted chestnuts, and eggplant.

Bacon   **Red wine**   Roasted chestnut

BEER

From modern craft beer to ancient ale, beer has long reigned as the most popular alcoholic beverage. Whether hoppy or bitter, earthy or fruity, sweet or spicy, there is a beer for every occasion.

Beer is made by fermenting cereal grains, typically malted barley. This is barley that has been soaked, germinated, and then kiln-dried in a process. Starches are broken down into simple sugars, which provide food for alcohol-producing yeast.

Malting the grain contributes to the toasty, caramel, and nutty notes of the beer. Also key to the flavor of beer is the hops, which are added to a boiling solution of the malted barley and water. Hops come in different varieties, largely defined by

WHEAT BEER
BEER BREWED USING MALTED WHEAT HAS FLAVORS OF BANANA, CLOVE, AND TOFFEE.

LAGER
WITH A MORE SUBTLE FLAVOR THAN ALE, LAGER HAS FAR FEWER FRUITY ESTERS.

PALE ALE
PALE ALE HAS A HOPPY BITTERNESS FROM HIGH LEVELS OF ALPHA ACIDS.

STOUT
STOUT HAS DEEP BURNT NOTES OF COFFEE AND CHOCOLATE FROM ROASTED BARLEY GRAINS.

their aroma and bittering qualities. Their aroma stems from the herb's aroma compounds, which can impart floral, citrus, and peppery flavors to beer, as well as contributing to its "hoppiness." Bitterness mainly comes from tasteless "alpha acids" in hops; boiling changes them into a form that tastes bitter.

The addition of yeast is central to the brewing process, turning into sugar, carbon dioxide, and ethanol during fermentation. With different fermenting temperatures and alcohol tolerances, yeasts can control the flavor, appearance, and alcohol content of beer. They also impact the amount of carbonation, which creates a foam head when poured. As these bubbles burst, they help draw the aromas of the beer from the glass and into your nose, providing a bright, refreshing flavor.

PICKING YOUR BEER

- **Pale ale:** Golden in color due to shorter kilning time with high levels of alpha acids imparting a hoppy bitterness. Aroma compounds such as myrcene provide a refreshing citrusy burst and herbal flavor. Pairs well with oily foods like fish and steak or with Asian spices to complement its aromatic notes.
- **India Pale Ale:** Stands alone from other pale ales for its strong hop flavor and fruitiness. Ester compounds provide tropical fruit flavors such as banana, apricot, and pineapple. Other aroma compounds like geraniol contribute a roselike fragrance with notes of citrus.
- **Lager:** A crisp beer with a clean taste and mouthfeel, brewed at a lower temperature using bottom-fermenting yeast (or "lager yeast"), which settles at the base of the tank and takes longer to ferment.
- **Stout:** Dark in color from lengthy, high-temperature kilning of the ungerminated barley. Moderate alpha acid levels give a balanced bitterness. Often aged to develop complex flavors of vanilla and dark fruit. A great pairing with desserts and strong cheese. Porter is similar to stout but is made with malted (germinated) barley, bringing out sweeter caramel flavors with no burnt qualities.
- **Wheat beer:** Brewed using mostly malted wheat, these beers have lots of body and some sweet and spicy flavors. Highly carbonated, producing a large foamy head when poured, with a cloudy appearance as it is usually unfiltered.

Common pairings
Lemon, lime, orange, basil, mint, and sage.

Lemon — **Ale | Lager** — Basil

Uncommon pairings
Oily fish, salad, blue cheese, ginger, and garlic.

Oily fish — **Ale | Lager** — Blue cheese

Common pairings
Strong cheese, coffee, caramel, and chocolate.

Coffee — **Stout | Porter** — Chocolate

Uncommon pairings
Bacon, banana, coconut, chile, and cinnamon.

Bacon — **Stout | Porter** — Chile

Common pairings
Sushi, ice cream, banoffee pie, seafood, pork, and poultry.

Ice cream — **Wheat beer** — Pork

Uncommon pairings
Donut, oyster, and shellfish.

Oyster — **Wheat beer** — Donut

SPIRITS

Central to cocktails and useful for giving dishes a boozy kick, spirits will get your taste buds tingling. These distilled concoctions offer warming spice and bold aromatics, with woody and caramel notes. The word "spirit" takes its name from the capturing of the essence of a heated liquid, such as alcohol, via a process called distillation. This reference and the knowledge of distilling liquids dates back hundreds of years to the practicing of medieval alchemy. As a beverage today, however, a spirit refers to an alcohol obtained via the distillation of fermented raw ingredients. Whether apples for calvados, barley for gin, or sugar cane molasses for rum, the fruits and plants used for fermentation are a big factor in the distinct characteristics of the resulting spirit.

Spirits have an alcohol (ethanol) content of 40 percent, far higher than that of beer (5 percent) and wine (12 percent). This is due to the art of distillation, which evaporates the alcohol from a vessel containing the fermented mixture, then condenses it into a new one, purifying the alcohol and increasing its percentage. This also produces a clear spirit, as seen with vodka, which is how all spirits start off. Spirits at this stage are fiery but bland; additional flavors are incorporated during the production processes. Gin is flavored through infusion with aromatic botanicals, a craft that has gained immense popularity over recent years both commercially and for the home enthusiast. Other spirits, such as rum and whiskey, acquire their depth of flavor and color from aging in oak barrels. These barrels are flame-treated to break down the wood's natural compounds, creating flavors of caramel and vanilla. Tannins from the wood also contribute bitterness and complexity.

VODKA
IS DISTILLED AND FILTERED TO REMOVE IMPURITIES, RESULTING IN A NEUTRAL FLAVOR.

ALL SPIRITS START AS CLEAR, COLORLESS LIQUIDS. DIFFERING COLORS AND AROMAS RESULT FROM AGING AND FLAVORING.

Types of spirits

Spirits are alcoholic drinks made through distillation. The most popular spirits are vodka, gin, whiskey, rum, and brandy. Vodka and gin are lighter spirits that pair well with seafood, while whiskey, rum, and brandy are heavy, more complex spirits and can be enjoyed with stronger, richer flavors.

VODKA
A clear spirit with little taste that can be made from various raw ingredients. These include grains, root crops, and fruits, imparting subtle notes of citrus and spice. It is considered the most versatile spirit for making cocktails, allowing mixers to bring the flavor while it delivers the alcohol warmth.

FLAVOR DIRECTORY 215

Common pairings
Fresh fruit, salmon, seafood, tonic water, pickles, and salads.

Salmon   **Vodka | Gin**   Fruit

Uncommon pairings
Cumin, cardamom, turmeric, and cucumber.

Cumin   **Vodka | Gin**   Cardamom

Common pairings
Steak, dark chocolate, pineapple, coconut, charcuterie, and blue cheese.

Steak   **Rum Whiskey**   Dark chocolate

Uncommon pairings
Vanilla ice cream, gingerbread, and banoffee pie.

Vanilla ice cream   **Rum Whiskey**   Gingerbread

WHISKEY
BARRELS HAVE OFTEN BEEN USED FOR OTHER SPIRITS BEFOREHAND, WHICH AFFECTS ITS COLOR AND TASTE.

GIN
Distilled with the infusion of botanicals, which must include juniper berry to deliver the signature piney flavor of pinene. Other herbs, spices, citrus peels, and barks impart aromatic compounds such as minty cineole, floral linalool, and woody bornyl acetate. Enjoyed in cocktails partnered with tonic, it pairs well with the delicate flavors of seafood and salads.

WHISKEY
Amber in color with flavors of vanilla and dark fruits. Lactones from barrel aging provide woody notes. Made with malted barley, which is often peat heated to provide smoky phenolic compounds such as guaiacol. Makes a great pairing to grilled steaks or after the meal with dark chocolate. A smoky variety blends well with blue cheese.

RUM
Made from molasses and aged in oak casks, imparting notes of brown sugar and butterscotch. High in fruity esters such as ethyl propanoate. Available as dark or white, where the coloration is removed via filtering through charcoal. Impurities are also removed, creating a smoother drink. Rum is a great companion to any desserts featuring tropical fruit and nuts.

INDEX

Page numbers in **bold** refer to main entries

A

acetic acid **84**, 85, 206
acids 22, 208
  acidity levels **31**
  in apples and pears 123
  and astringency 80
  chiles and 180
  cooking with **32–33**
  Maillard reaction and 76
  and sourness 30–31
acrolein 40
acrylamide 79
Adrià, Ferran 70
agave syrup **21**
age, effect on taste 60–61
aging foods 151, 211
alcohol 24, 81
  beer **212–13**
  and bitter tastes 24
  cooking with alcohol 149
  fermentation 85
  spirits **214–15**
  wine **210–11**
alcohols (aroma compound) 57, 67, 208
aldehydes 57, 67, 79, 83, 208
ale 213
alkali foods 33, 76
allicin **44**, 96, 97
allspice **187**
almond milk 173
almonds 172, **173**
alpha acids 24

amaranth **99**
amino acids 26, 75, 143
amygdala 48, 53
androstenone 152
anticipation, and flavor **52–53**
antioxidants 174, 175
aonori 144, 145
Apicius, Marcus Gavius 50
appearance 48, 49
  effect on flavor **50–51**
appetite 52
apples 59, **122–23**, 138
apricots 71, 124, **125**, 173
aroma 10, 53
  aroma compounds 57, 66, 72, 82, 106
  perception through life **60–61**
  receptors 57, 59
  temperature and 72, 73
arrangement of food **54–55**
artificial sweeteners 19
arugula 139
astringency 11, **80**, 81

B

babies 15, 60
bacon 152
bacteria 136, 165
bananas **128**, 129
basil **193**
bay leaves **202**
beans **114–15**
  soybeans 114, **116–17**
béchamel sauce 148, 149, 165

beef 98, **146–47**, 161, 183
beer 75, **212–13**
beet greens 99
beets 108, **109**
bell peppers **90–91**, 92, 118
Benzi, François 68
berries 37, **126–27**
beta-carotene 101
bisques 161
bitter tastes 12, **22–25**, 31, 60, 208
  bitterness in cooking **24–25**
  garlic 96
  kale 99
  pungency and 42
  salt and 14, 16, 92
  sound and 62
  taste receptors 13, 22
black-eyed beans 115
black foods 51
black pepper **176–77**
blackberries 127
blood-sugar levels 20
blue foods 50
blueberries **126**
Blumenthal, Heston 68
bok choy 99
Boston butt 153
Bourdain, Anthony 38
the brain, flavor and the **46–63**
brain (offal) 157
brassicas 23, **99**, 108
  broccoli and cauliflower **110–11**

cabbages and Brussels sprouts **112–13**
Brazil nuts **173**
bread 102, **134–37**
  enriched dough 137
  salt in 15, 135
  sandwiches **138–39**
  sourdough 136
  whole grain bread 134, 135
Brillat-Savarin, Jean-Anthelme 26
brines 16, 151
broccoli **110–11**
brown food 50
brown sugars **20**, 137
Brussels sprouts 23, **112–13**
butter 38, 41, 77, **166–67**
  clarified butter 41, 167
  cultured vs. sweet cream 166–67
  flavor compounds and pairing 167
  pastries 137
  production 166
  regional varieties 167
  salted vs. unsalted 166
  sandwiches 138, 139
  whey butter 167
butter beans 115
buttermilk 166

C

cabbages 99, **112–13**
cacao 23, 209
calcium 81, 99

cannellini beans 115
capsaicin 42, 43, **45**, 81, 91, 180
caramelization 32–33, **78–79**, 95
carbon dioxide 80, 85
carotenoids 170
carrots 100–101
casein 43
cashews 172
cassava 107
cassia 186
cauliflower 99, **110–11**
celeriac 109
cereal **36–37**
ceviche 159
chard 98, 99
cheese 29, 72, 85, 139, **168–69**
cherries 124, **125**
chestnut flour 173
chia seeds 37
chicken 118, 150–51, 161
chickpeas 114, **115**
chile peppers (capsicum) 91
chiles 45, 119, **180–81**
pungency **42–43**
Chinese cabbage 99
Chinese cuisine 29, 118
chips 62
chives 95
chlorogenic acid 92, 93
chocolate 36, 62, 72, **208–209**
bitterness in 22, 23, 24
flavor compounds 66, 68
cholesterol 174
cilantro **188–89**

cinnamaldehyde **45**
cinnamon 45, **186**
citrus fruit 33, **120–21**, 150
clarified butter 41, 167
cloves **179**
cockles 162
coconut **129**
coconut milk 182, 183
coconut oil 40, 41
coffee 22, 24, 75, **206–207**
cold foods 72
collard greens 99
color **50–51**
acids and 32–33
carrots 100
crustaceans 160
egg yolks 170
game meat 156
olives 175
combining food **68–69**
compounds, flavor **66–67**, 68, 70, 74
preservation **82–83**
cooling sensations 80
copper 81
coriander **188–89**
corn **132–33**
corn syrup 20
crab 160, 161
cranberries **126**
cravings, for sweetness **20–21**
cream **164–65**
creaminess 63
crispness 37
crudo 159
crunch 36, 37, 49, 62
crustaceans **160–61**
cucumber 103
cumin **185**

curcumin 184
curing 152, 159
curry **182–83**
curry leaves **203**
cyclopropanones 79

D
dairy: butter **166–67**
lactose **19**
milk and cream **164–65**
yogurt, kefir, and cheese **168–69**
deafness, and flavor 62
dessert wine 211
diacetyl 78, 79
dill **192**
dopamine 18, 20, 42, 180
dressings 102, **103**
drinks: beer **212–13**
coffee **206–207**
spirits **214–15**
tea **204–205**
wine **210–11**
drying **82, 83**, 159
duck 150–51
duck eggs 171
dulse 144, 145
durum wheat **135**

E
eating speed 63
edamame 116, 117
effervescence 11, **80**
eggplants **92–93**
egg substitutes 170
eggs 77, 137, **170–71**
emotions 49, 52, 53
emulsification **103**
endives 23
endorphins 42, 43, 180

enriched dough **137**
enzymes 11, 38, 164
esters 57, 67, 208
ethanol 81
ethyl acetate 78
ethylene gas 88

F
fat 36–37, **38–41**
adding to bread dough 137
beef fat 146
and bitterness 22, 24
in cashews 172
chiles and 180
cocoa fat 209
in cooking 39
goose fat 151
lamb fat 154
milk fat 164, **165**
pork fat 152
smoke point 40, 118
types of **40–41**
why we need it **38–39**
fat tastes 12, 31, 38, 39
fattoush 103
fatty acids 39
fava beans 114–15
fennel **190**
fermentation **84–85**
beer 212
dairy 168
eggs 171
soy sauce 117
wine 211
fish 29, **158–59**
dried fish flakes 82–83
mineral levels 161
oily fish 158, 159
preserving 159

raw fish varieties 159
white fish 158, 159
fish sauce 29
5-methylfurfural 79
flavonoids 22
flavonols 23
flavor: activating **64–85**
and the brain **46–63**
flavor pairing **68–71**
vs. taste 12
where flavor begins **10–11**
fleur de sel 17
flour 135, 173
food combinations **68–71**
fortified wine 211
frontal lobe 48, 52
fructose **19**, 20, 21
caramelization 78
Maillard reaction 75, 76, 77
fruit 103
berries **126–27**
citrus fruit **120–21**
stone fruits **124–25**
tropical fruits **128–29**
see also individual types of fruit
fufural 79
fungi **142–43**
furanone 75
furans 67, 75, 78
furfural 79, 206

G

galactose **19**
game meat **156**
garlic 44, **96–97**, 119, 183
genetics, and taste 58
ghee 41, 166

gin 214, **215**
ginger 23, 44, 45, 119, **176–77**
gingerol 44, **45**, 176, 177
gizzards 157
glass sizes and shape 210
glazes 77, 171
gliadin 134
glucose **19**, 20, 21
caramelization 78
Maillard reaction 75, 76, 77
glucosinates 23
glucosinolates (GTCs) 108, 111
glutamate 12, 26, 27
in MSG 28
in mushrooms 143
in tomatoes 88
and umami tastes 28–29
gluten 134, 137, 140, 141
glutenin 134, 141
goat **154–55**
goat's milk 165
goose **150–51**
goose fat 151
grains 37
grapefruit 24, 120, **121**
grapes **126**
wine **210–11**
green beans 115
green food 50
green onions 95, 119
green tea 205
gros sel 17
guanylate (GMP) 28–29

H

ham, dry-cured 29

hanging meat 151
hazelnuts 172, 173
heart 157
heat: mint 198
pungency 11, 42
Scoville heat scale **180**
hemicellulose 32
herbs: basil **193**
cilantro **188–89**
dill **192**
fennel **190**
mint **198–99**
oregano **194–95**
parsley **191**
rosemary **197**
sage **196**
thyme **194–95**
Himalayan pink salt 17
homogenization 164
honey 19, 21, 36, 77
hops 24
hot foods 72, 73
hunger 52–53
hydrogen ions 30
hydrogen sulfide 170
hydroxytyrosol 174
hypothalamus 53

I

Ikeda, Kikunae 26
India Pale Ale 213
ingredients **86–215**
flavor pairings **68–69**
inosinate (IMP) 28–29
Irish moss 145
iron 98
iso-maltol 79
isothiocyanates 43, **44**, 45
Italian cooking 29

J

jalapeño 180, 181
Japanese cuisine 29, 37, 71, 81, **82–83**
juglone 172

K

kale 98, 99
katsuobushi 83
kefir **168–69**
kelp seaweed 29
ketones 57, 67, 83, 208
kidney beans 114, 115
kidneys **157**
kokumi 81
kombu seaweed 29, 144, 145
Korean cuisine 71

L

lactic acid 30
lactofermentation **84**, 85
lactones 67, 74
lactose **19**, 76, 164, 168
lager 212, 213
lamb **154–55**
lamian noodles 141
lard 41
lasagna **148–49**
leafy green vegetables **98–99**
leeks 95
legumes **114–15**, 172
lemon mint 199
lemons **121**
lentils 114, **115**
lettuce 103
limes **121**
lips 10
liver **157**
lobster 160, 161

M

mace **178**
mackerel 158
magnesium 81
Maillard, Louis-Camille 74
Maillard reaction 25, **74–77**
   acids and alkalis and 33
   beef 146
   bread 134
   and caramelization 78
   coffee 206
   eggs 171
   fat and 39
   how to control **76–77**
   mushrooms 142
   onions 95
   parsnips 108
   pork 152
   potatoes 104
   poultry 150
   and salt 74
   sugar 19, 75, 76
   wok hei 118, 119
malaxation 174
Maldon sea salt 17
maltol 78, 79
maltose **19**, 76
mangoes **124**
maple syrup **21**
marinades 151, 155
marjoram 194, 195
marrow 157
mawa (khoya) 166
meal planning and timing 52–53
meat: beef **146–47**
   game **156**
   lamb, mutton, and goat **154–55**
   offal **157**
   pork **152–53**
   poultry **150–51**
melon 128, **129**
memories 48, 49, 60
menthol 80, 198
metallic tastes 16, 80, **81**
milk **164–65**, 166
   yogurt, kefir, and cheese **168–69**
minerals 81, 161
mint 102, **198–99**
miso 29, 84, 85, 116–17
molasses 20, 137
mold 84, **85**, 169
mollusks **162–63**
monosodium glutamate (MSG) 26, **28**
mouthfeel 10, 11, **34–35**, 36, 49
   alcohol and 81
   fats and 39
mushrooms 26, 29, 85, 119, **142–43**
music, and speed of eating 63
mussels 162, 163
mustard 44, 45, 139, **176–77**
mutton **154–55**
myrosinase 44, 111

N

Napa cabbage 113
naringin 24
nectarines 125
noodles 118, **140–41**
nori 144, 145
noses 12, 56–57
numbing sensation 80
nutmeg **178**
nutritional yeast 29
nuts **172–73**
   nut oils 40

O

oats 37
octopus **162**
offal **157**
oils 39, 40
   emulsification 103
   and the Maillard reaction 74
   olive oil **174–75**
   preservation in **82**, 83
   smoke point 40, 118
   wok hei 118
oleic acid 174
oleogustus 38, 39
oleuropein 174
olfactory bulb 56, 60
olfactory epithelium 57
olive oil 40, 137, **174–75**
olives 174, 175
onions 44, **94–95**, 183
oolong tea 205
orange foods 51
orange wine 211
oranges 120, **121**
orbitofrontal cortex 48
oregano **194–95**
orthonasal pathway 56, 57, 60
oxidation 82
oxtail 157
oysters 162, **163**

P

pairing foods **68–71**
   see also individual ingredients
palate 10, 11, 34, **35**, 36
pale ale 212, 213
papillae **11**, 12, 35
paprika **180**
parietal lobe 49
parsley 102, **191**
parsnips **108**
pasta **140–41**
   lasagna **148–49**
pasteurization 164
pastries 137
peaches 124, **125**
peanut oil 40, 117, 182
peanuts 172, 182
pears **122–23**
peas 114, **115**
pectin 32, 114, 122
peppercorns 45, **176–77**
peppermint 198, 199
peppers **90–91**, 92, 118
Persian blue salt 17
personality types 61
pH scale 31
pheasant 156
phenols 57, 67, 174, 207
phyto-hemagglutinin 114
pickling 16, 171
picky eaters 58, 59
pimento **187**
pineapple **129**
pink foods 51
pinto beans 115
piperine **45**
placement 54
plant-based milks 165
plantains **128**, 129
plating food **54–55**
plums 124, 125, 173
poke 159
polyphenols 175

popcorn 132
pork **152–53**
pork fat 152
potatoes **104–107**, 182
   cooking 105–106
   pairings 106
   potato-like tropical roots and tubers 107
   sugar content 104
   varieties 104, 107
poultry **150–51**
   offal 157
pregnancy 60
preservation **82–85**, 159, 171
protein 26, 27, 32, 75
prunes 124
pu-erh 205
pulses **114–15**
pungency **42–45**, 81, 198
pyrazines 57, 67, 74, 75, 79, 208

Q–R

quail eggs 171
rabbit 156
radicchio 23
radishes 103, 108, **109**
ragù 148, 149
raisins 36
ramen noodles 141
raspberries **126**, 127
red cabbage 113
red foods 51
red kidney beans 114, 115
red wine 24, 72, 73, 80, 210–11
red currants 127
retronasal pathway 56, 57, 60, 66

ribonucleotides 28
rice **130–31**
rock salt 16, 17
root vegetables **108–109**
rosé wine 211
rosemary **197**
rugae 35
rum 214, **215**
rye **135**

S

saccharin 19
saffron **200**
sage **196**
salads **102–103**
saliva 10–11, 12, 81
   fat-digesting enzymes in 38
   sour tastes and 30
   tannins and 80
salmon 159
salt **14–17**
   adding salt to eggplants 92–93
   curing 152, 159
   dangers of 15
   how to salt **16**
   and the Maillard reaction 74
   masking and enhancing taste with 14
   MSG and 28
   presalting 14
   salt bread 135
   salt curing **82–83**
   salted vs. unsalted butter 166
   salting fish 159
   and texture 15, 16, 135
   types of **16–17**

salty tastes 12, 13, 42, 63
sandwiches **138–39**
sashimi 159
saturated fat 40, 41
sausages 152
scallions 95
scallops 162, 163
scarlet runner beans 115
Scotch bonnet chiles 180, 181
Scoville heat scale 91, **180**
sea bass 158
sea grapes 145
sea lettuce 144, 145
sea salt 16, 17
sea spaghetti 145
seaweed 29, **144–45**
sel gris 17
semolina (durum) 135, 140
serving food: plating **54–55**
   temperature **72–73**
shallots 95, 183
sheep breeds **155**
shiitake mushrooms 29, 119, 142
shogaol 44, 45
shrimp 160, 161
Simas, Tiago 70, 71
sinalbin 44
singrin 44
smell 48, 53, **56–57**, 60
smoke point 40, 118
smoked fish 159
smoked salts 17
snails 162
snout 153
soba noodles 141
sound 49, **62–63**

sour cherries 124
sour tastes 13, 42, **30–31**, 62
sourdough **136**
soybeans 114, **116–17**
soy sauce 29, **117**, 118
sparkling wine 211
spearmint 198, 199
spelt **135**
spices: bay leaves 202
   black pepper **176–77**
   cloves **179**
   cumin **185**
   curries 182
   curry leaves **203**
   ginger 23, 44, 45, 119, **176–77**
   mace **178**
   mustard 44, 45, 139, **176–77**
   nutmeg **178**
   saffron **200**
   turmeric **184**
   vanilla **201**
spicy foods **42–45**
spinach 98, 99
spirits **214–15**
sprouts **112–13**
squid **162**, 163
starches 32, 104, 105
stir-fries **118–19**
stock 151, 161
stone fruits **124–25**
stout 212, 213
strawberries **126**, 127
sucrose 21, 77, 78
sugar **18–21**
   acids and 32, 80
   adding to bread dough 137
   caramelization 25, **78–79**

Maillard reaction 75, 76
preservation in **82**, 83
types of **20–21**
sulfides 57, 111
sulfur compounds 67, 74, 83, 170
sun-drying **83**
supertasters **58–59**
sweet potatoes 107
sweet tastes 12, **18–21**, 60
and bitterness 22, 24
sound and 62, 63
taste receptors 13, 18, 20
sweet tooth 18, 20
sweetbreads 157
sweet corn **132–33**
sweeteners, artificial 19
Swiss (green) chard 98, 99
syrups **21**, 36

T
table salt 16
tamarind paste 183
tannins 24, 72, 80, 81, 208
taro 107
tastants 11, 12, 13, 66
taste 12–13, 25, 62
the brain and 48
differences in **58–59**
effect of age on **60–61**
and serving temperature 72, 73
vs. flavor 12
taste buds 11, 12, **13**, 35, 58
age and 60
bitter tastes and 22
fat and 38, 39
how they work 12
pungency and 42
salt and 14

sour tastes and 30
sweet tastes and 18, 19, 20
temperature and 72, 73
umami taste 26, 27
tea 24, 80, **204–205**
teeth 10, 30
Telefonica 70
tempeh 116, **117**
temperature 49, 74, 78
serving temperature **72–73**
terpenes 57, 67
texture 10, **36–37**, 49
fats and 39
and flavor pairings 71
papillae and 35
preferences for 34
salt and 15, 16, 135
Thai Massaman curry 182–83
thalamus 48
theobromine 23
thermophilic microbes 168
thiols 74, 75
thiophene 75
thoughts 49
thyme **194–95**
tofu 116, 117
tomatoes **88–89**, 103, 148
flavor pairings 71
how the brain experiences flavor 48–49
serving temperature 72
tongue 11, 34, **35**, 157
fat receptors 38, 39
papillae **11**
pungent compounds and 42–43

tastants 11, 12, 13, 66
touch 49
toxins 22, 114
tripe (stomach) 157
tropical fruits **128–29**
TRPV1 receptors 42, 43, 44, 45, 81
truffles **142–43**
turkey 138, 150–51
turmeric **184**
turnips **108**, 109
2-methyl-3-furanthiol 79

U
umami tastes 12, **26–29**
citrus fruit 120
crustaceans 160
enhancing **28–29**
salt and 15
taste receptors 13, 26, 27
unsaturated fat 40

V
vanilla **201**
vegetable oils 40
vegetables 103
leafy green vegetables **98–99**
root vegetables **108–109**
see also individual types
venison 156
vinaigrette 102
vinegar 84, 85, 103
vision 49, 50, 62
visual cortex 48, 49
vitamin A 101
vitamin C 33
vitamin D 142
vodka **214**, 215

W
Wagyu beef 146, 147
wakame 144, 145
walnuts **172**, 173
warm foods 72
wasabi 44
water spinach 99
watermelon **129**
waxy corn 132, 133
wheat 134, 135
pasta and noodles **140–41**
wheat beer 212, 213
wheat berries 134
whey butter 167
whiskey 71, 214, **215**
white foods 50
white wine 72, 73, 210–11
whole grain bread 134, 135
wild boar 156
wild garlic 96
wild mushrooms 119, 142–43
wild rice 130, 131
William of Orange 100
wine 72, 73, **210–11**
wok hei 118–19

Y–Z
yeast 29, 85, **136**, 137, 212, 213
yellow foods 51
yogurt 37, **168–69**
zingerone 176

ABOUT THE AUTHOR

Dr. Stuart Farrimond is a medical doctor, science communicator, food science expert, and award-winning author of the DK bestsellers *The Science of Cooking* (2017), *The Science of Spice* (2018), *The Sunday Times* bestseller *The Science of Living* (2020), and *The Science of Gardening* (2023). Dr. Farrimond makes regular appearances on popular science TV and radio shows, such as *Inside the Factory* and *Food Unwrapped* (both BBC) and at public events. His writing appears in national and international publications, including *The Independent*, the *Daily Mail*, *BBC Science Focus*, and *New Scientist*.

ACKNOWLEDGMENTS

AUTHOR'S ACKNOWLEDGMENTS

The scope of this book is vast—exploring the flavor science behind everyday ingredients as well as the latest research—and it could not have been brought to life without a kitchen brigade of immensely talented creatives. Led by our wonderful head sous-chefs, senior editors Lucy Sienkowska and Sophie Blackman, editors Susan McKeever, Clare Double, and Nicola Hodgson worked tirelessly to transform my overly generous servings into this refined, finished dish. Immense gratitude also goes to the talented designers Alison Gardner and Sarah Snelling, who crafted the stunning designs and artworks that make this book visually delicious.

This, my fifth book, is particularly meaningful and I hope it isn't my last. Midway through its writing, the cancerous brain tumor that first set up home inside my skull nearly two decades ago once again decided to reawaken, nibbling into my gray matter and needing drugs and radiotherapy to keep it at bay. It is through the unrelenting love and support of my wife, family, friends, and church that this book ever made it to the printers. This book is dedicated to you.

I am deeply indebted to writers Josh Smalley, Robin Sherriff, Nicola Temple, and Laura Gladwin— the chefs de partie—who stepped in during the closing weeks of my cancer treatment, ensuring the manuscript reached the printer's platter on time.

The book also benefited from the insights of experts who helped fill gaps in my knowledge. My heartfelt thanks go to Professor Charles Spence, a world leader in sensory science, and Dr. Ni Yang (Nicole), Associate Professor at the University of Nottingham, who kindly shared her cutting-edge research into how aroma compounds create flavor as we chew, drink, and swallow. Dr. Yalda Moayedi at NYU College of Dentistry generously discussed her recent discovery of a new type of nerve cell in the mouth—the starburst ending cell—pivotal to our understanding of texture and mouthfeel. Tea chemistry expert Professor Michelle Francl also offered invaluable insights into the science behind the world's favorite hot drink.

Finally, my agent Jonny Pegg continues to be a friend and steady rock, deftly handling the complexities of the book industry so I can focus on the creative process. To the entire DK team, particularly Lucy and Clare, thank you for your genuine compassion, patience, and unflagging support during our family's darkest days. This book would not exist without you, and I sincerely hope it will not be the last we work on together.

PUBLISHER'S ACKNOWLEDGMENTS

DK would like to thank Josh Smalley for expertly reviewing the manuscript; and Laura Gladwin, Robin Sherriff, Josh Smalley, and Nicola Temple for contributing to the text. The publisher would like to thank Tobias Sturt for visualization work; Sunil Sharma for photographic retouching; Ellie Jarvis for food styling; Elpida Magkoura for prop styling; Thomas England for consulting on the US edition; Kathryn Glendenning for proofreading; and Vanessa Bird for providing the index.

BIBLIOGRAPHY

To access a full list of research citations supporting the information in this book, please visit:
www.dk.com/science-of-flavor-biblio

PICTURE CREDITS

The publisher would like to thank the following for their kind permission to reproduce their photographs:

(Key: a-above; b-below/bottom; c-center; f-far; l-left; r-right; t-top)

15 National Academy of Sciences: Adapted from- Gillette, Marianne. "Flavor effects of sodium chloride." Food Technology (1985). (b). **17 Getty Images / iStock:** FotografiaBasica (t, c). **19 MDPI:** Adapted from- Chen, E.; Zhao, S.; Song, H.; Zhang, Y.; Lu, W. Analysis and Comparison of Aroma Compounds of Brown Sugar in Guangdong, Guangxi and Yunnan Using GC-O-MS. Molecules 2022, 27, 5878. https://doi.org/10.3390/molecules27185878. **20 Getty Images / iStock:** SUNGMIN. **21 MDPI:** Adapted from- Chen, E.; Zhao, S.; Song, H.; Zhang, Y.; Lu, W. Analysis and Comparison of Aroma Compounds of Brown Sugar in Guangdong, Guangxi and Yunnan Using GC-O-MS. Molecules 2022, 27, 5878. https://doi.org/10.3390/molecules27185878. **24 Adobe Stock:** NIKCOA (br). **28 MDPI:** Adapted from -Yu, Hang Yu et al. "Monosodium Glutamate Intake and Risk Assessment in China Nationwide, and a Comparative Analysis Worldwide. Nutrients 15 (2023): n. pag. (bl). **31 Adobe Stock:** NIKCOA (bl). **34 National Library of Medicine:** Adapted from- Food texture assessment and preference based on Mouth Behavior, Melissa Jeltema et al. 2014 (bl). **58 MDPI:** Adapted from- Melis, M.; Sollai, G.; Mastinu, M.; Pani, D.; Cosseddu, P.; Bonfiglio, A.; Crnjar, R.; Tepper, B.J.; Tomassini Barbarossa, I. Electrophysiological Responses from the Human Tongue to the Six Taste Qualities and Their Relationships with PROP Taster Status. Nutrients 2020, 12, 2017. https://doi.org/10.3390/nu12072017 (br). **60-61 ResearchGate:** Adapted from- Richard L. Doty et al. ,Smell Identification Ability: Changes with Age.Science226,1441-1443(1984)_. **63 Semantic Scholar:** Adapted from- Effect of background noise on food perception. / Woods, A.T.; Poliakoff, E.; Lloyd, D.M. et al. (cra). **68 Getty Images / iStock:** Floortje (bc/Cheese); Adam Smigielski (bc/Chocolate). **70 Getty Images / iStock:** Tim UR (br). **71 Springer Nature Limited:** Adapted from- Ahn, YY., Ahnert, S., Bagrow, J. et al. Flavor network and the principles of food pairing. Sci Rep 1, 196 (2011). https://doi.org/10.1038/srep00196. **73 ResearchGate:** Adapted from-Talavera Perez, Karel & Ninomiya, Yuzo & Winkel, Chris & Voets, Thomas & Nilius, B. (2007). Influence of temperature on taste perception. Cellular and molecular life sciences : CMLS. 64. 377-81. 10.1007/s00018-006-6384-0. . **79 ResearchGate:** Adapted from- Davies, Cathy & Labuza, Theodore. (2000). The Maillard Reaction Application to Confectionery Products. . **81 Getty Images / iStock:** jorge-imstock (br). **90 Getty Images / iStock:** Andrey Elkin (t). **92 Getty Images / iStock:** A-S-L (cl). **96 Depositphotos Inc:** sommaill (tr). **104 Chapingo University:** Adapted from- Morales-Fernández, S. D., Mora-Aguilar, R., Salinas-Moreno, Y., Rodríguez-Pérez, J. E., Colinas-León, M. T., & Lozoya-Saldaña, M. T. (2015). Growth, yield and sugar content of potato tubers at different physiological ages. Chapingo Journal Horticulture Series (tr). **120 Shutterstock.com:** grey_and. **121 Adobe Stock:** NIKCOA (l). **125 Getty Images / iStock:** Tim UR (bl). **131 Getty Images / iStock:** AlasdairJames (tc); valio84sl (tl); LeventKonuk (tr). **132 Getty Images / iStock:** Napoletana (l). **142 Dreamstime.com:** Eyeblink (br); Lcc54613 (bl); Tananuphong Kummaru (bc/Enoki); Akepong Srichaichana (fbr). **Getty Images / iStock:** y-studio (bc). **Shutterstock.com:** Jangqq (fbl). **143 Dreamstime.com:** Kaiskynet (fbl); Tarog8 (fbl/Button); Nevinates (bl). **Getty Images / iStock:** Gago-Image (fbr); YinYang (bc); hsvrs (bc/Chanterelle, br). **166 Dreamstime.com:** Viktorfischer (ca); Kevkhiev Yury (cra). **171 Adobe Stock:** SerPhoto (ftr). **Dreamstime.com:** Isselee (tc/Goose Egg). **Getty Images / iStock:** Geshas (tl/x2, tr); koosen (tc/Duck Egg). **177 Dreamstime.com:** Ajafoto (bc); Feldarbeit (fbl, bc/Brown Mustard); Marilyn Barbone (bl); Troichenko (fbr). **Getty Images / iStock:** milanfoto (br). **178 Dorling Kindersley:** James Young (cb). **180 Depositphotos Inc:** Maks_Narodenko (br). **181 Depositphotos Inc:** Wavebreakmedia (bl). **Getty Images / iStock:** hongquang09 (fbl). **186 Depositphotos Inc:** alexlukin (crb). **Dreamstime.com:** Valentyn75 (clb). **187 Adobe Stock:** GSDesign (tc). **Shutterstock.com:** Koko Foto (c). **194 Getty Images / iStock:** Floortje (c); timsa (cr). **195 Getty Images / iStock:** Everyday better to do everything you love (cl). **196 Getty Images / iStock:** malerapaso (cb). **197 Getty Images / iStock:** LICreate (cr). **198 Getty Images / iStock:** JPC-PROD (cr). **200 Dreamstime.com:** Ludmila Makarova (crb). **201 Getty Images / iStock:** FRANCOIS-EDMOND (tr). **202 Depositphotos Inc:** mayakova (crb). **205 Depositphotos Inc:** nenovbrothers (clb). **Dreamstime.com:** Alexey Borodin (bl); Anna Kucherova (tl, cl); Deryabinka (cla). **207 Shutterstock.com:** pongpinun traisrisilp (t/Data reference) **214 Getty Images / iStock:** grynold. **215 Dreamstime.com:** Francesco Marzovillo (c). **Getty Images / iStock:** Kateryna Kolesnyk (cr); subjug (cl). All other images © Dorling Kindersley

DK LONDON

Editorial Director Cara Armstrong
Managing Editor Clare Double
Senior Editors Sophie Blackman and Lucy Sienkowska
US Senior Editor Jennette ElNaggar
Senior Designer Barbara Zuniga
Production Editor David Almond
Senior Production Controller Stephanie McConnell
DTP and Design Coordinator Heather Blagden
Jackets and Sales Material Coordinator Emily Cannings
Publishing Director Stephanie Jackson
Art Director Maxine Pedliham

DK DELHI

Rights and Permissions Specialist Priya Singh
Consultant, IPR & Imagery Taiyaba Khatoon

Managing Art Editor Sarah Snelling
Editorial Susan McKeever and Nicola Hodgson
Design Alison Gardner
Photography Neil Watson, Sun Lee,
Stephanie McLeod, and Stuart West
Illustration Sally Caulwell

First American Edition, 2025
Published in the United States by DK Publishing,
a division of Penguin Random House LLC
1745 Broadway, 20th Floor, New York, NY 10019

Text copyright © Dr. Stuart Farrimond 2025
Copyright © 2025 Dorling Kindersley Limited
25 26 27 28 29 10 9 8 7 6 5 4 3 2 1
001–340340–Aug/2025

All rights reserved.
Without limiting the rights under the copyright reserved above,
no part of this publication may be reproduced, stored
in or introduced into a retrieval system, or transmitted, in any form,
r by any means (electronic, mechanical, photocopying, recording, or otherwise),
without the prior written permission of the copyright owner.
DK values and supports copyright. Thank you for respecting intellectual property
laws by not reproducing, scanning, or distributing any part of this publication by any
means without permission. By purchasing an authorized edition, you are supporting writers and
artists and enabling DK to continue to publish books that inform and inspire readers. No part of
this publication may be used or reproduced in any manner for the purpose of training artificial
intelligence technologies or systems. In accordance with Article 4(3) of the DSM Directive
2019/790, DK expressly reserves this work from the text and data mining exception.

Published in Great Britain by Dorling Kindersley Limited

ISBN 978-0-5938-4424-3

Printed and bound in China

www.dk.com

This book was made with Forest
Stewardship Council™ certified
paper—one small step in DK's
commitment to a sustainable future.
Learn more at www.dk.com/uk/
information/sustainability